UNDOING AESTHETICS

Theory, Culture & Society

Theory, Culture & Society caters for the resurgence of interest in culture within contemporary social science and the humanities. Building on the heritage of classical social theory, the book series examines ways in which this tradition has been reshaped by a new generation of theorists. It will also publish theoretically informed analyses of everyday life, popular culture, and new intellectual movements.

EDITOR: Mike Featherstone, *Nottingham Trent University*

SERIES EDITORIAL BOARD
Roy Boyne, *University of Durham*
Mike Hepworth, *University of Aberdeen*
Scott Lash, *Lancaster University*
Roland Robertson, *University of Pittsburgh*
Bryan S. Turner, *Deakin University*

THE TCS CENTRE
The Theory, Culture & Society book series, the journals *Theory, Culture & Society* and *Body & Society*, and related conference, seminar and postgraduate programmes operate from the TCS Centre at Nottingham Trent University. For further details of the TCS Centre's activities please contact:

Centre Administrator
The TCS Centre, Room 175
Faculty of Humanities
Nottingham Trent University
Clifton Lane, Nottingham, NG11 8NS, UK e-mail: tcs6@ntu.ac.uk

Recent volumes include:

The Social Construction of Nature
Klaus Eder

Deleuze and Guattari
An Introduction to the Politics of Desire
Philip Goodchild

Pierre Bourdieu and Cultural Theory
Critical Investigations
Bridget Fowler

Re-Forming the Body
Religion, Community and Modernity
Philip A. Mellor and Chris Shilling

The Shopping Experience
edited by *Pasi Falk and Colin Campbell*

UNDOING AESTHETICS

Wolfgang Welsch

Translated by
Andrew Inkpin

SAGE Publications
London • Thousand Oaks • New Delhi

First published 1997

Published in association with *Theory, Culture & Society*,
Nottingham Trent University

SAGE Publications Ltd
6 Bonhill Street
London EC2A 4PU

SAGE Publications Inc.
2455 Teller Road
Thousand Oaks, California 91320

SAGE Publications India Pvt Ltd
32, M-Block Market
Greater Kailash – I
New Delhi 110 048

British Library Cataloguing in Publication data

A catalogue record for this book is available
from the British Library

ISBN 0 7619 5593 3
ISBN 0 7619 5594 1 (pbk)

Library of Congress catalog card number 97–061790

Typeset by Mayhew Typesetting, Rhayader, Powys
Printed in Great Britain by The Cromwell Press Ltd,
Broughton Gifford, Melksham, Wiltshire

For Katharina,
who undoes things her own way

CONTENTS

PREFACE

The lectures and essays collected here originated in the years 1990–5. They develop further perspectives from my *Aesthetic Thinking*, which appeared in German in 1990, but with new accentuations.

My work is guided by the conviction that thinking aesthetically in a new way is essential in grasping our condition today. Modern thought, since Kant, has subscribed to the insight that the nature of the underlying condition we call reality is aesthetic. Reality has proven itself again and again to be constituted not 'realistically' but 'aesthetically'. Where this insight has penetrated – and by now that is just about everywhere – aesthetics has lost its character as a special discipline relating solely to art and become a broader and more general medium for the understanding of reality. This has resulted in a general significance for aesthetic thinking today and in a need for change in the structure of the discipline of aesthetics, so that it becomes an aesthetics beyond traditional aesthetics comprising the whole range of *aisthesis* in everyday life, science, politics, arts, ethics, and so on. The essays collected here seek to explore this new relevance and configuration of the aesthetic.

A first group of considerations is dedicated to general questions. It deals with the particular relevance of the aesthetic for contemporary thinking, critically considers today's global aestheticization, explains relationships between the aesthetic and the ethical, and addresses the question of how contemporary aesthetics should be comprised.

A second group of contributions contains diagnoses regarding modern architecture and art in public space and then asks how art might – beyond traditional and modern one-sidednesses – be understood. The subsequent outlooks are then concerned with cities of the future, with the criticism of our culture's traditional visual primacy, as well as with the new dominance of electronic media and their repercussions for our conventional worlds of experience.

Undoing Aesthetics refers to aesthetics' new issues, configuration and tasks. Aesthetics has to be broadened beyond questions of art to daily life, perceptive attitudes, media culture, and the ambivalence of aesthetic – and anaesthetic – experience. These are pressing present-day areas for the questions addressed by traditional aesthetics as well as for the new competences of contemporary aesthetics. One of the most interesting points is that this opening up of aesthetics beyond art proves fruitful for every adequate analysis of art itself too.

These essays originated for particular occasions – sometimes in professional philosophical, sometimes in popular, forums. As they are closely connected with each other, they contain some overlap and repetition. I decided to retain this so as to ensure the independent readability of the pieces – and apologize to those readers who go through the volume in one session.

My thanks go to all of those who have encouraged these thoughts through discussions: the colleagues and students of different universities at home and abroad, as well as the participants of the congresses, conferences, and symposia at which I first presented these thoughts. They will recognize themselves in one or two of the arguments here. I would like to thank especially Arthur C. Danto, who helped me with distinctions in matters of aestheticization, Hanno Birken-Bertsch, who supported me untiringly in preparing these essays, Robert Rojek, with whom it has been a pleasure to work, as well as Andrew Inkpin, who – even when the texts sometimes took on a different form from week to week – was a patient and circumspect translator at all times.

Wolfgang Welsch

I NEW SCENARIOS OF THE AESTHETIC

1

AESTHETICIZATION PROCESSES
Phenomena, Distinctions and Prospects

Live with your country, but do not be its creature; render to your contemporaries what they need, not what they praise.

Friedrich Schiller, *On the Aesthetic Education of Man*

Perhaps, however, it would be altogether improper to see an aesthetic problem being taken so seriously

Friedrich Nietzsche, *The Birth of Tragedy*

The following deliberations are comprised of four parts. To begin with I want to sketch a tableau of contemporary aestheticization processes. As this contains quite different aspects, I shall secondly have to clarify what is meant by the term 'aesthetic' in these variant uses and how this term is to be dealt with correctly. In the third section I shall attempt a more in-depth explanation of aestheticization processes. The fourth section will then undertake an assessment of aestheticization processes and identify critical perspectives.

I. A tableau of contemporary aestheticization processes

We are without doubt currently experiencing an aesthetics boom. It extends from individual styling, urban planning and the economy through to theory. More and more elements of reality are being aesthetically mantled, and reality as a whole is coming to count increasingly as an aesthetic construct to us.

The following tableau attempts firstly to achieve some overview of partially known, but bewilderingly discussed phenomena. Secondly, and above all, it should become clear that in addition to a surface aestheticization there is a deep-seated aestheticization. The former has been much discussed and copiously derided; the latter is less well known, although more significant, and to criticize this validly ought to prove more difficult.

Whoever, as unfortunately most often occurs, speaks only in a superficial sense under the heading 'aestheticization' and fails to consider deep-seated aestheticization remains below the diagnostic level which is today necessary.

1. Surface aestheticization: embellishment, animation, experience

Aesthetic furnishment of reality

Aestheticization is at its most obvious in the urban space, where just about everything has been subjected to a face-lift over the last few years. Shopping areas have been fashioned to be elegant, chic and animating. This trend has long since affected not only city centres, but also the outskirts of towns and country refuges. Hardly a paving-stone, no door-handle and no public place has been spared this aestheticization-boom. Even ecology has largely become a further branch of enhancement. In fact, if advanced Western societies were able to do completely as they wish, they would transform the urban, industrial and natural environment *in toto* into a hyper-aesthetic scenario.

With this the world is becoming a domain of experience. 'Experience' is a central heading in these processes of enhancement or embellishment.[1] Every boutique and every café is today designed to be an 'active experience'. German railway stations are no longer called stations, but rather, following their artistic garniture, call themselves a 'world of experience with rail connection'. Every day we go from the experience-office to experience-shopping, relax with experience-gastronomy and finally end up at home for some experience-living. Suggestions have been made that even memorials – for example those to Nazi atrocities – should be staged as 'experience-domains'.

The art business too has interposed itself into the machinery of experience and continues its production in accord with the dialectics of such pseudo-experiences: the disappointment with those experiences, which in truth are nothing of the sort, drives people from one experience to the next. The 1992 Documenta art exhibition in Kassel demonstrated this afresh: it was described as being worse than all those preceding it, and in general worse all round – but, yet again, the number of visitors exceeded all expectations. It was the first Documenta to close without having made a loss. The worse it is, the more successful it is – this law of the entertainment industry also seems to apply to its sub-sphere of art.

At this first, foreground level aestheticization means furnishing reality with aesthetic elements, sugar-coating the real with aesthetic flair. This certainly takes up an old and elemental need for a more beautiful reality corresponding to our senses and feeling for form. On top of this, particularly in the provinces, comes the symbolism of progress: 'See, you don't just find these aesthetic productions in the metropolises, but here too – and here it's better, because it's on a human scale.' The old dream, that of improving life and reality through the introduction of aesthetics, seems to be being brought to bear. However, we cannot ignore the fact that only the most superficial elements have been carried over from art and then realized in a broadbrush form. Beautiful ensembles drift into prettiness at best, and the sublime descends into ridicule – Napoleon had already pointed out that the sublime is only one step away from the ridiculous.

This everyday aestheticization is not, as some theoreticians believe, about an accomplishment – albeit an unsatisfying one – of the avant-garde programmes to extend and break down the limits of art. On the contrary: when Beuys or Cage pleaded for an extension of the concept of art and a breaking down of its boundaries they were thinking that something which wasn't art should be understood as art – and that the conception of art would thereby be altered or extended. In today's aestheticization, however, it is quite the reverse: traditional artistic attributes are being carried over into reality, daily life is being pumped full of artistic character. This corresponds not to the programmes of the avant-garde, but at best to older aestheticization programmes à la Schiller, the System-Programme of German idealism, Werkbund, and so on. Admittedly, in the current aestheticization these too seem only to be being accomplished as a programme to further the kitsch.

Hedonism as a new cultural matrix

In surface aestheticization the most superficial aesthetic value dominates: pleasure, amusement, enjoyment without consequence. This animatory trend today reaches far beyond the aesthetic enshroudment of individual everyday items – beyond the styling of objects and experience-loaded ambiances. It is increasingly determining the form of our culture as a whole. Experience and entertainment have become the guidelines for culture in recent years. A society of leisure and experience is served by an expanding culture of festivals and fun. And whilst some of the all too strident offshoots of aestheticization, or singular aspects of the cosmetics of reality, might raise a smile, with its extension to culture as a whole, this is no longer a laughing matter.

Aestheticization as an economic strategy

Much of this everyday aestheticization serves economic purposes. The bond with aesthetics renders even the unsaleable saleable, and improves the already saleable two or three times over. And nowhere, as aesthetic fashions are particularly short-lived, does the need for replacement arise as quickly and assuredly as with aesthetically styled products: even before the already in-built obsolescence leaves articles unserviceable they are aesthetically 'out'. Moreover, products which are becoming increasingly unsaleable on moral or health grounds are being rendered presentable and saleable once again through aesthetic ennoblement. The aesthetic aura is then the consumer's primary acquisition, with the article merely incidental.

This has been recognized above all by the cigarette industry, which has long since been describable as aesthetically advanced. When direct advertising of its products was banned in Britain in the eighties it developed forms of advertising which got by without either the product's or the firm's name, but in which the allure was aesthetic refinement alone.

This process is revealing. From it two transpositions can be inferred which are of general significance, reaching out beyond economics. First comes an exchange of commodity and packaging, essence and appearance, hardware and software. The article, formerly the hardware, is now just an accessory; on the other hand, the aesthetics, formerly the software, becomes the main issue. Secondly, these advertising strategies betray the fact that aesthetics has become an autonomous guiding value – if not to say the main currency – of society. If an advert succeeds in associating a product with aesthetics which interest the consumer, then the product will be sold, whatever its real qualities may be. You don't actually acquire the article, but rather, by its means, buy yourself into the lifestyle with which the advert had associated it. And, as lifestyles themselves are today predominantly aesthetically forged, aesthetics altogether has become not just the vehicle, but rather the essence.

2. *Deep-seated aestheticization: transposition of hardware and software –*
the new priority of the aesthetic

The spread of aestheticization today is no longer merely superficial, but reaches into deeper tiers as well. Both of the processes named – the switching of hardware and software and the new priority of the aesthetic – characterize not only the superficial processes, but also the deeper processes of aestheticization, which are now to be addressed.

Changes in the production process: new materials technologies

New materials technologies should be commented upon first. In the wake of microelectronics, the classical hardware, matter, is also increasingly becoming an aesthetic product. The conception and testing of new industrial materials is today purely computer-simulated all the way through to final manufacture. Simulation – an aesthetic process which is enacted on the monitor's screen – has no longer an imitational, but rather a productive, function. So, here too, aesthetics shifts to the fore, namely in what concerns the process as well as the desired results. The reality which was once thought of as being hard, proves itself to be mutable, newly combinable and open for the realization of arbitrary aesthetically contoured wishes. When technology experts today say that it's unbelievable what we're able to do, this 'unbelievable' no longer means, as formerly, a self-confident plenitude, but the astonishment that material reality offers so little resistance. Through intelligent interference with its microstructure it is changeable down to the last fibre. Reality is – viewed from today's technological standpoint – of the most pliable, lightest stuff. More extreme materials' strengths are an effect of soft, aesthetic procedures.

Aesthetic processes don't only shroud already completed, given substances, but even determine their structure, affect not only the cover, but even the core. Aesthetics thus no longer belongs merely to the superstructure, but to the base. It can be seen that today's aestheticization is by no means merely a thing of *beaux esprits*, or of the postmodern muse of amusement, or of superficial economic strategies, but results just as much from fundamental technological changes, from the hard facts of the production process.

This material aestheticization, as I want to call these processes, entails an immaterial aestheticization at the same time. The daily interaction with microelectronic production processes effects an aestheticization of our consciousness and of our whole *apprehension* of reality. Whoever works constantly with computer-aided design knows the virtuality and manipulability of reality; she has learnt how barely real reality is, how it is so aesthetically modellable. – Perhaps the older generation still understands too little how easily a younger generation is beginning to establish itself in artificial worlds.

Constitution of reality through the media

The next aspect is connected to this. Social reality too, ever since it has been primarily mediated and forged by the media, particularly televisionary media, is subject to radical derealization and aestheticization processes. Our old belief in reality must definitively break down when faced by television, the main bestower of reality. For televisionary reality is no longer binding and inescapable, but rather in contrast, selectable, changeable, disposable, can be fled from. If something doesn't suit you, you simply change channel. In zapping and switching between channels, the advanced television consumer practises the derealization of the real – which also applies otherwise. The media's pictures no longer offer a documentary guarantee of reality, but rather are largely arranged and artificial and are being increasingly presented according to this virtuality.[2] Reality is becoming a tender through media, which down to its very substance is virtual, manipulable and aesthetically modellable.[3]

I set out, in my tableau of contemporary aestheticization processes, from the increasing furnishing of reality with aesthetic elements, from its sugar-coating with aesthetic flair. Then I pointed out that this surface aestheticization not only concerns singular elements within reality, but also affects the form of culture as a whole, and that it is becoming increasingly universal. In addition to surface aestheticization – key word universalization – there is a profound expansion – key word fundamentalization. With this, the exchange of position between hardware and software and the new priority of the aesthetic, which was first to be inferred from economic and advertising strategies, attain their full bearing. On the material as well as the social level, reality is revealing itself, in the wake of the new technologies and televisionary media, to be increasingly determined by aestheticization processes; it is becoming an ever more aesthetic affair – 'aesthetic' here of course being meant not in the sense of beauty, but rather of virtuality and modellability. A new, on-principle aesthetic consciousness of reality then reacts to these processes. This immaterial aestheticization reaches deeper than that literal, material aestheticization. It affects not just singular constituents of reality, but reality's mode of being and our conception of it as a whole.

3.   *Styling of subject and forms of life: on the way to* homo aestheticus?

Comparable observations are to be made when one goes from material and social reality over to subjective reality, to the form of individuals' existence. Here too there is a superficial and obvious aestheticization, but this too is underlain by a deeper aestheticization.

The current aestheticization could even be said to attain its perfection in individuals. We are experiencing everywhere a styling of body, soul and mind – and whatever else these fine new people might want to have (or acquire for themselves). In beauty salons and fitness centres they pursue the aesthetic perfection of their bodies, and in meditation courses and Toscana seminars the aesthetic spiritualization of their souls. Future generations should have it easier straight away: genetic engineering will already have come to their aid, this new branch of aestheticization which holds out the prospect of a world full of perfectly styled mannequins.

Individuals' interaction with one another is also increasingly being aesthetically determined. In a world in which moral norms are disappearing, table manners and etiquette – the correct choice of glass and of the suitable accompaniment to the respective occasion – still seem to hold firm the most easily. Aesthetic competence – propagated by lifestyle magazines and acquired in etiquette courses – offsets the loss of moral standards.

In such processes, *homo aestheticus* is becoming the new role-model.[4] He is sensitive, hedonistic, educated and, above all, of discerning taste – and he knows that you can't argue about taste. This affords new security amidst the insecurity which exists all around. Free of fundamentalist illusions, casually distanced, he enjoys all life's opportunities. The Kierkegaard literature waxes once again.[5]

But these superficial narcissisms also have a more profound background. All forms of life, means of orientation and ethical norms have long since assumed an aesthetic quality of their own to the modern consciousness. Since the historicism of the nineteenth century, at the latest, they have no longer been viewed as binding standards, but rather as historical, social or individual conceptions which are at best situationally appropriate – that is, for a particular location and time-span. There are always other conceptions opposing these, and every one of them can be altered or replaced. Morals pass as constructs of a near artistic order – but again are fluctuant rather than of binding validity. Even when their declarations are rigid, their constitution on the whole bears aesthetic traits. And the criteria, on the basis of which one chooses between different morals, will also ultimately be of an aesthetic nature.

It is, however, true that this on-principle aestheticization of our attitudes to life's practicalities and moral orientation is today leading to excessive manifestations, but it cannot be ignored that the underlying form of thinking has long since been valid. And again, although it's easy to mock this or that outward manifestation, it's extraordinarily difficult to raise even a single genuinely reliable argument against the situation's deeper causes.

4.   Aestheticization as a general trend, but in varying ways

The cheapest form of behaviour towards the new and pressing topicality of the aesthetic consists of simply denying the phenomena – because what's not permissible cannot be; and because what one doesn't perceive doesn't exist. People all too easily make use of the conceptual trick of speaking of aesthetics *per definitionem* only with a view to art – already rid of pressing questions, you find yourself in the safe haven of traditional questioning. Such escapism may well be necessary for anxious souls. But it is of no good to the philosophical understanding of what is. It puts defence in the place of diagnosis and self-consolation in that of conceptual exertion. It adheres to the magical belief that by looking the other way these phenomena can be made to disappear, or to the mania of theory that things are to be decreed and not explained. – In contrast to this escapism, it is important to look at the diverse aestheticizations unabridged, to differentiate and to reflect. Only in this way can one arrive at well-founded options.

Let's look back again at the tableau of aestheticization processes. Aesthetic elements are on the advance at a superficial level in both objective and subjective reality: façades are becoming prettier, shops more animatory, noses more perfect. But aestheticization reaches deeper too, it affects foundational structures of reality as such: of material reality in the wake of new material technologies, of social reality as a result of its mediation through media, and of subjective reality as a result of the dissolution of moral standards by self-styling.

Taken collectively a general condition of aestheticization ensues. 'Aestheticization' basically means that the unaesthetic is made, or understood to be, aesthetic. This is exactly what we are currently experiencing all around. This aestheticization might not follow the same pattern everywhere, and the type of aesthetic glaze applied to the non-aesthetic can be different from case to case: in the urban environment aestheticization means the advance of what's beautiful, pretty, styled; in advertising and self-conduct it means the advance of staging and life-styling; with regard to the techno-logical determination of the objective world and the mediation of social reality through the media 'aesthetic' above all means virtualization. The aestheticization of consciousness ultimately means that we no longer see any first or last fundaments, rather that reality for us assumes a constitution which until now was only known to us from art – a constitution of having been produced, being changeable, unobligating, suspended, and so on. In its details, then, aestheticization results in varying ways, but taken collectively the result is a general condition of aestheticization.

II.   Clarification of concepts

1.   Is ambiguity synonymous with unusability?

But perhaps I should first answer a possible objection before proceeding further on the basis of this general condition. I have just spoken of how the expression 'aesthetic' did not have the same meaning in all of the previous examples. Sometimes it related to things beautiful, or merely pretty, sometimes to styling, sometimes to virtualization, and so on. Furthermore, its point of reference also varied: sometimes it was concerned with the characteristics of objects, sometimes with associative dimensions, sometimes with the manner of reality's being.

Is it actually permissible to deal with a concept in this way? Or, to put it another way, if such varying ways of usage do in fact belong to the grammar of the expression 'aesthetic', does this not condemn the expression to being unusable? Doesn't polysemy of this sort make this a fake concept? Is even the diagnosed universality of the aesthetic ultimately merely a result of the expression's many-sidedness, and therewith an illusion? Is 'aesthetic' a *passe-partout* word, which is suited to everything only because it says nothing? Ought one not then to drop the expression completely because inexactitude in a concept is synonymous with unusability?

The problem of the aesthetic's semantic ambiguity is as old as the dis-cipline called aesthetics itself. Baumgarten, its founder,[6] defined aesthetics as the 'science of sensitive cognition'.[7] Aesthetics was to be not primarily to do with art, but a branch of epistemology. Hegel, on the other hand, a good half-century later, understood aesthetics to be decidedly a 'philosophy of art', and, more precisely, 'of fine art'.[8] To this, again some decades later, an expert such as Konrad Fiedler took exception: 'Aesthetics', he said, 'is not the theory of art'; the 'joining of beauty and art' is rather the *protos pseudos in the realm of aesthetics*.[9] The catalogue of such contrary definitions of aesthetics can be continued almost without end. Sometimes it is to concern the sensuous, sometimes the beautiful, sometimes nature, sometimes art, sometimes perception, sometimes judgement, sometimes knowledge; and 'aesthetic' should mean in alternation sensuous, pleasurable, artistic, illusory, fictional, poietic, virtual, playful, unobligating, and so on.

This ambiguity could indeed lead one to despair of the sense and usability of the expression. Every aesthetic theorist says something interesting, but each says something different. 'Anything – and nothing – is right', 'this is the position you are in if you look for definitions [. . .] in aesthetics'[10] – this is how Wittgenstein once described the situation.

2.   Family resemblance

Wittgenstein's example

Wittgenstein, however, shows us a way out of this difficulty. He demonstrates that, although coherence in usage is necessary for terms with variant uses, this coherence need not be due to a unitary essence, but can come about in a different way: through semantic overlap between one usage and the next. The differing meanings then have, as Wittgenstein says, 'no one thing in common'[11] – that is, no element which enables one to decree what *the* aesthetic is – rather their relationship results from these overlaps alone. Wittgenstein called a structure of this sort 'family resemblance'.

It is in exactly this way, in my view, that the term 'aesthetic' is constituted. Family resemblances determine its grammar. Borrowing a famous passage from Wittgenstein's *Philosophical Investigations*, you could almost use the formulation:

> Instead of producing something common to all that we call aesthetic, I am saying these phenomena have no one thing in common which makes us use the same word for all, – but they are *related* to one another in many different ways. And it is because of this relationship, or these relationships, that we call them all 'aesthetic'.[12]

In the quote I have only replaced the word 'language' with 'aesthetic'.

'Aesthetic' – a term characterized by family resemblances: semantic elements, semantic groups, overlaps

In the following I want to set out the extent to which 'aesthetic' is a term characterized by family resemblances. To this end I shall run through different ways of using the expression.[13] In doing so it will be analytically helpful to distinguish three points of view. What are – first of all – the different meanings and fields of reference of the expression? Secondly (and above all), which semantic elements of meaning can be identified with these different usages, and how do varying combinations of these elements result in the diverse meanings of the expression? And thirdly, in what way does the occurrence of the same semantic elements in the different usages lead to overlaps, links and transitions between these? How then – as a consequence of which semantic elements – do you get from one meaning to the next, and hence successively through the whole scale of usages of 'aesthetic'?

The sensuous semantic group: the aisthetic and the elevatory semantic element

Very generally the expression 'aesthetic' refers to the sensuous. 'Aesthetic' can be used more or less synonymously with 'sensuous'.[14] All the same, strictly speaking we do not call everything sensuous 'aesthetic'. We do this far more – in demarcation from the rough-sensuous – only with regard to the cultivated sensuous. For example, we do not denote the gourmand's attitude to pleasure, but only that of the gourmet, as 'aesthetic'. A tendency to mantle, surmount and ennoble the sensuous belongs to the aesthetic. It can reach as far as to connotations of the over-refined, the sublime, even the aethereal.

Whilst I call the first semantic element, which refers generally to the sensuous, the *aisthetic* semantic element, I call this second element, which is introduced for greater specification, the *elevatory* element. It expresses a setting aside, a distancing of the vulgar-sensuous, the ascent to a higher form of the sensuous. Only both elements together – the aisthetic and the elevatory element – comprise the full semantics of the semantic group of 'aesthetic' referring to the sensuous. Of course, through this doubling a peculiar tension inheres in the expression right from the start: 'aesthetic' refers to the sensuous – and yet carries out a distancing from it at the same time; it aims for the sensuous not as this ordinarily is, but for a higher and distinguished, an especially cultivated attitude towards the sensuous. A whole series of shifts and variations is thereby enabled.

The double character of aisthesis: sensation and perception

Within the aisthetic semantic element a further differentiation is to be observed straight away. For *aisthesis* has two sides; it is characterized by a bifurcation of *sensation* on the one side and *perception* on the other. Sensation is related to pleasure and is emotional in nature; perception, on the other hand, is related to objects and is cognitive in nature. Subjective evaluation forms the focus of sensation, objective ascertainment the scope of perception. Corresponding to this bifurcation 'aesthetic' can assume a *hedonistic* meaning with a view to sensation's accentuation on pleasure, and a *theoreticistic* one with a view to perception's observational attitude.

Sensation: the hedonistic semantic element

With respect to sensation the elevatory semantic element asserts itself again straight away. We do not call – just as previously, not everything sensuous – every sensation or pleasure 'aesthetic': not, that is, the lower, vital sensation of pleasure which is determined through life-interests, but only a higher type of pleasure which directs itself either to vitally irrelevant aspects of vitally pleasurable objects or to such objects as are, vitally viewed, neither pleasurable nor non-pleasurable from the outset. The specifically aesthetic pleasure refers, for instance, to the arrangement of meals – instead of their substance; or to the act of love – instead of the satisfaction of instinct; or to the form of a speech – in place of its content.

Whilst the vital pleasure could be compared with the ground floor of a building, the aesthetic pleasure corresponds to a storey situated above this, a *piano nobile*, where, once elementary needs have been satisfied, a reflexive pleasure is enjoyed, one which judges its objects not as necessary or useful, but as beautiful, harmonic, sublime or superior. This *piano nobile* is the *beletage par excellence* of the aesthetic faculty of judgement, of 'taste'. Hence 'aesthetic' is often used in the sense of 'tasteful' or 'corresponding to cultivated' taste.

This higher pleasure is, admittedly, strictly hedonistically oriented too. Pleasure is its central determination. The pleasure of taste is due namely to 'a sensation that is connected directly with the feeling of pleasure and displeasure'[15] – just that now it is concerned not with the pleasure of the mere 'taste of sense', but with the higher pleasure of the 'taste of reflection'.[16]

A certain reduction in distance between the two 'storeys' can admittedly be ascertained at present. Formerly, higher demands had to be fulfilled for one to speak of 'aesthetic'; today, lower ones suffice. Hence already an arrangement which pleases the senses is called 'aesthetic'. The elevatory element is thus reduced and aesthetic demands are already getting close to the vital sphere, even being raised within this. All the same the opposition of elite versus ordinary is still largely linked with the expression 'aesthetic'. A sort of distancing always belongs to the aesthetic.

Semantic elements of aesthetic perception: form- and proportion-related, theoreticistic, phenomenalistic

Likewise on the other side of *aisthesis*, on the side of perception, the elevatory semantic element is again the first to assert itself. When we designate a perception 'aesthetic', then we do not have the ordinary sort of perceiving in mind, but rather a particular and higher-level perception, which directs itself to specific aspects and objects – for example, not, like simple perception, to that which is red, but to the fact that this red is in a complementary contrast to the green or that it is emphasized particularly well by the surrounding colours.

This aesthetic perception refers generally less to elements than to relations between elements: to connections and contrasts, harmonies and correspondences, counter-supports or analogies. Aesthetic perception is interested in their concordance and accomplishment. Questions of form and proportion constitute its domains. Thus, wherever 'aesthetic' refers to such perceptions, a *form- and proportion-related* element shifts into the foreground.

Additionally, a *theoreticistic* semantic element is characteristic for such perception: aesthetic perception is executed in the form of contemplation. It is not interested in the immediate being of things as it is, and it even enjoys the objects peculiar to it at distance – precisely in the manner of contemplation. Aesthetic perception is not practice-oriented but contemplative, not pragmatic but theoreticistic. This can lead to connotations such as 'removed from practice', 'unrealistic' or 'unworldly'. The person who perceives aesthetically directs her gaze exclusively towards specifically aesthetic aspects and relations of objects, without being drawn into the real ones. She does not soil her hands, but contemplates aesthetic conditions without paying attention to the antagonisms of the real.

Following on from this, 'aesthetic' can target chiefly the *phenomenalistic* semantic element. With this is foregrounded the idea that aesthetic perception directs itself only to the surface, to the skin of things, thus dedicating itself to appearances and not their essence. It revels in the outers of things without worrying about their inners. Hence 'aesthetic' is often linked with connotations such as 'appearance', 'apparentness', 'emphasizing the surface', 'outward' and 'superficial'.

The 'subjective' semantic element

It is frequently said that aesthetic sensation is subjective – one person is pleased by this, another by that. Hence the use of the expression 'aesthetic' is often dominated by the *'subjective'* semantic element. This is understandable insofar as pleasure is a subjective determination in general (pleasurable character is attached not to objects as such, but is acquired by them only in relation to a subject) and this is particularly conspicuous with aesthetic pleasure, since it depends entirely on a specific attitude: its objects (say the successful form of a composition or the harmony of a colour palette) only reveal themselves at all in the perspective of taste, whereas they don't exist at all for ordinary sensing and perceiving.

The 'reconciliative' semantic element

'Aesthetic' sometimes expresses a *reconciliation perspective*. Structures are designated 'aesthetic' precisely to the extent that, within them, diverse things are wonderfully joined, brought into harmony, are made to agree or accord with one another. What clashes harshly and irreconcilably in everyday life seems to dovetail aesthetically as if by itself. The transition from elementary to aesthetic sensibility is at the same time one from disparity to accommodation, from conflict to harmony, from divergence to reconciliation.

Analytically viewed, several of the semantic elements already mentioned are asserted in this anew: the setting aside of everyday experience of reality as well as the elevatory, the form- and proportion-related and the phenomenalistic semantic elements. The varying elements of meaning can obviously be combined with one another too. Or, put more precisely, although the varying ways of using – that is, the meanings of – the expression 'aesthetic' are mostly concentrated on a particular semantic element, they can also incorporate other semantic elements as additional viewpoints. The singular semantic elements always seem, even structurally, to imply other semantic elements too.

The callistic semantic element

'Aesthetic' is often used synonymously with 'beautiful', that is, in a callistic sense.[17] Beauty is even widely considered to be the aesthetic predicate *par excellence*. This is linked with the fact that 'beautiful' is able to assimilate all elements relating to the sensuous and summarizes them in a reconciliative perspective. For beauty denotes the perfecting form of the sensuous, and this perfection consists of a free joining of the pieces to a whole, that is, of reconciliation. With this, the aisthetic just as the elevatory, the hedonistic and the form- and proportion-related semantic elements, and especially that signalling reconciliation, belong to the structure of the callistic semantic element.

The cosmetic and poietic semantic element

In a more pragmatic accentuation, 'aesthetic' can refer to design – especially to good design, to design in the sense of 'good form'. The elevatory, the form- and proportion-related, the callistic and the reconciliation-related semantic elements again participate. Additionally a *cosmetic* meaning of the aesthetic shifts to the fore: the formation arrives at the result's representation being accomplished and enjoyable for aesthetic consideration not through a change in substance, but through skilful arrangement and capable overforming of its materials and objects. This cosmetic semantic element is obviously close to the phenomenalistic one.

But above all here a new semantic element appears: the *poietic* element, the element of production. Whereas the preceding usages of 'aesthetic' referred to the aesthetic *consideration* of existing things (whereby the production side would be limited to the generation of the aesthetic attitude, of the aesthetic type of perception), the concern here is with the *production on the object level*, the generation of objects of aesthetic character. This can concern everyday objects just as it can works of art.

The artistic semantic element

'Aesthetic' is often more or less definitionally referred to art, thus having specifically *artistic* meaning. The widespread nature of this usage can be explained by the fact that the art-related meaning is able to gather almost all the elements previously mentioned within it: the sensuous, its transcendence and perfection, the enjoyment of observation, the distancing from the real, the perfection of forms and proportions, the distancing from practice, phenomenalism, the wonderful joining of elements to the reconciled whole, and equally of course the accent on subjectivity and beauty, as well as the cosmetic and the poietic moment.

The semantic element 'conforming with aesthetics'

'Aesthetic' can ultimately be used synonymously with 'according with the theory of the aesthetic', that is, mean as much as 'conforming with aesthetics'. Put briefly, the expression then signals competence in aesthetic matters.

In contrast to the meanings of the expression 'aesthetic' just named, which are more restricting, three more meanings are cited to conclude, which, in comparison, extend the expression.

The 'sensitive' semantic element

When a person is called 'aesthetic' this does not (following on from meanings already mentioned) have to refer to his or her appearance or aesthetic deportment, but one can also mean that this person is *able to feel* in a particular way, is peculiarly *'sensitive'*. Such a person is able to perceive things which others oversee.

This usage follows on from the peculiarity of aesthetic perception, noticing things different and farther-reaching (say the harmony of colours) wherever ordinary perception perceives only the ordinary (say colours). The meaning 'sensitive' transfers this structure of the aesthetic to other fields which are not primarily sensuous, but rather ethical, moral or political. Whoever, for instance, is able to perceive the aggressiveness in a gesture of friendliness, or the oppression within a deportment of tolerance, is then considered 'sensitive'. And so when we speak of an 'aesthetic culture' we do not have to have in mind a particularly high artistic level of the culture concerned, but can mean with this designation culture's extraordinarily developed sensitivity in moral and political matters.

The 'aestheticistic' semantic element

'Aesthetic' often stands for an extreme case of the aesthetic, for the shaping of life according to exclusively aesthetic criteria, for an aesthetic type of existence.[18] 'Aesthetic' here means as much as *'aestheticistic'*.

The aestheticistic attitude describes the path back to the vital, initial demarcational ground of the aesthetic. The question was always open in a certain sense as to whether aesthetic feats come along to supplement the vital ones, or seek ultimately to absorb or replace them. The aesthetic type of life chooses the latter, the far-reaching solution.

A universalization of the aesthetic is linked with the aestheticistic attitude, and 'aestheticistic' is, as was 'artistic' previously, capable of assimilating almost all of the semantic elements explained until now. One difference from the integration in the case of art, however, consists in that the poietic moment refers not outwardly (to the generation of works), but inwardly, to the design of one's own life – that it has, so to speak, become reflexive.

What is new (alongside the element of enjoyment's becoming reflexive too, since the aestheticist is ultimately concerned with enjoying his or her self) is, then, above all, the dominance of the playful as well as the priority of the possible over the real. The *homo aestheticus* is a virtuoso of the 'sense of possibility' (Musil) and of virtualization.

The 'virtual' semantic element

This leads on to the last semantic element that I want to mention here: to *virtuality*. It denotes a specifically aesthetic grasp of reality, which makes its entry wherever aesthetic consideration is made the guiding model for the relationship towards reality. This aesthetic world-view directs itself (in continuation of the phenomenalistic semantic element) entirely towards surfaces and appearances. For it the coherence of the world is no longer one of things, but of phenomena; the purely aesthetic observer will even tend to the viewpoint that 'there is nothing behind the phenomena: they themselves are the lesson'.[19]

In this view of reality neither single things nor the singular aesthetic manifestations are decisive, but their connection, their relationship, their constellation within the whole. This has the consequence that all definitions – the objective references as it is, but equally the aesthetic manifestations – drift into a peculiar suspension. The aesthetic world on the whole then mediates an impression of lightness, of changeability and of suspension.

Such definitions have, of course, the 'real' world as their counterfort. The gravitas of the real is the dark sediment against which the aesthetic world shapes up so brilliantly. It is in opposition to the real that the aesthetic assumes the character of the virtual, of the dissolution of reality, of being silhouetted and tending to unreality. The aesthetic world appears in contrast to be superior, light and luminous, and comparatively unreal – somehow cloud-like. This can lead through to negative associations like 'alien to reality', 'hovering', 'apparent', 'ephemeral', 'unobligating', 'irresponsible' or 'groundless'. It is to such meanings – encircling the central predicate 'virtual' – to which 'aesthetic' refers when a mode of being is meant.

Conclusion: family resemblances and the relationship between the diverse meanings of 'aesthetic'

What is the result of this run through the main usages of the expression 'aesthetic', one which has allowed us to identify a whole series of meanings and semantic elements for the expression?

Firstly, it was demonstrated that there is neither a single obligating meaning of the expression 'aesthetic' nor is there a semantic element which would be common to all its diverse meanings – one which would hence represent something like the essential element of the aesthetic or comprise a continuous thread through all the meanings.[20]

Secondly, it became clear that the diverse usages were nevertheless not simply disparate. To be sure, if 'aesthetic' has the meaning 'theoreticistic' in the group referring to perception and the meaning 'pleasurable' in the group referring to sensation, then these are highly differing meanings and you will in no way be able to substitute one for the other. Something similar applies for predicates such as 'form- and proportion-related', 'phenomenalistic', 'subjective', 'poietic' or 'virtual'. Nonetheless other transitions obviously do exist between these predicates. Hence the groups of meanings determined by them display not merely lasting differences (chiefly with respect to their leading predicates), but a number of links and transitions at the same time.

Such entanglements are due especially to the fact that the semantic elements do not represent 'radicals' in the strict sense (are not constituted like atoms), but rather display a complex structure. The semantic architecture of a single semantic element can include several other semantic elements. Such a networking of the semantic elements displayed itself time and time again in the run through the usages. The elements do not represent autonomous semantic positions, but are to be understood as being particular points within a mesh of semantic elements.

Insofar as other semantic elements can belong to the structure of a single semantic element, meanings of this type might superficially appear to be disparate; they are, however, linked with one another in a subterranean – and constitutive – manner. So the hedonistic and the theoreticistic element, for instance, sprout from the different branches of *aisthesis* – one on the branch relating to sensation, the other on that relating to perception – but an elevatory component is effective in both of them; hence they are, in spite of their superficial difference, linked both by the double matrix of *aisthesis* and by this elevatory component. This structure has the result that you can transfer from one meaning to the next within the duct of such common elements. And this certainly doesn't cancel out their difference, but – quite the contrary – in effect makes it more understandable. In making clear to oneself how the hedonistic and theoreticistic meanings sprout from the different branches of *aisthesis* as a consequence of the same elevatory dynamics one can understand both the origin of their difference and the mechanism which makes them both members of the array of meanings of 'aesthetic'. – Or a predicate such as 'sensitive', although sharing with 'relating to form' the element of setting aside ordinary perception and of superiority over this, applies this element to completely different material (not to an aisthetic one, but to, say, a political or moral one). Thus 'sensitive' is far from 'relating to form' in a conceptual manner, since the premises of the form-related meaning (the aisthetic components) do not even occur in the chromosome set of 'sensitive'; but, insofar as both have in common an element of distancing, a link exists between them and both belong plausibly to the array of meanings of 'aesthetic'. – Or 'virtual', which links on to numerous other elements ('elevatory', 'theoreticistic', 'phenomenalistic'), by no means includes all others (like 'callistic', 'conforming with aesthetics' or 'sensitive').

Thirdly, then, an analysis which penetrates through to the substructure of meanings teaches us why and how we can transfer from one meaning to another. Precise consideration is able to reveal the overlaps and links as well as the differences and shifts between the diverse usages of 'aesthetic' and, by doing so, to make the network of their relationships on the whole understandable. It leads us piece by piece through the entire, wide-branching scale of diverse usages of the expression 'aesthetic'.

With this the transition from one usage to the next takes place more or less as expressed by Wittgenstein through comparison with the formation of a thread: 'we extend our concept [. . .] as in spinning a thread we twist fibre on fibre'.[21] If we consider the singular usages or semantic elements, then we do 'not see something that is common to *all*' of them, rather we see 'similarities, relationships, and a whole series of them at that'.[22] 'And the result of this examination is: we see a complicated network of similarities overlapping and criss-crossing: sometimes overall similarities, sometimes similarities of detail.'[23]

Fourthly, the point – Wittgenstein's just as, following on from him, that of this analysis – lies in that family resemblances of this sort are fully sufficient for the coherence and efficacy of a concept like 'aesthetic'. In no way is an 'essence' which is uniform throughout necessary for this. The suitability and durability of a concept (like, analogously, that of a thread) depends on the overlapping of different meanings, not on the continuity of a single basic meaning.[24] All that's necessary is that links exist from piece to piece – but these themselves can conform to different patterns so that the chain of meanings displays richly differing aspects in the different sections and continually shifts other predicates or semantic elements into the foreground.

Fifthly, it follows from this that a concept of this sort is not strictly closed, but can be 'spun further'. Not only historical shifts in meaning, but also new variants of meaning are possible.

In summary: the different usages of the expression 'aesthetic' are held together by family resemblances. There exist significant differences as well as overlaps and cross-connections between the diverse meanings. Hence the polysemy of the expression 'aesthetic' is not, say, objectionable or threatening, but can be well understood; moreover the family resemblances guarantee a – loose – coherence of the expression 'aesthetic' as a whole.

3. Consequences

What consequences does this have in dealing correctly with this expression?

1   In spite of its ambiguity, the expression is serviceable. The variety in usages doesn't disavow a concept, but can – in correct usage – even form

the basis of its particular serviceability. 'Inexact' is not synonymous with
'unusable'.[25] You only need to know how to differentiate precisely, with
which semantic versions or which combination of semantic elements you
are dealing with, and how to switch from one to the other. If this is
guaranteed then you can be extremely precise with respect to singular
usages as well as do justice to the concept's polyvalency as a whole.

2   Proceeding in this way is not only legitimate and purposeful, but
necessary. Whoever wants to develop an aesthetics in the full sense of the
word must be able to do justice to *all* usages of the expression.[26] Anything
but this would result merely in a partial aesthetics. A comprehensive, truly
complete aesthetics – whose development I advocate – cannot take random
selections as its point of departure. Philosophically, or rather in aesthetic
theory, it would be wrong and antiquated to give, or want to dictate, a
single, ultimate concept of the aesthetic. The meaning of a word is not what
enamours theoreticians, or what they decree – 'the meaning of a word is its
use in language', as Wittgenstein pointed out.[27] To decretorially exclude
those parts which don't suit one's own preferences, or to declare one certain
meaning the basic, or the only legitimate, meaning amongst the diverse
meanings of the aesthetic conflicts with the phenomena. Such an imperial
gesture suggests clarity, but *de facto* misrepresents the field of the aesthetic.
Bad philosophy flirts with the traditional expectation that one must reduce
the multitude of meanings to one basic meaning in all circumstances. It
thereby fulfils its own desire for mastery, as well as that of those who prefer
conceptual bulldozing to the analysis of complex problems.

3   An aesthetics which faces up to the reach of the aesthetic demands
greater far-sightedness and ability to differentiate than does a partial
aesthetics. Put briefly, it is more difficult. It demands the consideration of
the varying semantic provinces, versions and groups of the aesthetic with
their intersections and entanglements, and the ability to state respectively
with which semantic element one is operating and which intersections one
is making use of. Only in this way can justice be done to the complexity of
the aesthetic.

4   The point of these comments is found in objecting to the most
conventional of all constrictions relevant to aesthetics, which today seems
to be becoming popular again: the restriction of the aesthetic to art.
Whoever links the concept of the aesthetic exclusively to the province of art
and wants to border it off completely from daily life and the living world
partout practises aesthetic-theoretical provincialism.[28] He or she thematizes
a single province of the aesthetic whilst ostensibly addressing the aesthetic
world, and thereby fall short not only of the full and legitimate concept of
the aesthetic, but also – in objective irony – even of the concept of that
which he or she is ostensibly serving: that of art. For modern art no longer
longs to be locked within the golden cage of autonomy, but rather
renounces such aesthetic-theoretical ghettoization.[29]

Art is certainly a particularly important province in the universe of
meanings of the aesthetic. But it is not the only one. Today's topicality of

the aesthetic results from just this, the fact that the conventional equation of aesthetics and art has become untenable, and that other dimensions of the expression have shifted into the foreground. That's why – for the benefit of the full concept of aesthetics – one must take steps against the narrowing of the aesthetic to the artistic, why one must keep aesthetics clear of this obsolete constriction.[30]

III.   Epistemological aestheticization

Among the convolution of aestheticization processes portrayed in section I many ominous manifestations are found, in view of which it would be foolish to want to maintain that everything is bettered through aestheticization. We can no longer share this hope, that of aestheticization programmes from the late eighteenth century onwards. On the contrary, proclamations such as Schiller's that only the aesthetic man would be a complete human being,[31] or that of Hegel–Schelling–Hölderlin that 'truth and goodness become kindred only in beauty',[32] reveal themselves to be dubious in view of the forms in which such aestheticization programmes are acquitting themselves today.

But how is the line separating the positive from the negative in aestheticization to be drawn, and how might criticism of singular manifestations of aestheticization be substantiated? Generally speaking, either criteria of truth, or those of morality, or aesthetic criteria, come into consideration for this purpose. One can seek the assistance of science, ethics or aesthetics.

The attempt to expect criticism of aesthetics from aesthetics of all things sounds paradoxical from the start. In the same way, ethics is not the best authority today for a critique of aestheticization, since ethics itself – from Neoaristotelian bases through to Foucault's followers – is currently on its way to becoming a subdiscipline of aesthetics. Obviously, then, only science remains to be backed and therewith the perspective of truth.

1.   A critique of aestheticization in the name of truth?

And indeed, many intellectuals are taking to the battlefield against aestheticization in the name of truth. They say a universal aestheticization would result in the dissolution of truth and the destruction of science, the Enlightenment and reason. The sciences would be threatened with being undermined if rhetorical brilliance were to become more important than the justification of assertions. The Enlightenment would totter aimlessly should the aesthetic law of fiction step in in place of truth, and plurality in the place of obligation. Finally, should fundamental questions become questions of taste, then reason would be being juggled with in a scandalous manner.

These warnings, however, are reprises. In them the old contest between truth and beauty, being and appearance, fundamentalist obligation and fictional freedom is revived once again – a contest which has permeated the Occident in multifarious forms since Plato's critique of poets, Bernard of Clairvaux's polemics against Gothic style, and ever since the conflict between idealism and romanticism.

However, I think that the fundamental principles in this dispute have changed. It is increasingly settled. And what's more – other than believed by our forebears – it is settled in favour of aesthetics. My thesis is that this came about in consequence of the development of scientific rationality itself, through which truth has to a large extent become an aesthetic category. Following the introductory tableau of aestheticization processes, I have yet to mention the most incisive and profound aestheticization: the aestheticization of our categories of knowledge and reality, including the category of truth as ordained by the guiding authority of modernity, by science. Through this, allegedly 'rational' defences against aestheticization have long since been losing ground on their own territory.

2.   Epistemological aestheticization

Hence I must append this point, although of course I can only recount the history of this modern aestheticization of knowledge as a short story, since it already began around two hundred years ago.[33] Here too Kant, the revolutionary of modern philosophy, forms the point of departure.

Kant: aesthetics as a fundamental epistemological discipline

Kant showed in the *Critique of Pure Reason*, under the title 'Transcendental Aesthetic', that aesthetic elements are foundational for our knowledge. According to Kant's 'revolution of the way of thinking' we know '*a priori* of things only what we ourselves put into them',[34] and what we first put into them are *aesthetic* stipulations, namely space and time as forms of intuition. Only in space and time can objects first be given to us. And our cognition and reality reach just so far as these forms of intuition stretch. To this extent, aesthetics has for Kant – as the theory of these forms of intuition, that is, as a *transcendental* aesthetic (not, say, as a theory of art) – become epistemologically fundamental.[35] Since Kant we have known of the aesthetic fundaments of all knowledge, of a principal protoaesthetic of cognition.

Nietzsche: the aesthetic-fictional character of cognition

Nietzsche took this Kantian foundation further and rendered it so convincing that ever since, though one may address the question of our cognition's aesthetic constitution, scarcely anything can be brought forward against it.

Nietzsche showed that our representations of reality not only contain fundamental aesthetic elements, but are wholly aesthetic in nature. Reality is a construct which we produce, like artists with fictional means – through forms of intuition, projections, phantasms, pictures, and so on. Cognition is a foundationally metaphorical activity. The human is an *animal fingens*.

In 'On Truth and Lies in a Nonmoral Sense' (1873), Nietzsche writes:

> [. . .] one may certainly admire man as a mighty genius of construction, who succeeds in piling up an infinitely complicated dome of concepts upon an unstable foundation, and, as it were, on running water. Of course, in order to be supported by such a foundation, his construction must be like one constructed of spiders' webs: delicate enough to be carried along by the waves, strong enough not to be blown apart by every wind.[36]

This is how cognition is depicted in an aesthetic perspective. Like artists or virtuosic constructors we create forms of orientation, which must be as movably and elastically constituted as reality itself is fluid and changeful. All our forms of orientation are aesthetic in a threefold sense: they are produced poietically, structured with fictional means, and in their whole mode of being of that floating and fragile nature which had traditionally been attested only to aesthetic phenomena and had only been considered possible with these.

The suffusion of epistemological aestheticization in the twentieth century

Philosophy of science and philosophy

Is such an aesthetic view of cognition advocated only by exquisite – or seemingly eccentric – aestheticians such as Nietzsche? No. Nietzsche's views became increasingly commonplace in the twentieth century. Even this century's philosophy of science has gradually become 'Nietzschean'. Thus, Otto Neurath described our situation in a manner quite similar to Nietzsche's: 'We are like mariners who must rebuild their ship on the open sea, without ever being able to disassemble it in dock and reassemble it with the best components.'[37] This sentence from Neurath became the guiding maxim for the analytic philosopher Willard Van Orman Quine.[38] And even with Karl Popper we read that, 'just when we believed that we were standing on firm and safe ground, all things are in reality insecure and unstable'.[39] It can be seen that even philosophers of science, who certainly don't want to be Nietzscheans, cannot avoid sounding Nietzschean when addressing basic questions. The aesthetic constitution of reality is the view not just of a few aestheticians, but of all theoreticians reflecting on reality and science in this century. This is an insight which is indeed *due*.

More recent analytic (or post-analytic) philosophy – like Nietzsche and modern philosophies of science – is of the view that we have to operate 'upon an unstable foundation, and, as it were, on running water'. This is a consequence of the fact that the talk of a reality-in-itself has become empty of meaning on principle since there exists only 'reality-under-a-certain-description'[40] – and that means: in the spectrum of problematic (never absolutely justifiable) premises and as one version of reality alongside others.

Paul Feyerabend's was the most provocative formulation of the aesthetic character of truth when he pointed out that the sciences basically proceed no differently from the arts,[41] since both operate according to a style, and truth and reality in science are just as relative to style as in art: 'If one examines namely what a particular form of thought understands by these things, then one encounters not something which lies beyond the style of thought, but its own foundational assumptions: truth is whatever the style of thought says truth is.'[42]

Richard Rorty draws a revealing conclusion from these views from philosophy of science. He appeals for a 'poeticized culture'. By this he means a culture which knows that our 'fundaments' are all aesthetically constituted, are namely 'cultural artifacts' throughout which can only ever be scrutinized against other cultural artefacts but never against reality itself. A poeticized culture acknowledges this situation instead of further insisting in vain that 'we find the real wall behind the painted ones, the real touchstones of truth as opposed to touchstones which are merely cultural artifacts'. It appreciates the fact 'that *all* touchstones are such artifacts'.[43]

Scientific practice

Researchers in the natural sciences too have long since become aware of the importance of aesthetic elements for their pursuit of knowledge. Thus Bohr, Dirac, Einstein and Heisenberg had already argued aesthetically in critical passages, and Poincaré even bluntly explained that aesthetic and not, say, logical potency is a good mathematician's central skill.[44] More recently the effect was ground-breaking when Watson pointed out that he had only succeeded in deciphering the structure of DNA because he had assumed from the start that the solution would have to be of the utmost elegance – only with this aesthetic premiss did he manage to find the appropriate solution in reasonable time amongst the large number of those remaining theoretically open.[45] Today conscious and systematic attempts are being made to bring aesthetic factors to bear in the cognitive process. Recent approaches in the philosophy of science even attribute a causal function to changes in the aesthetic canon for scientific revolutions.[46] When confronted with theories such as that of the 'Big Bang' or the never-ending story of quarks you can scarcely do anything but take into account the great relevance of aesthetic and fictional factors.

An awareness of cognition's and reality's foundational aesthetic character is currently permeating all academic disciplines. Whether semiotics or system theory, whether in sociology, biology or microphysics, everywhere we are recognizing that there is no first or last fundament, rather that it's precisely in the dimension of 'fundaments' that we run into an aesthetic constitution. Thus the semioticians tell us that chains of signifiers always refer to other chains of signifiers and not, say, to an original signified; system theory teaches us that 'instead of having recourse to final unities' we only ever observe observations and describe descriptions;[47] and microphysics finds that wherever it tries to revert to things elementary it always encounters not the elementary, but new complexity.[48]

This basic aesthetic awareness has also long since pervaded the pores of society and the minds of individuals – in any case, much more than the prevalent academic anxiety and defensive public rhetoric would like to admit. Individuals' ability to deal with current aestheticization depends on an awareness of this on-principle aestheticization.

Conclusion

I shall summarize the development outlined here: truth, knowledge and reality have increasingly assumed aesthetic contours over the last two hundred years. Firstly, it has become evident that aesthetics' participation is foundational for our knowledge and our reality. This began with Kant's transcendental aesthetics and extends to the self-reflexion of today's natural sciences. Secondly, the view that cognition and reality are aesthetic in the nature of their being has increasingly established itself. This was Nietzsche's discovery, which has subsequently been expressed by others, above all with recourse to nautical metaphors, and which reaches through to today's constructivism. Reality is not a fixed given quantity, independent of cognition, but the object of a construction.

If earlier it was thought that aesthetics was concerned only with secondary, supplemental realities, then today we are recognizing that the aesthetic belongs to knowledge and reality directly at a base level. Traditional knowledge of reality sought to be objective, that is, fundamentalist; only the laws of genuine production were clarified through aesthetic phenomena. But, at the same time, categories for the understanding of the production of reality were actually being developed on the quiet. Since it has become clear to us that not only art, but other forms of our conduct too, through to cognition, exhibit the character of a production, these aesthetic categories – categories such as appearance, manoeuvrability, diversity, groundlessness or suspension – have become fundamental categories of reality.

And all of this was decreed not by some aestheticians or other, but was a recognition called for by science, the guiding authority of modernity itself. It prescribed an *epistemological aestheticization* – an on-principle aestheticization of knowledge, truth and reality – by which no question remains unaffected. This epistemological aestheticization is the legacy of modernity. If one is to talk of the contemporary standing of aesthetics, then one must keep in mind this protoaesthetics and face up to its assertions.

Today there is no single argument which is able to engage this aestheticization effectively.[49] Irrespective of whether one values it or not –

all thinkable objections will themselves be subject to it. If you go back to the foundations of argumentation then you regularly run into aesthetic options. Because, in modernity, truth has revealed itself to be an aesthetic category, defences rooted in truth are no longer able to beat back aestheticization. Science cannot keep us from the aesthetic wanton, it has itself switched to the latter's camp – not through flippancy, however, but through the pressure of insight.

3.   The relationship of the diverse forms of aestheticizations to one another

How are we to view the relationship to one another of the different levels of aestheticization addressed in the course of my account?[50] How do, firstly, the embellishing everyday surface aestheticization, secondly, the more profound technological and media aestheticization of our material and social reality, thirdly, the equally deep-reaching aestheticization of our practical attitudes in life and of moral orientation, and, fourthly, epistemological aestheticization relate to one another?

I have expanded on epistemological aestheticization so extensively because it is obviously the most fundamental of all the aestheticizations with which we're today concerned. It seems to me to form the actual substratum of current aestheticization processes and to explain their conspicuous acceptance. It operates as foil and engine, and also as counsel for these aestheticization processes. In that cognition and reality have turned out to be basically aesthetic, we have become generally prepared for aestheticization. That's why we are increasingly acceding to the transposition of former hardware into software, as is determining daily life in the wake of technological and media aestheticization. And for the same reason, we are enacting this deep-seated aestheticization in a sweeping surface aestheticization, realizing it, as it were, through to and within the skin of appearances, demonstrating it to ourselves *ad oculos*, practising it daily.

IV.   Perspectives of aesthetic criticism of aestheticization processes

In the meantime we appear, however, to have lurched into an extremely awkward situation with regard to the question raised at the beginning of section III, the question as to criteria which are capable of impeding aestheticization or of permitting criticism of certain of its manifestations. Truth, the criterion on which all hopes had been concentrated, is obviously unfit to intervene against aestheticization, since truth itself has largely become an aesthetically forged category in modernity. I had cast aside ethical criteria straight away for the same reason – ethics is today in the process of transforming itself into a subdiscipline of aesthetics. Does this mean that we have now been gratuitously handed over to aestheticization without any criteria?

Aesthetic criteria, nonetheless, remain. Although I previously set these aside before all else, this only *appeared* to be right. For, firstly, the fact that there are aesthetic criteria cannot be disputed. Aesthetics has always differentiated between the accomplished and the unaccomplished, better and worse, exemplary and digressive. And, secondly, it is precisely in a situation of global aestheticization that one expects aesthetic criteria to become especially relevant, and have the chance to attain particular regard. To back aesthetic criteria in a situation of universal aestheticization is thus more consistent than paradoxical.

Which individual aesthetic criteria are conceivable? Or to put it another way: how can Adorno's promise, that aesthetic sensitivity is always also an organ of its own self-criticism, be brought to bear in today's conditions?[51]

1. An objection to the turmoil of aestheticization

A basic aesthetic law states that our perception needs not only invigoration and stimulation, but delays, quiet areas and interruptions too. This law condemns to failure the presently epidemic trend for enhancement. Total aestheticization results in its own opposite. Where everything becomes beautiful, nothing is beautiful any more; continued excitement leads to indifference; aestheticization breaks into anaestheticization. It is, then, precisely aesthetic reasons which speak in favour of breaking through the turmoil of aestheticization.[52] Amidst the hyperaestheticization aesthetically fallow areas are necessary.[53]

Aesthetic reflexion will not allow itself to become the agent of an aestheticization which in truth is tantamount to an anaestheticization – of the production of insensitivity, of the stupor arising through being constantly aesthetically overwrought. Aesthetic thinking opposes the turmoil of aestheticization and the pseudo-sensitivity of an Experience Society.

2. In favour of a blind-spot culture

What is currently important is not a hyperaestheticization of culture of this sort, but – running more counter to this – the development of a *blind-spot culture*. What is meant by this? Reflected aesthetics always encourages one to be aware of the twofold relationship between heeding and excluding. To see something is constantly to oversee something else. There is no vision without a blind-spot. Developed sensibility is attentive of this and addresses the consequences.[54]

These consequences reach far beyond the narrow realm of design or aesthetics.[55] The indications here – unlike those in the superficial trend of embellishment – are of a societal consequence of aestheticization which is worth pursuing. A genuinely aestheticized culture would be sensitive to differences and exclusions – not only in relation to the forms of art and design, but equally in daily life and towards social forms of life.

Of course that is not to say that regular museum visits would make us better social beings. Firstly, it is not the enjoyment of art as such, but only a reflected aesthetic consciousness according to today's conditions that affords the potential for sensibility which can also become socially relevant; and, secondly, its effect is to be understood not as a direct, but as an indirect one. What is made possible, however, is a transfer of aesthetic sensibility to social issues through a specific analogy between conditions in art and in life. Their common denominator is denoted by the watchword 'plurality'.

Modern societies are characterized by a plurality of divergent forms of life within one and the same society. They do not form a uniform band, but represent a loose network of highly varying forms of life. Their recognition is called for both democratically and in terms of civil rights. What matters in practice is to pay attention to each of these forms of life's own logic and to safeguard their own rights – instead of wanting to rate them *partout* according to a single measure and cut them to shape. This societal problem structure and assignment is obviously analogous to that of art, for twentieth-century art is also characterized by a plurality of highly varying paradigms. Artists do not simply rinse off a well-defined programme by the name of 'art', rather they produce different versions of art. Duchamp's Ready-Mades cannot be measured against Picasso's cubism, nor this against Malewitsch's suprematism or Kandinsky's abstraction. Hence for aesthetic judgement from the standpoint of modernity a broad knowledge of, and adequate practice in, these paradigms and their varying sets of criteria is called for. It would be an elementary categorial mistake to want to judge a surrealist work according to constructivist criteria, or conversely a constructivist work according to surrealist criteria – in general: one work according to the set of criteria of a type alien to it, or all works according to a single set of criteria. Such a method characterizes the philistine.

What is increasingly self-evident with respect to art ought to be elevated to a social standard too. For here too the same aspects of plurality, of specifity and partiality apply, as well as the tendentious blindness of perspectives for one another, and here too recognition and justice are called for. In that reflected aesthetic consciousness is sensitized for fundamental differences as a matter of principle it is able to recognize and to respect the peculiarity and irreducibility of forms of life more easily than widespread social consciousness, which denies alterities rather than acknowledging them. Hence an aesthetically sensitized awareness can also become effective within the life-world by illuminating, clarifying and helping out. The readiness is constituively built in to be critically attentive of borders and exclusions, to see through imperialisms and – being, as a matter of principle, allergic to injustice – to intervene wherever excessive domination is found and wherever the rights of the oppressed must be espoused.[56] To this extent aesthetic culture is also capable of contributing indirectly to political culture.

The extent to which political culture is *de facto* dependent upon aesthetic culture can be made clear through the example of tolerance. Tolerance without sensibility would be merely an empty principle. Imagine just once a person who has made all of the maxims of tolerance their own perfectly, yet who in everyday life lacks the sensibility even to notice that the intuitions of others are different on principle and not just a matter of some arbitrary lapse, that is, that it's a case not of a deficit, but of a cultural difference. Such a person would never be embarrassed by so much as having to make use of his fine maxims of tolerance, but rather would incessantly practise imperialisms and oppressions – but with the clearest of consciences and in the securest of beliefs that he's a tolerant person. Sensibility for differences is thus a real condition for tolerance. – Perhaps we live in a society which talks too much of tolerance but possesses too little sensibility.

Through its sensitization effects aestheticization can intervene in societal processes. I see chances here in aestheticization which I don't see in the tendencies to embellish which are mostly in the foreground where the talk is of aestheticization.

3. Résumé

The current aestheticization is neither to be affirmed nor to be rejected without qualification. To do either of the two would be equally cheap and wrong. In the thought of epistemological aestheticization I have tried to name an on-principle reason which makes the modern inevitability of aestheticization processes comprehensible. If we look at this profound aestheticization, then we are concerned with a form of aestheticization which seems to be irrefutable. Its non-fundamentalism forms our modern 'basis'. If, however, we look at surface aestheticization, much cause for criticism exists. The on-principle justification of aestheticization processes in no way means that every form of aestheticization is to be sanctioned. I have lastly made clear that it is precisely from an aesthetic standpoint that objections to current manifestations of aestheticization are both possible and necessary. Finally, if we look at the social and political implications of an aestheticized culture, that is, at the sensitization for differences and the development of a blind-spot culture, then the indications in this respect are of the chances and responsibilities of a new topicality of the aesthetic. Only the on-principle justification of aestheticization processes, together with specific criticism of certain forms of aestheticization and the development of the opportunities for sensitization, will permit us to bring about something just from the midst of aestheticization.

Notes

This essay was originally published as 'Ästhetisierungsprozesse – Phänomene, Unterscheid-ungen, Perspektiven', *Deutsche Zeitschrift für Philosophie*, 41(1), 1993, pp. 7–29, and first appeared in English in an abridged form, in *Theory, Culture & Society*, 13(1), February 1991, pp. 1–24. It has been revised for this volume.

1. Cf. Gerhard Schulze, *Die Erlebnisgesellschaft. Kultursoziologie der Gegenwart* (Frankfurt a.M.: Campus 1992).

2. In the age of pixel technology the photo too, formerly a direct documentation of reality, has become unreliable as a matter of principle. In still being able to count on the old belief in reality, whilst at the same time availing oneself of newer, manipulatory technology, opportunities for perfect deception open up.

3. Video games are a case in point. They are an interactive form of television, definitively detached from any reporting obligations and references to reality. That they prevalently present not pleasant, but rather dramatic, warlike and shocking realities is an indication of a need resulting from aestheticization. In time, aestheticization as such makes everything arbitrary and stale and thus awakens the need for ever stronger stimuli. At the same time one believes it possible to deliver these innocuously in the aesthetic medium. Video games, therefore, by way of compensation, offer the hard reality which is increasingly receding from daily life through aestheticization processes. – A good share of today's art too sees its purpose in the mediation of hard reality, corporeality and drastic experiences – that is, all that which we have lost in reality as a result of aestheticization processes. In the same way, the everyday adventure industry seeks to present emergency without risk. Video war games, body art and bungee-jumping form a family.

4. Cf. here for a critical consideration: Luc Ferry, *Homo aestheticus* (Paris: Grasset 1990).

5. Its affirmative version today stems from Foucault, who is all too sweepingly rated as being subversive. Foucault's 'aesthetics of existence' is largely an acclamation of aesthetic self-styling in contemporary spirit. Of one's life one should make 'an oeuvre that carries certain aesthetic values and meets certain stylistic criteria' (Michel Foucault, *The History of Sexuality, Vol. 2: The Use of Pleasure*, trans. Robert Hurley, New York: Vintage 1990, p. 11). Although Foucault thinks that independent and resistant subjects would emerge in this way, *de facto* they instead turn out adapted and fit themselves into the objective aestheticization like decorative puppets. Robert Wilson and Botho Strauß introduced us to this new type of zombie. The aesthetic subjects of the brave new world are in truth less self-determined and wilful than they are adapted and controllable. Even their authenticity is either high-spirited or volitive in character. – The borders between these types and Foucault's maxims are at least fluid.

6. Baumgarten created the term 'aesthetics' in 1735, first lectured on the subject in 1742, and published the first book with this title in 1750.

7. Alexander Gottlieb Baumgarten, *Aesthetica* (Frankfurt a.d. Oder 1750; reprint: Hildesheim: Olms 1970), § 1.

8. Georg Wilhelm Friedrich Hegel, *Aesthetics. Lectures on Fine Art*, vol. 1, trans. T.M. Knox (Oxford: Clarendon Press 1975), p. 1.

9. Konrad Fiedler, 'Kunsttheorie und Ästhetik', in *Schriften zur Kunst*, ed. Gottfried Boehm (Munich: Fink 1991), vol. 2, pp. 9–24, here p. 9.

10. Ludwig Wittgenstein, *Philosophical Investigations*, trans. G.E.M. Anscombe (Oxford: Macmillan, 2nd edition, 1958), p. 36^e [77].

11. Ibid., p. 31^e [65].

12. Ibid.

13. For reasons of space I restrict myself to naming the main meanings – their number alone is large enough. The analysis should suffice to convey the peculiarity of the family resemblances, which will then also mark other meanings of the expression 'aesthetic'.

14. The German *Sinnenhaft* can be rendered only somewhat awkwardly in English. Hence 'sensuous' is meant here, and for the remainder of this passage, as 'of, relating to, or derived from the senses', but not as containing reference to the appreciation, or otherwise, of what's perceived (trans.).

15. Immanuel Kant, 'First Introduction to the Critique of Judgment', in Kant, *Critique of Judgment*, trans. Werner S. Pluhar (Indianapolis: Hackett 1987), pp. 385–441, here p. 413 [H 30].

16. As Kant called this distinction (ibid., pp. 57f. [B 22]).

17. In the Introduction to his *Aesthetics* Hegel discusses the understanding of aesthetics as 'callistics' – as the science of the beautiful.

18. This meaning has been in circulation ever since Schiller, Hegel and Kierkegaard, and was exemplarily embodied by artists like Baudelaire and Wilde.

19. Johann Gottfried Goethe, *Maximen und Reflexionen; Goethes Werke* (Hamburger Ausgabe), 7th edition, vol. 12 (Munich 1973), pp. 365–547, here p. 432 [488].

20. The elevatory semantic element could most easily give the impression of being such an essentialistic candidate. But there are versions of the aesthetic which direct themselves precisely against this element in pleading for a turn back to the raw, primary sensuous as a countermove to the standard transcending of the primary sensuous – think, say, of *art brut*. What's more, even if it were in fact to inhere in all meanings, the elevatory element as such would not be enough to constitute the concept of the aesthetic. It is, taken by itself, in no way specific enough to generate by itself the meaning 'aesthetic'; it occurs in equal measure in other spheres which are nonetheless far from being able to be called aesthetic – such as, for example, in the moral or cognitive sphere. A second moment at least – such as the aisthetic one – must come on top of the elevatory one for the meaning 'aesthetic' to arise.

21. Wittgenstein, *Philosophical Investigations*, p. 32^e [67].

22. In Wittgenstein the corresponding passage reads, in context, 'Consider, for example, the proceedings that we call "games". [. . .] if you look at them you will not see something that is common to all, but similarities, relationships, and a whole series of them at that.' (Ibid., p. 31^e [66].)

23. Ibid., p. 32^e [66].

24. 'And the strength of the thread does not reside in the fact that some one fibre runs through its whole length, but in the overlapping of many fibres.' (Ibid., p. 32^e [67].)

25. Wittgenstein explains this with reference to the concepts 'language' and 'game': '[. . .] I can give the concept "number" rigid limits [. . .], that is, use the word "number" for a rigidly limited concept, but I can also use it so that the extension of the concept is not closed by a frontier. And this is how we do use the word "game". [. . .] What still counts as a game and what no longer does? Can you give the boundary? No. You can draw one; for none has so far been drawn. (But that never troubled you before when you used the word "game".) But then the use of the word is unregulated, the "game" we play with it is unregulated. – It is not everywhere circumscribed by rules.' (Ibid., p. 33^e [68].) Concluding this consideration, Wittgenstein then says that hence every explanation of such a concept – corresponding to its manifoldness and overlapping structure – must be inexact, and to this he adds: 'Only let us understand what "inexact" means. For it does not mean "unusable".' (Ibid., p. 41^e [88].)

26. Already Meier – Baumgarten's student, who had brought the latter's new ideas into circulation, even before the publication of the *Aesthetica*, with his text *Anfangsgründe aller schönen Wissenschaften* (Halle a.d. Saale 1748–50) – demanded: 'One must know all the meanings of an expression which it has already received through common and educated usage' (Georg Friedrich Meier, *Auszug aus der Vernunftlehre*, Halle 1752, quoted from *Kant's gesammelte Schriften*, Akademie Ausgabe, vol. 16, Berlin 1924, pp. 3–872, here p. 818 [§ 446]).

27. Wittgenstein, *Philosophical Investigations*, p. 20^e [43]).

28. As is well known, Karl Heinz Bohrer has lamented political provincialism in the Federal Republic of Germany and called for more aesthetics in politics. Conversely he himself supports a form of provincialism in aesthetics: a decidedly artistic provincialism. Bohrer argues for the limitation of the aesthetic to art, even to great art or emphatic art (cf. Karl Heinz Bohrer, 'Die Grenzen des Ästhetischen', in *Die Aktualität des Ästhetischen*, ed. Wolfgang Welsch, Munich: Fink 1993, pp. 48–64). He hereby declares the artistic province to be the world of the aesthetic as such. I call this aesthetic-theoretical provincialism, since one is a provincial not in that one is at home in a particular province, but in holding this province for unique and mistaking it for the world. – Bohrer's options, incidentally, don't simply differ, but contradict one another. When he adjures more aesthetic politics, he himself has a transartistic sense of the aesthetic in mind in which the aesthetic is understood 'not only as a criterion for artistic imagination, but far more for the way in which people deal with each other too' (Karl Heinz Bohrer, *Nach der Natur. Über Politik und Ästhetik*, Munich: Hanser 1988, p. 19).

However, when he talks of aesthetics in relation to art, he favours autonomy without reference to practice. As such his political aesthetics and his artistic aesthetics mutually contradict.

29. If taken absolutely, the autonomy-theorem has always been subject to misunderstanding. This could be learned even with Baudelaire, who proclaimed *l'art pour l'art* to be, at the same time, the only remaining existential ideal for the few; Gehlen and Adorno (each in his own way) have theoretically formulated the connection between autonomy and societal reference in showing how autonomy always has a precise societal function as its reverse side. – A detailed portrayal of the dialectic of autonomy can be found in my *Vernunft. Die zeitgenössische Vernunftkritik und das Konzept der transversalen Vernunft* (Frankfurt a.M.: Suhrkamp 1995, stw 1996), pp. 464–484.

30. Furthermore, one has cause to do this even for the sake of a sufficient understanding of art. For art today, even where it sets itself against everyday aestheticization, is etched by it all the same. Art opposes, filled with hope, strenuously or desperately – often too, in vain. It cannot, as it is, be overlooked in general that art has reacted very consciously to the societal state of the aesthetic time and time again. Wherever in the world sensibility has been under threat, art – heedful of its old bond – understands itself as the harbinger and rescuer of the sensuous (Dubuffet); where embellishment is rife, it can see its responsibility in countering this and behaving decidedly demurely (*arte povera*, concept art) – just as earlier, in an aesthetically more sparing world, it had championed the Elysium of beauty. Art reacts not only to art, but constantly to reality and particularly to the state of the aesthetic therein.

31. Schiller said 'it is play, and play alone, that makes Man complete and displays at once his twofold nature'; 'Man [. . .] is only wholly Man when he is playing' (Friedrich Schiller, *On the Aesthetic Education of Man*, trans. Reginald Snell, Bristol: Thoemmes 1994, here 15th Letter, pp. 79 and 80).

32. 'The "Oldest System-Programme" of German Idealism', in *Hegel Selections*, ed. M.J. Inwood (London/New York: Macmillan 1989), p. 87.

33. The next essay in this edition, 'Basic Aesthetic Features in Current Thinking', contains a more detailed account of the considerations presented here in section III.2. I have, however, retained the brief account here so as to safeguard the completeness of the tableau for which the current essay aims.

34. Immanuel Kant, *Critique of Pure Reason*, trans. Norman Kemp Smith (New York: St Martin's Press 1965), here p. 19 [B XI] (modified) and p. 23 [B XVIII].

35. Incidentally, Kant pondered, at the beginning of this transcendental aesthetic, whether or not it might be better to comply with the meaning of aesthetic as had just been developed by Baumgarten – that is (as Kant understood Baumgarten) as the attempt 'to bring the critical treatment of the beautiful under rational principles', thus reserving the title aesthetics for 'that doctrine [. . .] which is true science' (ibid., p. 66 [B 35 f.]). In the 'General Observations on Transcendental Aesthetic' Kant additionally underlines that his Transcendental Aesthetic should have 'that certainty and freedom from doubt which is required from any theory that is to serve as an organon' (ibid., p. 85 [B 63]). For Kant the legitimacy and necessity of denoting epistemological aesthetics 'aesthetics' was beyond question. That should be a warning to those who are far too rash in wanting to short-circuit definitionally aesthetics and art.

36. Friedrich Nietzsche, 'On Truth and Lies in a Nonmoral Sense', in *Philosophy and Truth. Selections from Nietzsche's Notebooks of the Early 1870's*, trans. and ed. Daniel Breazeale (Atlantic Highlands, NJ: Humanities Press 1979), pp. 79–91, here p. 85.

37. Otto Neurath, 'Protokollsätze', in *Erkenntnis*, 3, 1932/3, pp. 204–214, here p. 206.

38. It forms the epigraph to his *Word and Object* (Cambridge, Mass.: MIT Press 1960), p. vii.

39. Karl Popper, 'The Logic of the Social Sciences', in Popper, *In Search of a Better World*, trans. Laura J. Bennett (London/New York: Routledge 1992), pp. 64–81, here p. 65.

40. Richard Rorty, *Philosophy and the Mirror of Nature* (Princeton: Princeton University Press 1979), p. 378.

41. Cf. Paul Feyerabend, *Wissenschaft als Kunst* (Frankfurt a.M.: Suhrkamp 1984).

42. Ibid., p. 77.

43. Richard Rorty, *Contingency, Irony and Solidarity* (Cambridge/New York: Cambridge

University Press 1989), pp. 53f. For the concept of this poeticized culture, see also pp. 65, 67–69.

44. Cf. *On Aesthetics in Science* (Boston: MIT Press 1981) edited by Judith Wechsler as well as the collected works of Subrahmanyan Chandrasekhar entitled *Truth and Beauty. Aesthetics and Motivations in Science* (Chicago: University of Chicago Press 1987).

45. Cf. James D. Watson, *The Double Helix. A Personal Account of the Discovery of the Structure of DNA* (London: Penguin 1970).

46. Cf. James W. McAllister, 'Truth and Beauty in Scientific Reason', in *Synthese*, 78, 1989, pp. 25–51, as well as Mary Hesse, 'The Explanatory Function of Metaphor', in Hesse, *Revolutions and Reconstructions in the Philosophy of Science* (Bloomington: Indiana University Press 1980), pp. 111–124.

47. Niklas Luhmann, *Die Wissenschaft der Gesellschaft* (Frankfurt a.M.: Suhrkamp 1990), p. 717.

48. Incidentally, Montaigne too had already said that we only ever make comments on comments: 'Our opinions are grafted upon one another' (Michel de Montaigne, *The Complete Essays of Montaigne*, trans. Donald M. Frame, Stanford: Stanford University Press 1965, here III.13, p. 818).

49. Similarly Rüdiger Bubner observes: 'In fact no sufficient means are available to designate truth as truth and appearance as appearance without taking the risk of becoming involved in the turmoil. In the aestheticization of daily surroundings portrayed, categories critical for knowledge, as those for deceipt are being desolated.' ('Mutmaßliche Umstellungen im Verhältnis von Leben und Kunst', in Bubner, *Ästhetische Erfahrung*, Frankfurt a.M.: Suhrkamp 1989, pp. 121–142, here p. 139.) Bubner also records the key role of modern scientific knowledge in the irrefutability of aestheticization processes: 'The long-since effected breakdown of the undoubted dependability of the scientific picture of the world enforces [. . .] aestheticization [. . .]. Scientific progress unintentionally refutes the naive prospect of finality which accompanies it.' (Ibid.)

50. In *Ästhetische Zeiten? Zwei Wege der Ästhetisierung* (Saarbrücken: Deutscher Werkbund 1992) I concentrated on the presentation of two aestheticization paths. The one – corresponding to traditional aesthetics – has beauty, the other – corresponding to the epistemological aestheticization – truth as its focus. The first concerns the shaping, the second the apprehension of reality. Both paths began in the eighteenth century, but in terms of their outset and their results they are highly different, in philosophy and art as well as in reality. Philosophy soon applied the aesthetics of beauty for its own ends. This can be inferred from Kant's third critique, Schiller's *Letters on the Aesthetic Education of Man* and 'The "Oldest System-Programme" of German Idealism'. This line (through which philosophy was promoted to philosophy's top position within a few years) seemingly amounts to a eulogy of beauty, of aesthetics and art. In reality, however, what's concerned is an act of philosophical usurpation – with highly dubious results. Aesthetics was now to achieve what philosophy had been traditionally striving for, but with which it had increasingly experienced problems: achieving totality and universal reconciliation. Later on this beauty-related aestheticization was continued in the theories of the total work of art (Gesamtkunstwerk) and in the Arts and Crafts, Werkbund and Bauhaus movements. Aestheticization, as is still believed, was to bring improvement, because beautification brings about totality. Today all of this – along with the misrecognized problematic that total aestheticization in truth can amount to aesthetic terror and anaestheticization – is running into the aestheticization of the everyday. In critical opposition to this I drew attention to epistemological aestheticization as another path of aestheticization. This effects the structure of our understanding of reality – prior to all design. This line of development seems to me to be the more important and more promising. At the same time it is the line which is commonly overlooked in usual debate on aestheticization. Having both lines in mind is a condition for a sufficient understanding and a suitable evaluation. The tandem approach thus named can be used as a dependable probe in diagnosing both historically and in the present day. – Incidentally it is interesting that in art of the twentieth century, although some movements continue to work towards the beauty-like aestheticization, important outsets – from cubism, Dada and surrealism through to concept art

– leave this path and have turned to aesthetic ideals which obviously correspond to epistemological aestheticization. David Rabinowitsch provides a revealing example of how present-day artists can comprehend Kant's *Critique of Pure* Reason as the breakthrough towards the world of ideas on which their artistic deeds are based. He states that 'Kant's first "critique" created [. . .] the basic conditions for the revolutionary developments in the visual arts' (David Rabinowitsch, 'Bemerkungen zu den "Gravitational Vehicles"', Opening Speech for the exhibition 'Gravitional Vehicles', Gallery St Stefan, Vienna, 9 June 1990, manuscript p. 4). Kant is to have showed there that 'already the physical world is a product of the human constitution' (ibid., p. 3) and the artistic constructivism of the twentieth century as well as Rabinowitsch's own work are to have moved within the track of this discovery (ibid.).

51. 'It is precisely the nerves most highly-developed aesthetically that now find self-righteous aestheticism intolerable.' (Theodor W. Adorno, *Minima Moralia. Reflections from Damaged Life*, trans. E.F.N. Jephcott, London/New York: Verso 1974, p. 145 [95].)

52. That provides the opportunity to point out an alternative possibility of aestheticization. In contrast to the usual one, which carries out the spectacular furnishing of reality with designer gems, this concentrates not on singular objects and their superficial appearance, but on their cultural and functional context. It attempts a total design which seeks to optimize the relationship between the urban, functional, emotional and cultural aspects. With this, the result – unlike with embellishment – can be wholly inconspicuous. A particularly convincing example of this is Robert Irwin's project for the airport in Miami (1986), about which Arthur C. Danto writes: 'One of the goals of art in such projects is [. . .] to "heighten awareness". Not to heighten awareness of art as art, but of the dimensions and features of life that art raises to the highest powers of enhancement while remaining invisible, directing the viewer's sensibilities with a kind of aesthetic Hidden Hand. [. . .] Anything can be art without having to look like art at all.' (Arthur C. Danto, 'Art in Response', in *Robert Irwin*, ed. Russell Ferguson, Los Angeles: Museum of Contemporary Art 1993, pp. 129–151, here p. 151.)

53. Cf. the essay 'Contemporary Art in Public Space: A Feast for the Eyes or an Annoy-ance?' in the present volume.

54. I detailed this more closely in 'Ästhetik und Anästhetik' in my *Ästhetisches Denken* (Stuttgart: Reclam 1990), pp. 9–40. (Forthcoming in English as 'Aesthetics and Anaesthetics', in *Aesthetic Thinking*, trans. John Bailiff, Atlantic Highlands, NJ: Humanities Press 1998.)

55. I have discussed consequences relevant for this in my *Ästhetische Zeiten? Zwei Wege der Ästhetisierung* (see note 50).

56. Cf. for the ethical implications of aesthetic awareness the essay 'Aesthet/hics: Ethical Implications and Consequences of Aesthetics' in the present volume.

2

BASIC AESTHETIC FEATURES IN CONTEMPORARY THINKING

I. A due revision?

If, as this essay's title suggests aesthetic elements were in fact not merely decoration and accessories, but were rather to determine the basic features of thinking, then Plato and his successors would not have triumphed in the Occident. In Book X of the *Republic* Plato banished all poets, including Homer, from the state. Poetry and art brought too much danger, they allured people to the wrong things, both cognitively and emotionally. Philosophy, on the other hand, would show us the right way. Whereas art ensnares us in appearance and deception and makes us hostages to our passions, philosophy would raise us above our passions and allow us to glimpse the true and unchanging.

Hence nothing would endanger this Platonic project and the Platonic veneration of philosophy more than if philosophy should prove itself to be artistic in nature by exhibiting basic aesthetic features. Philosophy's well-being depends on the separation from the aesthetic; being mixed up with the aesthetic means its woe.

This Platonic constellation was very influential in the Occident. We find it again for instance – under a Christian auspice – in the twelfth century with Bernard of Clairvaux's polemics against abbot Suger of Saint-Denis.[1] And it is still effective – under the auspices of rationality theory – in the late twentieth century when Jürgen Habermas accuses Derrida of levelling the 'genre distinction between philosophy and literature'.[2] Although this no longer leads to an exile from the state, it still suffices for an exile from philosophy. The institutionally sanctioned concept of philosophy demands a clear line of demarcation from the aesthetic.

If I'm right in what the title suggests, this tradition must in the meantime have become questionable and flawed. The aesthetic would have to be not just occasionally and outwardly appended to thought – as ornamentation or an aid, as may (for reasons of presentation, for the sake of clarity, for educational purposes, and so on) sometimes be desirable – rather aesthetic elements would have to belong to the *core* of philosophy, would have to be inherent within it. Then, however, an axiom would indeed have fallen: a traditional philosophical, in fact a basic occidental, model would have become decrepit.

Now I actually do think that there is cause to speak of such a revision. And I even defend my claim, that basic aesthetic features are inherent in today's thinking, in a doubly strong sense.

Firstly, I would like to make plausible the idea that basic aesthetic features determine our notions of *truth*. The salient point of the more recent situation seems to me to be characterized precisely by the fact that the aesthetic has gained the right to residence in the centre of philosophical claims to validity, in the perspective of truth. The aesthetic has, so to speak, forced its way into the sanctum of philosophy.

Secondly, I link this thesis with the further-reaching claim that truth, strictly speaking, has always been aesthetically founded, just that traditionally one didn't want to admit this. I don't think I'm actually saying anything new with regard to the *status* of truth, but only with regard to the *apprehension* of truth. What was discovered some considerable time ago and what I propose to defend is an aesthetic – or semi-aesthetic – constitution of truth. You cannot adequately speak of truth at all without taking into consideration foundational aesthetic elements in the configuration of what we call 'truth'. Every thorough analysis uncovers, in the constitution of truth itself, what once counted as its enemy and counterpart: the aesthetic. This is to be shown. Thus the theme of the following deliberations is a *cognitive*, that is, an *epistemological aestheticization*.

This epistemological aestheticization is not to be confused, or even equated with the beauty-based or artistic aestheticization prevalent today.[3] Whereas the latter assumes the foremost position in the convolution of current aestheticization processes (as the previous essay attempted to show), the foundational rank belongs to the epistemological aestheticization. Hence this – in addition to the short account in the previous essay (section III.2) – is to be set out here expressly.

II.   What do we call 'aesthetic', and what does the term mean?

Above all, however, more precise clarification is needed of what we actually mean when we say 'aesthetic'. Obviously all sorts of things – and things quite different from each other.[4]

1.   Standard semantics

Firstly, there is the meaning *relating to art*. The usual talk of the aesthetic refers to art; and more closely to art *as* art (in contrast, say, to art as a commodity); and, closer still, to art as the object of our esteem and evaluation. But this art-related – I also call it the *artistic* – meaning of the aesthetic is not the only one, let alone the original one.

With Baumgarten, the founding father of aesthetics who gave it its name, aesthetics by no means had art as its object. Its point of reference was far more the cognitive faculty. In particular it was to serve to improve the lower, the *sensuous* cognitive faculty. This sense-related – this *aisthetic* (from the Greek *aisthetos* = 'sensuous', 'perceptible') – meaning of the aesthetic was the first historically. The name 'aesthetics' is also derived from it.[5]

A third point of reference for the aesthetic is the *beautiful*. We call something aesthetic which exhibits superior form, and whose highest graduation we usually denote as beauty. Viewed historically this third meaning – you could call it the callistic one – forms the bridge between the two initially named, that is, between the artistic and the aisthetic concepts of the aesthetic.[6] Other aspects which we associate with the term 'aesthetic' can effortlessly be added to this third element of meaning, in which beauty stands in the foreground: aspects of reforming, of cultivation, of refinement, of artificiality.

Besides which, beauty is not traditionally the only noble predicate of art. A tendency towards the constriction to the beautiful exists only so long as you cling to comprehensibility for the senses as the definiens of the aesthetic. But art has always sought to transcend the power of the senses to comprehend – therein lies the significance of the category of the sublime. The aesthetics of the sublime does not bow down before the dictate of sensibility, but would rather be an aesthetics of the intellect. Kant called the sensation of the sublime an 'intellectual feeling' (*Geistesgefühl*).[7]

With this the most common semantic areas of the term 'aesthetic' ought to have been outlined: the *artistic*, the *aisthetic* and the *callistic-sublime*. In the following I shall call these predicates the *standard predicates* of the aesthetic. As can be seen, three quite different definitions are concerned. They do, of course, exhibit overlaps and possible associations too, but an all-pervading uniform 'essence' of the aesthetic does not exist.

2. The aesthetic as a type

But the *brisance* of the aesthetic lies not in the palette listed until now, that is, neither in the areas of reference named (art, the senses) nor in the singular predicates named (beautiful, sublime, or stirring, comical, and so on). It results far more from the fact that the aesthetic can evolve into a universal *type*. This occurs for instance wherever it is declared to be a type of life. This is known to us under the heading 'aestheticism' – say with Charles Baudelaire or Oscar Wilde. Aestheticism is an attitude which considers, evaluates and shapes *everything* in accordance with the measures of aesthetic criteria.[8]

That the aesthetic does not remain restricted to one region but becomes a potentially universal type is made possible by the dynamics of modernity – by its differentiation and autonomization of aspects of validity. In the wake of this it is almost to be expected that the autonomization will, at least occasionally, develop through to absolutism. That this is actually the case with the aesthetic is due, amongst other things, to the factual development of modernity. For modernity – contrary to its idea of the equiponderance of the cognitive, practical and aesthetic – had theoretically led to a dominance of the cognitive and practically established a dominance of the economic. Against the tank of modernity which thus arose, against this 'steely housing'[9] of modernity, people then backed the explosive power of the aesthetic time and time again. In unliveable conditions the aesthetic alone was to be able to make a decent life possible again. In such ways the modern aesthetic became a potentially universal type, in whose language everything can be said, according to whose grammatical models everything can be declined and conjugated.

3.   Semantics of state: the aesthetic as a mode of being

In the transition to the aesthetic as a type the aesthetic's semantic chromosome set reforms itself at the same time. The senses, art, beauty, the sublime, and so on – that is, the standard predicates of the aesthetic – can still be spoken of, but other outlooks now take first place: the poietic, the imaginative and the fictional as well as designations such as appearance, mobility, suspension. In the following I shall call these the aesthetic's *predicates of state*. They characterize the aesthetic as a mode of being. That these are now coming to the fore is due to the fact that the autonomized aesthetic can no longer be understood with recourse to a preordained reality, but must be determined from its own conditions alone. As something autonomous it can no longer be something imitating reality or culminating in ideals. Hence the principle of the 'production of reality' is becoming the aesthetic's new guide.[10] It's to precisely this that the aesthetic's predicates of state refer. They express what's specific about aesthetic realities.

4.   The primary character and universality of the aesthetic

The aesthetic could certainly have been apprehended much earlier – from antiquity onwards – as a mode of being. To this extent the use of predicates such as 'appearance', 'poiesis' and 'fiction' with a view to the aesthetic is not unfamiliar. In modern conditions, however, two important changes come about. Firstly, these predicates of state – precisely because the aesthetic is now conceived of as original and no longer as derived – become the primary predicates of the aesthetic. And secondly, the aesthetic mode of being becomes relevant no longer only to aesthetics, but is understood as a general mode of being. A particular contribution to this is made by the conception – one general to the modern age and specifically idealist-romantic – that reality is not something given, but a fabrication – that reality exhibits the character of a construct. The aesthetic's predicates of state are hence capable, so far as it is precisely fabrications' mode of being that they characterize, of now advancing to being fundamental predicates of the understanding of reality in general. To modern aesthetics belongs a tendency towards poeticization and aestheticization – and to the modern world, a tendency to apprehend reality increasingly as an aesthetic phenomenon.

This view was established in idealism and was advocated for example by Hölderlin and Schelling.[11] In romanticism it then achieved widespread bearing, say with Friedrich Schlegel and Novalis.[12] But Nietzsche became the paradigmatic author for the understanding of the aesthetic as being both an elementary and comprehensive mode of being. He declared the aesthetic to be the paradigm for everything – for life, just as for truth and knowledge. Thus, as early as in 1872, in the *Birth of Tragedy*, he stated that 'only as an *aesthetic phenomenon* is existence and the world *justified*'.[13] Later he understood this increasingly as being a consequence of the constructed character of being, the world and reality. Thus, already in 1873 in 'On Truth and Lies in a Nonmoral Sense', he set out how all our notions of reality are underlain by 'freely inventive' human activity and hence by an '*aesthetic* relation'.[14] According to Nietzsche, aesthetics constitutes our most fundamental and outermost horizon. 'We can't get away from aesthetics [. . .] we have the essence of a world which *people* have gradually *created*: *their* aesthetics.'[15]

Traditionally the aesthetic mode of being had been conceived of as a particular and secondary one, which was firstly relevant only for objects of human origin and secondly to be subordinated to the foundational mode of being of the real. In modern conditions, however, a principalization and universalization of the aesthetic occurs. The notion that aesthetic categories could be suited to the understanding of even the elementary and general constitution of reality is suggesting itself more and more forcefully. The place of the classical ontological categories of being, reality, constancy, actuality, and so on, is now being taken by aesthetic categories of state such as appearance, mobility, baselessness and suspension. In previous centuries a second set of categories had been developed in the shadow, so to speak, of the primary categories of reality (and only with regard to the secondary realities of human fabrication) which then suddenly – once reality itself had idealistically, romantically, historically, and so on, revealed itself to be a fabrication generally – proved itself to be suitable for the understanding of the primary and universal reality too.

To what extent is this transition – through which aesthetic categories become the basic categories of reality and our cognition – justified? And how exactly is it to be understood? This is what I would like to attempt to explain in the following.

5.   *Criticism of the hyperbolic claims of the aesthetic*

But before doing this, I don't want to hide the fact that the new apprehension and expansion of the aesthetic – well justified as it might be –

stands, at the same time, in the crossfire of criticism. The intrusion of the
aesthetic into the sphere of truth, its epistemological fundamentalization,
are considered dangerous and intolerable.

In this sense Habermas, for example, has criticized Nietzsche's universalization of the aesthetic and censured subsequent forms of this strategy. He
has done so even with regard to Horkheimer and Adorno. They are
supposed to have fatally allowed themselves to be inspired by Nietzsche's
primacy of aesthetics and his questioning of classical expectations of
reason. It's precisely because Nietzsche stands in the background of the
Dialectic of Enlightenment that Horkheimer and Adorno, in Habermas's
view, have arrived at 'an uninhibited scepticism regarding reason'.[16]

It would be both tempting and necessary to go into detail in this respect
– into lots of detail. This, however, is not the place to do so. I would just
like to express one suspicion – so as to follow up on this. I fear that
Habermas's distancing from the aesthetic sets out too late – too late by far.
The 'entry into postmodernity' may have taken place with Nietzsche,[17] the
fundamental aestheticization of reality and thinking, however, had already
begun far earlier. That is to say a hundred years before Nietzsche, and with
an author from whom Habermas would also not want to distance himself:
with Kant.

III. Epistemological aestheticization

My basic thesis reads: the new fundamentality and universality of the
aesthetic is the consequence of an *epistemological* aestheticization. In the
course of this the aesthetic has pushed its way into the core of knowledge
and truth. It is as a consequence of this process that recent thinking has
assumed basic aesthetic features.[18]

1. Kant 1781: aesthetics as a fundamental epistemological discipline

This epistemological aestheticization was initiated by Kant more than two
hundred years ago. He was the first to show that our knowledge is aesthetically moulded in an elementary and constitutive sense. The place for this
insight is not the *Critique of Judgment*, which alone is supposedly relevant to
aesthetics, but the *Critique of Pure Reason*, and specifically the 'transcendental aesthetic'.[19] Kant calls this deliberately and rightly 'transcendental'
insofar as it exposes the 'conditions of the *possibility of experience*' as well as
'the conditions of the *possibility of the objects of experience*'.[20] It demonstrates that aesthetic structures are indispensable for our experience because
they are constitutive of the objects of this experience.

This transcendental fundamentalization of the aesthetic is connected with
the basic thesis of Kant's theoretical philosophy – with his 'intellectual
revolution'[21] – according to which we know not things in themselves, but

appearances because 'we can know *a priori* of things only what we ourselves put into them'.[22] And it is just what we put into things first of all that are *aesthetic* stipulations: the forms of intuition of space and time. Only within space and time can objects first be given to us at all. Our cognition and our reality reach precisely so far as these forms of intuition extend.

This then is the first and elementary aestheticization factor: our reference to reality and our cognition include basic aesthetic components. A second aestheticization factor lies in the fact that the whole arrangement of knowledge and reality is simultaneously altered: they assume a fundamentally fictional, productive, poietic character. Kant himself was clearly aware of this. Thus when he pointed out the 'transcendental ideality' of space and time and, with this, of appearances in general,[23] he had exactly this fictional character in view (which isn't usually conspicuous because all people – at least so Kant thought – enact these fictions in the same way). The ideas, the genuine concepts of reason, Kant expressly designates as 'heuristic fictions'.[24] In the *Opus postumum* he says that the power of imagination, which he had already spoken of in the *Critique of Pure Reason* as 'a blind but indispensable function of the soul, without which we should have no knowledge whatsoever',[25] 'invents' wherever it is active *a priori*.[26] With reference to mathematics he even declares that it is nothing but 'pure invention'.[27] Finally he notes tersely: 'We make everything ourselves.'[28]

Kant, this assuredly temperate head, has taught us in a highly lucid and compelling manner to take note of the aesthetic components of truth, reality and knowledge. He pointed out to us the foundational aesthetic character of cognition, demonstrated a base meaning of aesthetic components for our cognition.[29] With Kant aesthetics – namely as *transcendental* aesthetics (not, say, as a theory of art) – became epistemologically fundamental.[30] Since then it has hardly been possible to talk about knowledge, truth and science without taking aesthetic components into consideration. It was precisely the failure to recognize the aesthetic dependency of our cognition which was traditional metaphysics' basic mistake. From then on the following rule applied: no cognitive discourse can succeed without the awareness of its fundamental aesthetic elements; the grasp of aesthetics and cognitive competence are coextensive; no cognition without aesthetics.[31] – If Kant is a classic author for the present day then it's also precisely in consequence of this protoaesthetics of cognition which he revealed.[32]

2.   *A look back to Baumgarten: cognitive claims in the original project of aesthetics*

Retrospectively in this context another reminder might be helpful that Baumgarten had already launched the new discipline named 'aesthetics' not artistically but epistemologically. Already Baumgarten's outset had aimed for a cognitive meaning of the aesthetic.

Baumgarten had defined aesthetics, as I've said, as the 'science of sensitive cognition'.[33] The task of the new science was to be the improvement of our knowledge by means of the systematic extension of the previously neglected lower, sensible cognitive faculty. Baumgarten's concept of aesthetics set out to be knowledge-related from the start.

In the wake of this epistemological project aesthetic predicates came to be seen as pertaining to truth in a fundamental way for the first time. The newly founded aesthetics aimed ultimately for an aesthetic reinterpretation of cognition. This was the catalyst by means of which it then became philosophy's new career-discipline and rose within a few decades from being the Cinderella to the queen of epistemology. The clearest evidence of this is 'The "Oldest System-Programme" of German Idealism' (from around 1796), in which it is stated that the 'highest act of reason [. . .] is an aesthetic act' and that 'the philosophy of the spirit is an aesthetic philosophy'.[34] In a dazzling career, aesthetics, which was originally to concern only the lower cognitive faculty, had acquired the peak position in philosophy.

At the start, when Baumgarten presented his aesthetics project, such high-flying impulses were admittedly hardly noticeable. On the contrary, Baumgarten introduced aesthetics with the promise of pure usefulness and in a gesture of servility. The new science, in cultivating the previously neglected sensuous cognitive faculty, was to prove a welcome service for our cognition as a whole. Aesthetics was to produce material, to guarantee distinctness, improve representation and comprehensibility. To begin with, then, aesthetics seemed to make no claims of its own, but merely to serve the improvement of cognition in general. Baumgarten leads it to the court of the scientific mistress as a personal maid ready to serve.

Towards the end of the *Aesthetica*, however, Baumgarten suddenly strikes a completely different tone. The new aesthetics now openly revolts against the received cognitive ideal. Conceptual truth is abstract and impoverished and unable to do justice to reality, which is always individual.[35] For the individual a different organ is needed: aesthetics, which from then on was to become the attorney of the individual.[36] Since pure logical truth remains closed to us humans anyway, as sensible-logical beings,[37] we would, moreover, in the event of a conflict between the traditional ideal of logical, abstract-general truth and the new ideal of aesthetico-logical truth, have to decide for the latter – that is, for an ideal which in the name of reality and with an appeal to the *conditio humana* shifts aesthetic aspects to the fore.[38] And since such conflicts always come about, aesthetically moulded cognition is largely to be given preference over the merely logical.[39] – This is a noteworthy change compared with the beginning of the text and compared with the traditional notion of truth, cognition and science.

Baumgarten might not yet understand the aesthetic to be transcendental, but he already conceives of it as indispensable. He emphasizes that for us humans *every* truth – not, say, just in its sensualistic origin, but enduringly

– possesses an aesthetic component or inclusion. In doing so he had introduced a motif which was to assert itself successively. Even in this first design aesthetics – with which Baumgarten had, so to speak, infiltrated the fortress of science as a kind of Trojan horse – leads to a change in the concept of science and knowledge: true knowledge would henceforward have to be aesthetico-logical knowledge, and true science could not be allowed to ignore its aesthetic determinants, but must do them justice. From here on it is not far to the unreasonable demand that science *on the whole* should reorganize itself aesthetically.

It is just this step which was taken by Kant in apprehending the distinction of the aesthetic, which for Baumgarten had remained an empirically anthropological one, as transcendental. The aesthetic is, according to Kant, more than an anthropological ideal, it is constitutive for our knowing the world and our behaviour in the world altogether.

3.   Nietzsche: the aesthetic-fictional character of knowledge and reality

Kant's foundation was resumed a hundred years later by Nietzsche and made so convincing that since then, although the question of the aesthetic grounding of cognition might still be addressed, hardly anything can be brought forward against it.

Nietzsche – possibly the aesthetic thinker *par excellence* – radicalized aestheticization in three ways. He showed, firstly, that reality altogether (not only in its transcendental structure) is *made*: facts are fact-*itious*. He pointed out, secondly, that this production of reality takes place with *fictional* means: through forms of intuition, basic images, guiding metaphors, phantasms, and so on. And, thirdly, he breached the threshold of the single and common world: if reality is the result of production, then the emergence of varying worlds must also be reckoned with.

Even in the early manuscript 'On Truth and Lies in a Nonmoral Sense' (1873), Nietzsche (significantly having just paraphrased Kant) points out that we bring forth reality everywhere with fictional means and by way of metaphorical activity. The talk of 'meta-phorical' activity is to be under-stood literally in this. We transfer an incipient nerve stimulus into an image, this into a sound, finally the sound into a concept. Through such transfer from one sphere to another emerge the cascades of reality, which, in everything which goes beyond the elementary physical stimulus, is a product of human artistry. The 'drive toward the formation of metaphors' is something which 'one cannot for a single instant dispense with in thought, for one would thereby dispense with man himself'.[40] The human is an *animal fingens*.

If reality usually appears to us to be not produced but as given, then this is the consequence of our habitually and almost systematically forgetting our active share. The human arrives at 'his sense of truth'[41] only 'by forgetting that he himself is an *artistically creating* subject'.[42] 'He forgets that the original perceptual metaphors are metaphors and takes them to be the things themselves.'[43] We do indeed produce our realities but we hide this from ourselves or forget about it – and the appearance of objectivity arises in this way.[44] The fabric of reality in general rests on primary aesthetic or poietic projections – it is founded on 'free inventive' human activity, and thus an 'aesthetic relation'[45] – but usually it's precisely this which we don't admit, but rather forget and suppress. It was Nietzsche who made us aware of this suppression of the basic aesthetic process.

In this way Nietzsche arrived at an ingenious assessment of our edifice of concepts:

> Here one may certainly admire man as a mighty genius of construction, who succeeds in piling up an infinitely complicated dome of concepts upon an unstable foundation, and, as it were, on running water. Of course, in order to be supported by such a foundation, his construction must be like one constructed of spiders' webs: delicate enough to be carried along by the waves, strong enough not to be blown apart by every wind.[46]

This is how cognition portrays itself to a state of consciousness which has become attentive of its basic aesthetic achievements. All elements of the new primary character of the aesthetic are gathered together in this characterization: like artists or virtuosic constructors we produce our systems of understanding, erect artistic constructions, which although they refer to reality, do so not through representation, but invention, and which take account of the non-fundamentalism of reality altogether: 'There is no "reality" for us [. . .].'[47]

So according to Nietzsche our sketches of reality not only contain foundational aesthetic elements, but are altogether aesthetically tailored: they are generated poietically, structured by fictional means, and in their entire mode of being of that suspended and fragile nature which one had traditionally attested to and thought possible only for aesthetic phenomena. With Nietzsche reality and truth in general became aesthetic. What Baumgarten had paved the way for and Kant had been the first to work out to some extent was developed to the extreme by Nietzsche.

4. The suffusion of epistemological aestheticization in the twentieth century

Philosophy of science

Is such an aesthetic view of cognition advocated only by exquisite – or seemingly eccentric – aestheticians such as Nietzsche? No. Nietzsche's views became increasingly commonplace in the twentieth century. Even this century's philosophy of science has gradually become 'Nietzschean'. Thus Otto Neurath (who nonetheless belonged to one of the hardest schools in the philosophy of science – the Vienna Circle) described our situation in a manner quite similar to Nietzsche's: 'We are like mariners who must rebuild their ship on the open sea, without ever being able to disassemble it

in dock and reassemble it with the best components.'[48] This sentence from
Neurath then became the guiding maxim for the analytic philosopher
Willard Van Orman Quine.[49] And even with Karl Popper we read that,
'just when we believed that we were standing on firm and safe ground, all
things are in reality insecure and unstable'.[50] – It can be seen that even
philosophers of science, who certainly don't want to be Nietzscheans,
cannot avoid sounding Nietzschean when addressing basic questions. The
aesthetic constitution of reality is the view not just of some aestheticians,
but of all theoreticians reflecting on reality and science in the twentieth
century. It is an insight which is indeed *due*.

Hermeneutics

A similar diagnosis is advocated by hermeneutic philosophy. Hans
Blumenberg pointed out that the old metaphor of a sea voyage has been
increasingly modified in the history of occidental thought, and hence
become the key modern metaphor for the *conditio humana*.[51] Once there
was a complement to the voyage and its dramatic culmination in the
catastrophe of being shipwrecked: a spectator who could observe everything from the safety of firm ground and who was himself unaffected by the
mishap. Increasingly, however, it has been appreciated that there is no such
neutral or higher ground, rather that the position of any given spectator is
fluctuant, unsecured and subject to its own voyage – put another way, that
we are all sitting in boats.[52,53] No option remains for us other than 'Ship-
building [our way] out of Shipwreck'.[54,55]

Recent analytic philosophy

More recent analytic (or post-analytic) philosophy – like Nietzsche,
modern philosophy of science and hermeneutics – is also of the view that
we must operate 'upon an unstable foundation, and, as it were, on running
water'. In the analytic context this is a consequence of the talk of a reality-
in-itself having become empty of meaning on principle because reality only
ever exists as 'reality-under-a-certain-description',[56] that is because we 'are
confined to ways of describing whatever is described'.[57] Hence we can only
ever talk of reality within the spectrum of premises which are in principle
problematic (never ultimately justifiable) and always of one version of
reality alongside others.

   Correspondingly Richard Rorty has set out in *Philosophy and the Mirror
of Nature* how traditional notions of representation and objectivism have
neglected the productive and aesthetic character of our cognitive
achievements. In *Contingency, Irony, and Solidarity* he then showed that
all our 'fundaments' are aesthetically constituted, that is to say, are cultural
artefacts through and through. From this insight he inferred a revealing
consequence. Rorty pleads for a 'poeticized culture'.[58] By this he understands a culture which knows that one is everywhere dealing with cultural

artefacts, which can be examined only against other cultural artefacts, not, however, against reality itself. And a 'poeticized culture' acknowledges this situation instead of continuing in vain to insist 'we find the real wall behind the painted ones, the real touchstones of truth as opposed to touchstones which are merely cultural artifacts'.[59]

Nelson Goodman had, in a manner similar to Rorty, already pointed out a parallelity between artistic and scientific activity.[60] His talk of 'ways of worldmaking' carries on from Kant's analytic basis and Nietzsche's insight into the fictional character of cognition and leads the way over to a general non-fundamentalism. Goodman shows that all symbolic systems – those of science just as those of perception or life-forms – are aesthetically, namely poietically, constituted. World versions do not simply exist, world versions are *made*.

It doesn't seem exaggerated to claim that the transition to an aesthetic interpretation of truth, reality and cognition represents the basic philosophical process of the last two hundred years.[61] The aesthetic is forcing its way more and more into the elemental layer of the cognitive. Proto-aesthetics is the subterranean *movens* of recent epistemology.

History of science

In the field of the history and philosophy of science too awareness of the primary aesthetic components of cognition has increased. This applies precisely with respect to the 'hard' sciences, the natural sciences.

Paul Feyerabend was the most drastic in this respect in standing for an equivalence of cognition and aesthetics. In *Science as Art* he pointed out that 'artistic methods' crop up 'everywhere in the sciences' and that this is particularly the case 'where new and surprising discoveries are being made'.[62] He says that basically the sciences proceed no differently from the arts.[63] Both operate within the constraints of a certain style – an artistic style in the one case, a cognitive style in the other. Truth and reality in science are thus just as relative to style as in art: 'If one examines namely what a particular form of thought understands by these things, then one encounters not something which lies beyond the style of thought, but its own foundational assumptions: truth is whatever the style of thought says truth is.'[64] Hence the sciences too, according to Feyerabend, are nothing but 'arts [. . .] in the sense of this advanced understanding of art'.[65]

In this Feyerabend extended theses of Thomas S. Kuhn,[66] who had shown in his *The Structure of Scientific Revolutions* that the history of science does not proceed, as scientists like to think, rationally, linearly and in keeping with the model of progress on a unitary basis, but rather that it – in just the same way as the history of art – is characterized by a sequence of revolutionary periods in which the basis is changed, and cumulative periods in which work continues on the basis which has been attained.[67] At the same time Kuhn confessed that he had been inspired to this understanding of the history of scientific development by looking at 'historians of literature, of music, of the arts, of political development, and of many other human activities'. In these spheres the 'periodization in terms of revolutionary breaks in style, taste, and institutional structure' have long since been among the 'standard tools'.[68] All he had done was transfer these perspectives, well proven in the aesthetic realm, to the sphere of the natural sciences.[69] By doing so Kuhn overcame the conventional separation between the cognitive and the aesthetic realms. Since then the history of science has to a considerable extent become an aesthetic history of science. And whereas Kuhn had initially asserted only a homologous developmental structure of the two realms, more recent theoretical approaches to science even ascribe changes in the aesthetic canon a causal function for scientific revolutions.[70,71]

Scientific practice

Researchers in the natural sciences too have long since been aware of the significance of aesthetic aspects for their cognitive work. For them it is almost a platitude that their cognition is more production than reproduction in type and that imaginative abilities are indispensable for research. Thus Bohr, Dirac, Einstein and Heisenberg had already argued aesthetically in critical passages, and Poincaré even bluntly explained that aesthetic and not, say, logical potency is a good mathematician's central skill.[72,73] More recently the effect was ground-breaking when Watson pointed out that he had only succeeded in deciphering the structure of DNA because he had assumed from the start that the solution would have to be of the utmost elegance – only with this aesthetic premiss did he manage to find the appropriate solution in reasonable time amongst the large number of those remaining theoretically open.[74] – Aesthetics obviously not only delivers intuitions but makes available criteria too.

Through such developments rationalistic barriers in people's heads have been increasingly broken down. Today one dares without inhibition to acknowledge aesthetic elements within the core of science. Historically they have always existed. Examples of this extend from the circle metaphors of ancient astronomy and Newton's concept of the natural law, through to the imaginative components in present-day symmetry research;[75] and the heuristic relevance of aesthetic intuitions is known of from Archimedes and Newton through to Kekulé in just the same way.[76] When confronted with theories such as that of the 'Big Bang' or the never-ending story of quarks you can scarcely do anything but take into account the great relevance of aesthetic and fictional factors. The difference between scientific and aesthetic rationality formerly held to be a matter of principle has turned out to be merely a difference in degree. Cognitive rationality is – whether understood in the manner of Kant or Feyerabend – interlaced with aesthetic elements at its base level.

An awareness of cognition's and reality's foundational aesthetic character is currently permeating all academic disciplines. Whether semiotics or system theory, whether in sociology, biology or microphysics, everywhere we are recognizing that there is no first or last fundament, rather that it's precisely in the dimension of 'fundaments' that we confront an aesthetic constitution. Thus the semioticians tell us that chains of signifiers always refer to other chains of signifiers and not, say, to an original signified; system theory teaches us that 'instead of having recourse to final unities' we only ever observe observations and describe descriptions;[77] and microphysics finds that wherever it tries to revert to things elementary it always encounters not the elementary, but new complexity.[78] All of this, however, is to be grasped not as an expression of resignation, but as an indication of the insight into the foundational aesthetic structure of reality.

This awareness of the foundational aesthetic character of our cognition, our reality and our forms of understanding is today asserting itself right through to everyday understanding.[79] Our orientations are increasingly assuming aesthetic features, and increasingly we are justifying our deviations from traditional norms with arguments of an aesthetic nature.

5.   Protoaesthetics: the aesthetic turn

The supposition at the outset of the deliberations in this section stated that the aesthetic had pushed its way into the core of philosophy, into the foundational dimension of truth and knowledge. In the meantime we have established that truth, according to the modern understanding, is permeated by aesthetic premises; our cognition is aesthetically configured in its foundational features.

This protoaesthetics has become increasingly explicit in the last two hundred years. Since Baumgarten's project of an aesthetic improvement of science, since Kant's transcendentalization of the aesthetic, since Nietzsche's aesthetic and fictional interpretation of cognition, and completely in the diverse forms in which the twentieth century's philosophy of science and scientific practice have discovered aesthetic elements within science, truth, cognition and reality have revealed themselves to be eminently aesthetic. Firstly, it became evident that aesthetic components are foundational for our cognition and our reality. This began – following Baumgarten's preparation – with Kant's transcendental aesthetic and today extends to the self-reflexion of the natural sciences. Secondly, the view that cognition and reality are aesthetic in their mode of being asserted itself more and more. This was Nietzsche's discovery, one which has since been expressed by others (often in a different terminology) and extends to the constructivism of our times. Reality is not a cognition-free, fixed preordained quantity, but the object of a construction. Whereas previously it was only the secondary, supplementary realities which were ascribed an aesthetic character, we have increasingly realized that our primary realities already exhibit a constitution which can best be decribed as aesthetic. Aesthetic categories have become fundamental categories.

What is particularly incisive about this is the fact that the aesthetic affects not only higher-level but even the elementary dimensions, the very foundations. 'Rationality', on the other hand – the other element essential for truth – is decisive only for the subsequent processes on the basis of the foundations which are aesthetic as a matter of principle. Rationality, conforming to the premises and consistent in procedure, acts out the consequences of the set of principles determined by aesthetic aspects. But rationality can neither establish nor justify these foundations. The aesthetic, then, does not cover the whole scope of truth; rationality is also indispensable. But the aesthetic is concerned with the base level, whereas rationality is first concerned with the subsequent structures. It is precisely this – precisely this primary character of the aesthetic – that one traditionally hasn't grasped or wanted to admit to. The modern development, however, has allowed us to recognize it enduringly.

And this was decreed not by some aestheticians or other, but was a recognition forced upon us by science, the guiding authority of modernity. It prescribed an *epistemological aestheticization* – an on-principle aestheticization of knowledge, truth and reality – by which no issue remains unaffected.[80] This epistemological aestheticization is the legacy of modernity. There is today no argument which is able to counter this effectively. One has not only every occasion, but the obligation to consider aesthetic elements in the core of truth, knowledge and reality. If one is to talk of the contemporary standing of aesthetics, then one must keep in mind this protoaesthetics and face up to its assertions.

In view of this development one could speak of an 'aesthetic turn'. Our 'first philosophy' has to a considerable extent become aesthetic. 'First philosophy' – this was the classic title for that part of the discipline which made the most general statements about reality. Formerly (in antiquity) these were derived from being, later (in the modern age) from consciousness, finally (in modernity) from language; today the transition to an aesthetic paradigm seems to be imminent. The further back we question, the more fundamentally we analyse, the more we come across aesthetic factors and structures of an aesthetic nature. In the foundations of argument as well as in the elementary descriptions of reality we are discovering aesthetic options over and over again. In today's context – in the context of non-fundamentality – 'fundaments' on the whole are displaying an aesthetic countenance.[81] Or, more precisely, non-fundamentalism means precisely that the foundations bear an aesthetic inscription. – This is not to be mistaken for an 'aesthetic fundamentalism'. The concern here is obviously its opposite: a departure from each and every fundamentalism. For an aesthetically contoured 'first philosophy' abandons not only the traditional occupation but also breaks through the form of a 'first philosophy' at the same time. If it is a 'first philosophy', then it is no longer in the manner of a 'first philosophy'. It no longer has the status of a fundamental discipline which can be developed autonomously so as to derive from it answers to all subsequent questions. Aesthetics does not constitute an underpinning and provides no fundament. It is exactly this which characterizes this change of paradigm, this *aesthetic turn*.

6.   *The aesthetic constitution of 'fundaments'*

In the interests of precision I would like to emphasize one distinction once again. Two factors belong to epistemological aestheticization. Firstly, the basic structures of our cognition contain *aesthetic components* in large measure – these extend from elementary forms of intuition and guiding metaphors, through to specific fictions. This was taught fundamentally by Kant's transcendental aesthetic or Nietzsche's metaphorological interpretation of cognition, and on the specific level scientific or philosophical analyses are always managing to uncover the function of basic aesthetic notions as guiding images.[82]

Secondly – and this is indeed the decisive point – the *aesthetic nature* of reality's *constitution* comes to light. Reality's mode of being is, from its defining forms onwards, of a kind which is to be designated aesthetic. For the respective supporting structures are specifically (not universally) tailored, and from a certain point onwards they are no longer justifiable, but stand there, so to speak, without foundation, exhibit a floating constitution. A constitution of this type was, as I've said, traditionally known from aesthetic phenomena alone. There it has long since been described with recourse to the aesthetic's predicates of state – to terms such as appearance, manifoldness, groundlessness or suspension. Hence it is consistent to designate the novel constitution of foundations as being aesthetic in nature.

The situation which has come about can be made clear in the following way: understandings of reality and forms of life might well internally exhibit a hierarchical structure – there is the more foundational and that which builds upon it, but the foundations themselves can no longer be ultimately accounted for. Hence neither the predicate 'rational' nor the predicate 'irrational' applies to them. Wittgenstein said of this: 'You must bear in mind that the language-game is so to say something unpredictable. I mean: it is not based on grounds. It is not reasonable (or unreasonable). It is there – like our life.'[83] Attempts at explanation here can only have the character of a clarification, no longer that of a justification. Ultimately they exhibit a circular structure.[84] In this respect Wittgenstein referred to the argumentative law of a door and its hinges: '[. . .] it belongs to the logic of our scientific investigations that certain things are *in deed* not doubted.' 'That is to say, the *questions* that we raise and our *doubts* depend on the fact that some propositions are exempt from doubt, are as it were hinges on which those turn.'[85] It is just that these 'hinges' in turn are themselves not above all doubt. They do not, by being evident and undoubtable, constitute absolutely dependable foundations, but represent only pragmatically, that is, functionally, requisite foundations. Hence they themselves can be made the object of inquiry (as it were, the 'door') in the next step of the

deliberations – by using a different 'hinge', which can, however, in principle be inquired after in just the same way in further steps. In summary
Wittgenstein characterized the situation thus: 'Nothing we do can be
defended absolutely and finally. But only by reference to something else
that is not questioned.'[86] In the regress through justifications you come
across no irrevocable ground, but only ever settlements which, in principle,
are themselves in turn problematic. This architecture of justification and
argument remains altogether fragile, relative and in suspension.

In the end this leads – as it did Wittgenstein – to the priority of aesthetic
operations once again. For since at the base level different settlements are
always possible, between which a 'rational' decision can no longer be made,
only an aesthetic choice remains. Wittgenstein, talking of 'style', once
expressed this in the following way: 'So with creation. God is one style; the
nebula another. A style gives us satisfaction; but one style is not more
rational than another.'[87]

7.   *Wittgenstein*

I want to conclude this section with some supplementary comments on
Wittgenstein. With respect to the aesthetic turn, Wittgenstein is as decisive
for the twentieth century as Nietzsche was for the nineteenth. Wittgenstein
described the constitution of language-games and forms of life according to
a pattern which is basically aesthetic – in a manner wholly similar to that
of the constitution of reality according to Nietzsche, Neurath, Goodman or
Rorty. Understanding Wittgenstein also requires the comprehension of
notes like the following (which dates from Reformation Day in 1946): 'Oh,
why do I feel as if I were writing a poem when I write philosophy?'[88]

Wittgenstein was an aesthetic thinker in many of his traits. Thus he
spoke in general of the 'queer resemblance between a philosophical investi-
gation [. . .] and an aesthetic one'.[89] He called this similarity queer because
it contradicts our usual notions;[90] for him however, as a master of analytic
precision, this similarity forced itself upon him. Thus he repeatedly brought
in aesthetic parallels for his own philosophical activity. Generally he stated:
'I may find scientific questions interesting, but they never really grip me.
Only conceptual and aesthetic questions do that.'[91] Wittgenstein compared
his philosophical activity with a reforming of taste: 'A present-day teacher
of philosophy doesn't select food for his pupil with the aim of flattering his
taste, but with the aim of changing it.'[92] In single cases Wittgenstein drew
parallels with music, architecture, painting and poetry: 'My style is like a
[. . .] musical composition.'[93] 'Working in philosophy – like work in
architecture in many respects – is really more a working on oneself.'[94] '[. . .]
[A] painter is basically what I am [. . .].'[95] 'What I invent are new *similes*.'[96]
'Philosophy ought really to be written only as a *poetic composition*.'[97,98]

In the preceeding sections I have attempted to provide an explanation as
to why Wittgenstein can speak in this way. In analysing the problems of

philosophy without illusions through to the so-called 'first questions' – that is, through to the point where you have 'exhausted the justifications', 'reached bedrock' and the 'spade is turned'[99] – he became aware of the basic aesthetic constitution of thought. This was initially an astonishing discovery for him too, but then an increasingly self-evident one.

IV.   A look back, a look forward

I began with Plato and at the end I want to look back to him once again. Plato banished the poets from the state and enthroned philosophy instead. Wittgenstein, on the other hand, thinks that you can only really write philosophy 'as a *poetic composition*'.

All the same, the contrast with Plato (and the tradition as a whole) is not as great as it seems. I said at the start that I am not of the view that today's thinking is the first to exhibit basic aesthetic features but that this has always been the case – just that one traditionally didn't want to admit this, that one warded off the very hint of such an aesthetic character and sought to distance oneself from such. At the end it is precisely Plato, the apologist of the separation of philosophy and poetry, whom I want to call as a witness of this.

Not only do biographical indications suggest that Plato, so to speak, bore in himself the link between philosophy and poetry and was converted to philosophy by Socrates only at the last moment – namely on the evening before he wanted to take his place in a contest as a tragic poet; but rather at the end of my reference passage, the polemics against poetry in Book X of the *Republic*, Plato himself says that his entire speech has been a spell which he must cast upon himself so as not to fall back into that old love of poetry which still attracts him.[100] Plato then even leaves a door ajar for poetry: if someone were to come along who was able to hold a convincing speech in defence of poetry, then he would want not only to listen, but to agree with such a person – it would, after all, be to our advantage.[101]

Finally, doesn't Plato himself also act in the manner of a poet? Montaigne at least viewed it this way. 'Have I not seen in Plato this divine remark, that nature is nothing but an enigmatic poem? [. . .] And indeed philosophy is but sophisticated poetry. [. . .] and the first [philosophers] were themselves poets, and treat of philosophy in their style. Plato is but a rambling poet.'[102] In fact Plato himself had – and what's more, in the *Republic* – characterized his philosophical deeds several times in the nature of an artistic activity. What, for instance, he asks does he do differently from a painter who constructs 'a theoretical paradigm of a good community'?[103] The philosopher is after all a 'painter of constitutions', one who produces 'a very beautiful painting'.[104] With this there leads almost a literal bridge to Wittgenstein, who observed: 'A thinker is very much like a draughtsman whose aim it is to represent all the interrelations between things.'[105]

So even with Plato himself there's no lack of hints that philosophical activity exhibits far more affinity with aesthetic and poetic procedures than it might superficially disclose. It was only later, with philosophizing's rationalistic turn, that one no longer wanted to know of such affinities. Today, however, we have started to listen out for the aesthetic elements of our thinking and our understanding of reality and are also discovering aesthetic signatures in older texts.

The fact that the aesthetic constitution of thinking as such is not new, but only the attentiveness to this, might well ease the step to recognition of the aesthetic-poietic character of thinking. All the same, this step is a difficult and unaccustomed one. Wittgenstein once noted: 'I still find my own way of philosophizing new, and it keeps striking me so afresh: that is why I need to repeat myself so often.'[106] But he continued: 'It will have become second nature to a new generation [. . .].'[107] Perhaps one might be allowed to relate this expectation to the insight into the basic aesthetic features in thinking too.

Notes

This essay was originally delivered as a lecture, 'Ästhetische Grundzüge im heutigen Denken', at Ludwig Maximilians University, Munich, Germany (18 July 1991). It has been revised for this volume. (First English publication.)

1. See 'S. Bernardi Abbatis Apologia ad Guillelmum Sancti Theoderici Abbatem', in *Patrologia Latina*, ed. J.-P. Migne, vol. CLXXXII (Paris: Migne 1862), pp. 895–918, here esp. 914–916.

2. Jürgen Habermas, *The Philosophical Discourse of Modernity. Twelve Lectures*, trans. F.G. Lawrence (Cambridge, Mass.: MIT Press 1993), pp. 185–210. – Derrida counters: 'I have tried to think beyond this traditional distinction between philosophy and literature. I work on this border. [. . .] The bonds between literature and philosophy are more complicated than the people who contradict me seem to believe.' (Interview with Florian Rötzer, in *Französische Philosophen im Gespräch*, ed. Florian Rötzer, Munich: Boer 1986, pp. 67–87, here pp. 79f.)

3. I am concerned with anything but a beautification action for philosophy. I've always had little sympathy for the concept of 'beautiful thought' (*ars pulchre cogitandi*), coined in the eighteenth century with the genesis of aesthetics – and can have less still in view of the present-day aestheticization mania in the life-world and culture. I don't want to advocate this aestheticization wave's splashing over into philosophy too. Indeed the beautification trend (which mostly gives rise to uglification effects) ought rather to be opposed outside of philosophy as well.

4. See the more complete analysis in the previous essay (section II). In the present context the concern is with different accentuations.

5. Baumgarten had formed the expression 'aesthetics' as a short form of *episteme aisthetike* (see Alexander Gottlieb Baumgarten, *Meditationes philosophicae de nonnullis ad poema pertinentibus*, Halle 1735, quoted from the German edition *Meditationes philosophicae de nonnullis ad poema pertinentibus – Philosophische Betrachtungen über einige Bedingungen des Gedichtes*, Hamburg: Meiner 1983, § CXVI, pp. 86 and 87).

6. Baumgarten understood perfect sensuous knowledge to be beautiful knowledge; on the other hand, beauty was traditionally considered the guiding predicate of art. Thus it was later possible, via beauty, to transform the aesthetics of the senses into an aesthetics of art.

7. Immanuel Kant, 'First Introduction to the Critique of Judgment', in Kant, *Critique of Judgment*, trans. Werner S. Pluhar (Indianapolis: Hackett 1987), here p. 440 [H 67].

8. See here Kierkegaard's depiction, dating from 1843, of the aesthetic as one of the basic types of existence (Søren Kierkegaard, *Either/Or*, ed. and trans. Howard V. Hong and Edna H. Hong, Princeton, NJ: Princeton University Press 1987).

9. Max Weber, 'Parlament und Regierung im neugeordneten Deutschland', in Weber, *Gesammelte Politische Schriften*, ed. Johannes Winckelmann (Tübingen: Mohr 1988), pp. 306–443, here p. 331.

10. Konrad Fiedler, one of the most perspicacious aesthetes of the nineteenth century, diagnosed that from then on 'the principle of the production of reality' would take the place of realism and idealism; art was to become 'one of the means by which people would first attain reality.' (Konrad Fiedler, 'Moderner Naturalismus und künstlerische Wahrheit' [1881], in Fiedler, *Schriften zur Kunst*, ed. Gottfried Boehm, 2 vols, Munich: Fink, 2nd edition, 1991, vol. 1, pp. 81–110, here p. 109.)

11. Hölderlin had conceived of the 'aesthetic sense' as that faculty which is able to overcome all conflicts – 'between the subject and object, between our selves and the world, indeed between reason and revelation too' (letter to Immanuel Niethammer, 24 February 1796, in Friedrich Hölderlin, *Sämtliche Werke*, vol. 6, Stuttgart: Kohlhammer 1954, pp. 202f., here p. 203). The proximity of this conception to 'The "Oldest System-Programme" of German Idealism' (of which, as has recently been asserted with new arguments, Hölderlin might well have been the author [see Eckart Förster, '"To Lend Wings to Physics Once Again": Hölderlin and the "Oldest System-Programme of German Idealism"', in *European Journal of Philosophy*, 3(2), 1995, pp. 174–198]) is obvious. In relation to Schelling, Odo Marquard has shown that his system of identity can be understood as 'an aesthetics of reality as a whole' (Odo Marquard, 'Gesamtkunstwerk und Identitätssystem. Überlegungen im Anschluß an Hegels Schellingkritik', in Marquard, *Aesthetica und Anaesthetica. Philosophische Überlegungen*, Paderborn: Schöningh 1989, pp. 100–112, here p. 105).

12. Cf. Schlegel's idea of an 'aesthetic revolution' (Friedrich Schlegel, 'Über das Studium der Griechischen Poesie', in Schlegel, *Kritische Ausgabe*, ed. Ernst Behler, vol. 1, Paderborn: Schöningh 1979, pp. 217–367, here pp. 269–272) as well as his concept of 'universal poetry' ('Athenäums-Fragmente', in Schlegel, *Kritische Ausgabe*, vol. 2, Munich: Schöningh 1967, pp. 165–255, here pp. 182f. [116]). Novalis interpreted poetry as the 'universe's self-consciousness' (*Novalis Schriften*, ed. Paul Kluckhohn and Richard Samuel, vol. 3 [Das philosophische Werk II], Stuttgart: Kohlhammer 1983, p. 640 [513]) and declared: 'Poetry is the genuinely absolute real. This is the core of my philosophy' (ibid., vol. 2 [Das philosophische Werk I], Stuttgart: Kohlhammer 1981, p. 647 [473]).

13. Friedrich Nietzsche, *The Birth of Tragedy*, in *The Complete Works of Friedrich Nietzsche*, vol. 3, ed. O. Levy (Edinburgh/London: Foulis 1909), here p. 50 (similarly pp. 8 and 152).

14. Friedrich Nietzsche, 'On Truth and Lies in a Nonmoral Sense', in *Philosophy and Truth. Selections from Nietzsche's Notebooks of the early 1870's*, trans. and ed. Daniel Breazeale (Atlantic Highlands, NJ: Humanities Press 1979), pp. 79–91, here p. 86. (N.B. The German 'frei dichtend und frei erfindend' is rendered here in abridged form as 'freely inventive', thus losing explicit reference to the poetic connotations of 'dichtend'; cf. also note 27 [trans.].)

15. Friedrich Nietzsche, 'Nachgelassene Fragmente. Anfang 1880 bis Sommer 1882', in Nietzsche, *Sämtliche Werke. Kritische Studienausgabe in 15 Bänden*, eds Giorgio Colli and Mazzino Montinari (Munich: Deutscher Taschenbuch Verlag 1980), vol. 9, p. 581 [Autumn 1881].

16. Habermas, 'The Entwinement of Myth and Enlightenment' (lecture V in *The Philosophical Discourse of Modernity*, pp. 106–130). – Nietzsche, according to Habermas's diagnosis, was 'the first to conceptualize the attitude of aesthetic modernity' (ibid., p. 122). Horkheimer and Adorno then 'let themselves be inspired by Nietzsche' precisely 'in drawing their criteria for cultural criticism from a basic experience of aesthetic modernity that has now been rendered independent' (ibid., p. 121). This has led, in Habermas's view, to a 'lack of

concern in dealing with the [. . .] achievements of Occidental rationalism', indeed to 'an uninhibited scepticism regarding reason' (ibid., pp. 121, 129 resp.).

17. Cf. Jürgen Habermas, *The Philosophical Discourse of Modernity*, Chapter IV, 'The Entry into Postmodernity: Nietzsche as a Turning-Point', pp. 83–105.

18. As we will see, the aesthetic's predicates of state play the decisive role in this; on the other hand, of the standard predicates only the aisthetic aspect of meaning participates. – I have developed the following thoughts in a similar manner in my *Vernunft. Die zeitgenössische Vernunftkritik und das Konzept der transversalen Vernunft* (Frankfurt a.M.: Suhrkamp 1995, 2nd edition stw 1996), esp. pp. 485–509.

19. In the twentieth century Heidegger was the first to point out the great significance of Kant's transcendental aesthetic – in a countermove to the neo-Kantian interpretation of Kant. (Cf. Martin Heidegger, *Phänomenologische Interpretation von Kants Kritik der reinen Vernunft* [Lecture Winter Semester 1927/28], in Heidegger, *Gesamtausgabe*, vol. 25, Frankfurt a.M.: Klostermann 1977, pp. 77ff.). With his interpretation, however, Heidegger targets more the relevance of this aesthetics for an analysis of *Dasein* than for epistemology. In his reading of Kant, he is looking for time (which, in 1927, he had just found) from the start. – Odo Marquard, with a view to the development of philosophy since the eighteenth century, noted in 1962 that with Kant a 'turn to aesthetics' had taken place insofar as '*aesthetics from the end of the eighteenth century onwards and, in its claims, through to the present day becomes the fundamental philosophy on duty*' (Odo Marquard, 'Kant und die Wende zur Ästhetik', in *Zeitschrift für philosophische Forschung*, 16, 1962, pp. 231–243 and 363–374; reprinted in Marquard, *Aesthetica und Anaesthetica*, pp. 21–34, here p. 21). However, Marquard sees a '*turn away from (exact) science*' as going along with the 'turn to aesthetics', which for him is a turn to art, namely to artistic aesthetics (ibid., p. 24), whereas the turn to an epistemological aestheticization which I am dealing with takes place precisely within science too. Furthermore Marquard fixes the 'turn to aesthetics' to the *Critique of Judgment* and not to the *Critique of Pure Reason*. Finally, in his 1962 essay, Marquard considers the boom in aesthetics to be merely a transitional stage between the old dominance of science and the future dominance of the philosophy of history ('*In view of the aporia of the emancipated human, aesthetics is deployed as a way out wherever scientific thinking no longer bears fruit and historical thinking has yet to do so*. That is the thesis' [ibid., p. 25]), whereas what I am concerned with is to point out a significance of the aesthetic which is not yet outdated. – For a fundamentally 'aesthetic' reading of Kant see also Gilles Deleuze, *Kant's Critical Philosophy*, trans. Hugh Tomlinson and Barbara Habberjam (London: Athlone Press 1984).

20. Immanuel Kant, *Critique of Pure Reason*, trans. Norman Kemp Smith (New York: St Martin's Press 1965), p. 194 [A 158].

21. Ibid., p. 19 [B XI].

22. Ibid., p. 23 [B XVIII].

23. Cf. ibid., pp. 72 [A 28], 78 [A 36] and 449 [A 506].

24. Ibid., p. 614 [A 771].

25. Ibid., p. 112 [A 78].

26. That is, 'dichtet'. (Immanuel Kant, *Opus postumum. Zweite Hälfte*, Akademie-Ausgabe vol. XXII, Berlin/Leipzig: de Gruyter 1938, p. 476.) – Lines 13–30 of the Academy Edition's page 476 are editorially omitted in the English translation.

27. 'It can be well united with poetry (for mathematics is pure invention [*Dichtung*])' (Immanuel Kant, *Opus postumum*, trans. Eckart Förster and Michael Rosen, Cambridge: Cambridge University Press 1993, p. 139 [22.490]). – *Dichtung* is a key concept in the development to be traced here. We have already met with it with Schlegel and will bump into it several times again – with Herder, Nietzsche, Rorty and Wittgenstein. (The German *Dichtung* denotes invention not *qua* invention, but as a poetic or fictional mode of invention. – It is the constancy of this 'poetically inventive' characteristic which is being highlighted here [trans.].)

28. Ibid., p. 189 [22.82].

29. In making this observation I wish not to defend the way in which Kant construed these forms of perception in detail, but rather to point out the matter-of-principle fact that, for

Kant, aesthetics became a fundamental discipline in theoretical philosophy. Certainly much of Kant's exposition is problematic and untenable: the unhistoricalness of the transcendental *a priori*, details of the explication of space and time, the restriction to these two forms of intuition alone. But the *idea* of this transcendental aesthetic – according to which reality is disclosed to us only in the context of fundamental intuitions and aesthetic elements are hence attributed basic significance – was an inciting thought which, through its later transformations – some of which are about to be named – assumed an increasingly tenable form.

30. For Kant, incidentally, this transcendental aesthetic remained the primary and undoubtable aesthetics. He explained in both editions of the *Critique of Pure Reason* that it alone is 'true science' (*Critique of Pure Reason*, p. 66 [A 21/B 36]). In the 'General Observations on Transcendental Aesthetic' he underlines that this transcendental aesthetic 'should have that certainty and freedom from doubt which is required of any theory that is to serve as an organon' (ibid., p. 85 [A 46/B 63]). The subsequent aesthetics of taste – the possibility of which he had in 1781 still judged extraordinarily sceptically (cf. ibid., p. 66 [A 21]) and which he then in 1790 developed in the *Critique of Judgment* – in no way managed to impinge upon or restrict the concept of this transcendental aesthetic – for the simple reason alone that the aesthetics of taste lies on a completely different level. With not one syllable did Kant ever retract the designation of his transcendental aesthetic as 'aesthetics' or his apprehension of the primary relevance of this aesthetics. This should be a warning to all those who think that this cognitive aesthetics can easily be excluded from the realm of legitimate aesthetic concepts. Kant's view was quite the reverse. He was still free of the later conjunction of aesthetics and art.

31. Incidentally a lesson can also be found in the later *Critique of Judgment* which points to the foundational significance of aesthetic feats for *every* form of knowledge. According to Kant, the aesthetic has *universal logical* significance. However, in keeping with the double prejudice that the 'Critique of Aesthetic Judgment' is concerned only with a particular faculty by the name of 'taste' and that things aesthetic are relevant only for issues of taste, this lesson has been as good as completely ignored. Yet, even under the conditions of this restriction, every cause existed to take notice of it, for Kant explicitly states there that this lesson contains 'the key to the critique of taste' and hence 'deserves full attention' (Kant, *Critique of Judgment*, § 9, p. 61 [B 27]). What is this about? Kant points out that in a judgement of taste the cognitive powers find themselves in the 'proportioned attunement which we require for all cognition' (ibid., p. 64 [B 31]). This proportioned attunement consists in that imagination and understanding 'harmonize' (ibid., p. 62 [B 29]). It is precisely as pleasure in a 'harmony of the cognitive powers' of this type, that is, in the 'free play' of 'imagination and understanding' (ibid.), that Kant now comprehends aesthetic pleasure. To this extent the judgement of taste represents, according to him, the pure form of the mental state as is 'required for cognition in general' (ibid.). Imagination and understanding find themselves here in 'an activity that is [. . .] accordant', and, moreover in 'the activity required for *cognition in general*' (ibid., p. 63 [B 31]). The judgement of taste realizes the pure basic form of cognitive judgement.

This alone would already mean a considerable revaluation of the aesthetic; does the latter not thereby lose the whiff of the irrational and come to be apprehended as the pure form of the cognitive event altogether? But Kant even goes one step further still and claims not only that aesthetic feats are analogous to cognitive ones, but conversely that they have a foundational function for them. Aesthetic action is not only, so to speak, the concentrate for cognitive action, rather it is a basic condition and a factual implicate of all cognitive feats. Why is this? Kant says that 'any determinate cognition [. . .] rests on that relation as its subjective condition' (ibid., p. 62 [B 29]), whereby with 'that relation' he means that in which 'imagination and understanding are in free play', insofar as in this imagination and understanding 'harmonize with each other as required for *cognition in general*' (ibid.). Kant was obviously thinking that no judgement, of whatever type it may be, gets by without a feeling of concordance which refers to the dovetailing or fitting of the sensible and conceptual aspect, that is, of material and structural components. But this 'concord' can ultimately only be observed aesthetically. To this extent an aesthetic act inheres in every judgement. Consequently, not only does aesthetic judgement correspond to the pure basic form of every act of judgement, but the reverse even applies too: every act of judgement includes an aesthetic feat.

In § 21 Kant re-emphasizes this point – and this in a form which ought finally to have made people listen. Having repeated that the aesthetic judgement's claim to universality is due to the fact that this judgement represents the pure basic form of an act of judgement altogether, he points out once again that no act of judgement and no knowledge gets by without this ultimately aesthetic aspect. He explains that a common sense, such as is required for 'the universal communicability of a feeling', generally represents 'the necessary condition of the universal communicability of our cognition'. Hence it is presupposed 'in any logic and any principle of cognitions' (ibid., § 21, p. 88 [B 66]). No knowledge is even conceivable without this innermost aesthetic sense known as the 'common sense' [*Gemeinsinn*]. It is a necessary element of every theory of cognition – mostly remaining implicit, but made explicit by Kant. Our cognition is aesthetically determined in both its propositional constitution and its communicative character. – To this extent Kant also in the *Critique of Judgment* developed a lesson which could be given the heading 'protoaesthetics of cognition'. The recently popular strategy of playing off the *Critique of Judgment*'s aesthetics of taste against the *Critique of Pure Reason*'s transcendental aesthetic and declaring the former to be the actual, the latter, however, to be a merely nominal or obsolete, aesthetics is thus doubly wrong (see the preceding note).

32. Even Husserl, who otherwise at least attempted to counter the consequences of epistemological aestheticization to be portrayed in the following, could not avoid the insight into this protoaesthetics. He too emphasized 'the protological function of the transcendental aesthetic' (Edmund Husserl, *Formale und transzendentale Logik*, ed. Paul Janssen, Husserliana vol. XVII, The Hague: Nijhoff 1974, p. 447).

33. Alexander Gottlieb Baumgarten, *Aesthetica*, Frankfurt a.d. Oder 1750 (reprint Hildesheim: Olms 1970), § 1, p. 1.

34. 'The "Oldest System-Programme" of German Idealism', in *Hegel Selections*, ed. M.J. Inwood (London/New York: Macmillan 1989), pp. 86–87, here p. 87.

35. Cf. Baumgarten, *Aesthetica*, §§ 559, 560, 564.

36. Cf. ibid.

37. Cf. ibid., § 557.

38. Cf. ibid.

39. Cf. ibid., § 565.

40. Nietzsche, 'On Truth and Lies in a Nonmoral Sense', pp. 88–89.

41. Ibid., p. 84.

42. Ibid., p. 86.

43. Ibid.

44. Herder had already adhered to a dynamic and pragmatic – instead of an 'objective' – apprehension of our cognitive forms: 'What fraction among you considers logic, mathematics, morality, physics for what they are – organs of the human soul, *tools*, with which one should work!' (Johann Gottfried Herder, *Auch eine Philosophie der Geschichte zur Bildung der Menschheit* [1774], Frankfurt a.M.: Suhrkamp 1967, p. 76.)

45. Nietzsche, 'On Truth and Lies in a Nonmoral Sense', p. 86.

46. Ibid., p. 85.

47. Friedrich Nietzsche, *The Gay Science*, trans. Walter Kaufmann (New York: Vintage 1974), p. 121 [57].

48. Otto Neurath, 'Protokollsätze', in *Erkenntnis*, 3, 1932/3, pp. 204–214, here p. 206. Incidentally Neurath was a particularly lively and versatile character. He urged his students to embark upon a new course in life every five years.

49. It forms the epigraph to *Word and Object* (Cambridge, Mass.: MIT Press 1960), p. vii.

50. Karl Popper, 'The Logic of the Social Sciences', in Popper, *In Search of a Better World*, trans. Laura J. Bennett (London/New York: Routledge 1992), pp. 64–81, here p. 65.

51. Hans Blumenberg, *Schiffbruch mit Zuschauer. Paradigma einer Daseinsmetapher* (Frankfurt a.M.: Suhrkamp 1979).

52. One might want to object that this is mere metaphorical parlance. But the concern is,

firstly, if with a metaphor at all, then with a metaphor for an elemental situation, and elemental situations are only ever explicable metaphorically. And, secondly, if recent thinking has increasingly apprehended reality as the product of metaphorical activity, then metaphors are not mere 'metaphors' but potentially valid descriptions of reality.

53. A comparison with Aristotle shows how fundamental this difference is opposed to older conceptions. He too made use of a nautical metaphor at an important point – but with a completely different aim in mind. In the *Protrepticus*, his appeal to philosophy, Aristotle says of philosophers: 'Like a good sea-captain he moors his boat to that which is eternal and unchanging, drops his anchor there, and lives his own master.' (*Aristotle's Proterepticus. An Attempt at Reconstruction*, ed. Ingemar Düring, Gothenburg: Acta Universitatis Gothoburgensis 1961, p. 69 [B 50]). – It is just this chance to drop anchor, this Archimedean point, which is no longer seen by modern thinking.

54. 'Schiffbau aus dem Schiffbruch': The title of Chapter 6 of Blumenberg, *Schiffbruch mit Zuschauer*, pp. 70–74.

55. It doesn't seem to me to be going too far to characterize hermeneutics – in Gadamer's version too say – as thought in the conditions of this view.

56. Richard Rorty, *Philosophy and the Mirror of Nature* (Princeton: Princeton University Press 1979), p. 378.

57. Nelson Goodman, *Ways of Worldmaking* (Indianapolis: Hackett 1978), p. 3.

58. Richard Rorty, *Contingency, Irony, and Solidarity* (Cambridge/New York: Cambridge University Press 1989), pp. 53, 67, 68, 69.

59. Ibid., p. 53.

60. Goodman has above all made clear the cognitive dimension of the aesthetic – to the benefit of aesthetics as well as epistemology. See Nelson Goodman, *Languages of Art. An Approach to a Theory of Symbols* (Brighton: Harvester Press 1981), esp. pp. 264f.

61. Goodman has expressed this in the following way: 'The movement is from unique truth and a world fixed and found to a diversity of right and even conflicting versions or worlds in the making.' (Goodman, *Ways of Worldmaking*, p. x.)

62. Paul Feyerabend, *Wissenschaft als Kunst* (Frankfurt a.M.: Suhrkamp 1984), p. 8.

63. Cf. ibid. – Incidentally Konrad Fiedler had already, in 1876, observed: 'Art is just as much research as is science, and science is just as much design as is art.' (Konrad Fiedler, 'Über die Beurteilung von Werken der bildenden Kunst', in Fiedler, *Schriften zur Kunst*, ed. Gottfried Boehm, Munich: Fink 1991, vol. 1, pp. 1–48, here p. 31).

64. Feyerabend, *Wissenschaft als Kunst*, p. 77.

65. Ibid., p. 78. – It is interesting in the context being pursued here that one of the first important natural-scientific Kantians, Johann Wilhelm Ritter, had already in 1806 held a lecture in Munich with the title 'Physics as Art'.

66. See Thomas S. Kuhn, *The Structure of Scientific Revolutions* (Chicago: University of Chicago Press 1962).

67. Kuhn carries on in this from Gaston Bachelard, who had taught already in the thirties that the development of science proceeds not continuously, but is characterized by crises and dramatic incisions ('coupures épistémologiques') each of which has 'a complete upheaval of the system of knowledge' as a result (Gaston Bachelard, *Die Bildung des wissenschaftlichen Geistes. Beitrag zu einer Psychoanalyse der objektiven Erkenntnis*, Frankfurt a.M.: Suhrkamp 1978 [original French edition, Paris: Vrin 1938], p. 49). Bachelard had first proposed his thesis of the discontinuity of scientific development in his dissertation *Essai sur la connaissance approchée* (Paris: Vrin 1928) and then developed this more precisely in *The New Scientific Spirit*, trans. Arthur Goldhammer (Boston, Mass.: Beacon Press 1984 [original French edition, Paris: PUF 1934]).

68. Thomas S. Kuhn, *The Structure of Scientific Revolutions* (Chicago: University of Chicago Press, 2nd enlarged edition, 1970), p. 208.

69. Cf. ibid. Elsewhere Kuhn reports that 'the similarities between science and art' had for him 'been a revelation', and he emphasizes 'that the scientist, just as the artist, allows himself to be guided by aesthetic viewpoints and is subject to the influence of prevailing ways of perceiving' (Thomas S. Kuhn, 'Bemerkungen zum Verhältnis von Wissenschaft und Kunst', in

Kuhn, *Die Entstehung des Neuen. Studien zur Struktur der Wissenschaftsgeschichte*, Frankfurt a.M.: Suhrkamp 1977, pp. 446–460, here pp. 449f. [Eng.: 'Comment on the Relation of Science and Art', in *Comparative Studies in Society and History*, 17, 1969, pp. 403–412.]

70. Thus Mary Hesse interprets scientific revolutions as 'metaphorical redescriptions' of nature (Mary Hesse, 'The Explanatory Function of Metaphor', in Hesse, *Revolutions and Reconstructions in the Philosophy of Science*, Bloomington: Indiana University Press 1980, pp. 111–124, here p. 111), and James W. McAllister points out that new paradigms are essentially brought about by a change in the aesthetic canon, that is, in aesthetic preferences (cf. James W. McAllister, 'Truth and Beauty in Scientific Reason', in *Synthese*, 78, 1989, pp. 25–51).

71. Of course different cognitive preferences can then exist corresponding to different cognitive preferences. The aesthetics of beauty and of harmony is not the only one possible. One can also adhere to an aesthetics of paradoxy, of break-up, of ambivalence or of openness. In the first case one would have the feeling of successful knowledge when everything fits together to form a whole, that is, becomes harmonic; in the second case, however, one would have such a feeling when ultimate rifts and incompatibilities come to light. The former was the case with scientists such as Kepler or Heisenberg. Kepler was only willing to believe in an aesthetics of harmony, and for many scientists even today the statement 'if it's not beautiful, then it can't be true' applies. Things are different with thinkers such as Benjamin or Lyotard. Lyotard views concordance as having been first achieved when paradoxes and conflicts come to light; and Benjamin was convinced that true cognition is like a bolt of lightning in character.

72. See here the reader *On Aesthetics in Science* (Cambridge, Mass.: MIT Press 1981) edited by Judith Wechsler; also the works of Subrahmanyan Chandrasekhar collected under the title *Truth and Beauty. Aesthetics and Motivations in Science* (Chicago: University of Chicago Press 1987); finally Gideon Engler, 'Aesthetics in Science and Art', in *The British Journal of Aesthetics*, 30(1), 1990, pp. 24–34 and James W. McAllister, 'Scientists' Aesthetic Judgements', in *The British Journal of Aesthetics*, 31(4), 1991, pp. 332–341. McAllister points out that the application of aesthetic categories to intellectual constructs was much more familiar in Shaftesbury's and Hutcheson's time than it is today to an aesthetics which is far too artistically restricted (cf. ibid., p. 339).

73. Poincaré's outlook is incidentally in no way an extravagant one, but had already been forwarded by less original minds. For instance in his inaugural lecture in Erlangen on 11 January 1930, 'On the Aesthetic Approach in Mathematics', Wolfgang Krull demonstrated that imagination is very important to mathematics and that mathematics and art are related in this respect: 'I wanted to show that the mathematician's imagination and creative principles are, in a certain respect, related to those of an artist.' 'It seems to me [. . .] to be of general importance that it is finally emphasized that aesthetic aspects play a great role for mathematicians.' 'I [. . .] would like to emphasize in all strictness: real mathematicians must above all else possess imagination, of course a particular, a "mathematical" imagination.' (Wolfgang Krull, 'Über die ästhetische Betrachtungsweise in der Mathematik', in *Sitzungsberichte der physikalisch-medizinischen Sozietät zu Erlangen*, 61, 1930, pp. 207–220, here pp. 211, 218, 208.)

74. Cf. James D. Watson, *The Double Helix. A Personal Account of the Discovery of the Structure of DNA* (London: Penguin 1970).

75. For Newton, for instance, an aesthetic distinction such as simplicity was in effect a criterion for the concept of a law of nature. It was not a discovery which was made with regard to nature, but an aesthetic precondition for that which was to count as a law of nature (cf. Dale Jacquette, 'Aesthetics and Natural Law in Newton's Methodology', in *Journal of the History of Ideas*, 51/4, 1990, pp. 659–666, here esp. pp. 661 and 666).

76. Herder had already diagnosed: 'Thus became *Newton* unwillingly in his world-building a poet, just as did *Buffon* in his cosmogony, and *Leibniz* in his doctrine of prestabilized harmony and monadology. Just as our whole psychology consists of pictorial words, so it was mostly *one* new picture, *one* analogy, *one* conspicuous simile, which gave birth to the greatest and boldest theories.' (Johann Gottfried Herder, 'Vom Erkennen und Empfinden der

menschlichen Seele', in Herder, *Sämmtliche Werke*, ed. Bernhard Suphan, vol. 8, Berlin: Weidmann 1892, p. 170).

77. Niklas Luhmann, *Die Wissenschaft der Gesellschaft* (Frankfurt a.M.: Suhrkamp 1990), p. 717.

78. Incidentally, Montaigne too had already said that we only ever make comments on comments: 'Our opinions are grafted upon one another' (Michel de Montaigne, *The Complete Essays of Montaigne*, trans. Donald M. Frame, Stanford: Stanford University Press 1965, here III.13, p. 818).

79. Of course these insights also lead to a departure from science's monopoly on truth. The proof that scientific truth at base level is no less aesthetically constituted than are other forms of orientation leads consistently to the relativization of the previously exclusive status of scientific truth.

80. It is almost superfluous to note once more that this aestheticization has nothing to do with beautification or the like. It is concerned not with objects' aesthetic predicates, but rather with an aesthetic characteristic of the state of our knowledge, our cognition and our apprehension of reality.

81. Even 'fundamentalisms', viewed closely, prove themselves to be constructs of an ultimately aesthetic nature. However, fundamentalisms must also concede their status as a construction. As long as they appeal to absolute, objective truth they are pursuing a legitimization strategy which has become untenable. This simultaneously identifies a demarcation line between acceptable and unacceptable fundamentalisms. What's deceitful is not that one constructs, but that one denies the contructive character.

82. Gaston Bachelard has demonstrated brilliantly how modern age science always moved within the grip of a certain imagery (see for example his comments on the sponge metaphor with Descartes, Réaumur and Franklin: Bachelard, *Die Bildung des wissenschaftlichen Geistes*, pp. 127–135). With regard to philosophy Rorty explains generally: 'It is pictures rather than propositions, metaphors rather than statements, which determine most of our philosophical convictions' (Rorty, *Philosophy and the Mirror of Nature*, p. 12) – and then, in particular, he subjected the image of consciousness as a mirror to incisive criticism. Italo Calvino has pointed out that, surprisingly, pictures are still met with in 'a language as distant from the visual imagination as that of modern scientific discourse': 'Even when you read the most specialized scientific treatise or the most abstract book on philosophy, you can suddenly come across a sentence which unexpectedly stimulates the power of visual imagination.' (Italo Calvino, *Sechs Vorschläge für das nächste Jahrtausend. Harvard-Vorlesungen*, Munich: Hanser 1991, p. 125 [Eng.: *Six Memos for the Next Millennium*, Cambridge, MA: Harvard University Press 1988].) With regard to his own work Calvino said that, although 'a visual image stood at the origin of every one of my stories' (ibid., p. 123), his procedure nonetheless aimed to 'unite the spontaneous generation of pictures with the intentionality of discursive thinking' (ibid., p. 125). Finally he comes to the conclusion: 'All the same the visual solutions remain decisive, and sometimes they enter the plan unawares, to decide situations which neither the conjectures of thinking nor the resources of language can resolve' (ibid., pp. 125f.).

83. Ludwig Wittgenstein, *On Certainty*, eds G.E.M. Anscombe and G.H. von Wright, trans. Denis Paul and G.E.M. Anscombe (New York: Harper 1972), p. 73^e [559]. At another point Wittgenstein details the way in which it makes no sense to ask after reasons for thinking. You can only 'describe the game of thinking, but not the reasons why we think. "Reason" only applies within a system of rules. [. . .] It is nonsense to ask for reasons for the whole system of thought. You cannot give justification for the rules.' (*Wittgenstein's Lectures 1930–1932*, ed. Desmond Lee, Oxford: Blackwell 1980, p. 88). '[. . .] rational only applies within the system' (ibid., p. 105).

84. Rorty has pointed this out under the heading 'contingency' (cf. Rorty, *Contingency, Irony, and Solidarity*) and the views of modern hermeneutics (considered by Rorty) point in the same direction.

85. Wittgenstein, *On Certainty*, p. 44^e [342, 341].

86. Ludwig Wittgenstein, *Culture and Value*, ed. G.H. von Wright, trans. Peter Winch (Chicago: University of Chicago Press 1984), p. 16^e.

87. Wittgenstein, *Wittgenstein's Lectures 1930–1932*, p. 104.

88. Quoted from *Ludwig Wittgenstein. Sein Leben in Bildern und Texten*, eds Michael Nedo and Michele Ranchetti (Frankfurt a.M.: Suhrkamp 1982), p. 316.

89. Wittgenstein, *Culture and Value*, p. 25ᵉ.

90. In this sense Frege, in a letter to Wittgenstein dated 16 September 1919, reproved that the *Tractatus* represented 'more an artistic than a scientific achievement' (quoted from Manfred Frank and Gianfranco Soldati, *Wittgenstein – Literat und Philosoph*, Pfullingen: Neske 1989, p. 42).

91. Wittgenstein, *Culture and Value*, p. 79ᵉ.

92. Ibid., p. 17ᵉ.

93. Ibid., p. 39ᵉ.

94. Ibid., p. 16ᵉ. 'You think philosophy is hard enough, but I can tell you it is nothing to the difficulties involved in architecture.' (*Recollections of Wittgenstein*, ed. Rush Rhees, Oxford/New York: Oxford University Press 1984, pp. 76f.)

95. Wittgenstein, *Culture and Value*, p. 82ᵉ.

96. Ibid., 19ᵉ.

97. Ibid., p. 483. – Incidentally Nietzsche had already stated: 'Before anything is "thought", something has already been [poetically] "invented" [. . .]'. (Friedrich Nietzsche, 'Nachgelassene Fragmente. Herbst 1885 bis Anfang Januar 1889. Teil 1: Herbst 1885 bis Herbst 1887', in Nietzsche, *Sämtliche Werke*, vol. 12, p. 550 [Autumn 1887].)

98. One might want to object that whereas this applied perhaps for the late Wittgenstein, that with the early Wittgenstein, the strict Wittgenstein of the *Tractatus logico-philosophicus*, things are different. Not even close. As early as 1912 in a dispute with Bertrand Russell Wittgenstein insisted on the *aesthetic* character of his philosophical method. Russell had warned him 'he ought not simply to *state* what he thinks true', but Wittgenstein replied that arguments 'would spoil [a thought's] beauty, and that he would feel as if he was dirtying a flower with muddy hands' (Bertrand Russell in a letter to Ottoline Morrell dated 28 May 1912, quoted from Brian McGuiness, *Wittgenstein – A Life: Young Ludwig 1889–1921*, London: Duckworth 1988, p. 104). Such a sentiment stayed with Wittgenstein through to the end. The previously quoted utterance, 'Oh, why do I feel as if I were writing a poem when I write philosophy?' continues 'it is [. . .] as if something tiny were here which has a magnificent significance. Like a leaf or a flower' (*Ludwig Wittgenstein. Sein Leben in Bildern und Texten*, p. 316).

99. Ludwig Wittgenstein, *Philosophical Investigations*, trans. G.E.M. Anscombe (New York: Macmillan 1958), p. 85ᵉ [217].

100. Cf. Plato, *Republic*, 607 e–608 b.

101. Cf. ibid., 607 b–e.

102. Montaigne, *Essais*, II 12, p. 223. – Quoted here from Montaigne, *The Complete Essays of Montaigne*, trans. Donald M. Frame (Stanford: Stanford University Press 1965), pp. 400–401.

103. Plato, *Republic*, 472 d–e.

104. Ibid., 501 c.

105. Wittgenstein, *Culture and Value*, p. 12ᵉ.

106. Ibid., 1ᵉ.

107. Ibid.

3

AESTHET/HICS
Ethical Implications and Consequences
of Aesthetics

Aesthetics is the mother of ethics.

Joseph Brodsky, 'Uncommon Visage'

Preliminary remark: on the relationship between aesthetics and ethics, and the concept of an aesthet/hics

Two of philosophy's subdisciplines have gained considerable impetus in recent years: ethics and aesthetics. With ethics the reason is obvious. The new and ever greater problems faced by industrial societies – North–South differentials, ecology, unemployment, genetic technology – are continually increasing the need for ethics. The reasons for the topicality of aesthetics, on the other hand, are quite different. Its boost is due not to external consequences, but to an internal factor of the rationalization process, namely the fact that truth, the guiding category of scientific rationality, has increasingly proven itself to bear an aesthetic signature; as a result aesthetics is on its way to becoming a kind of fundamental discipline.[1]

A change has occurred too in the relationship between the disciplines of ethics and aesthetics in recent years. If, traditionally and in modernity, they were contrasted with one another, then it's their connections which are currently coming to the fore.

Traditionally the aesthetic was considered dangerous; it was thought that ethical barriers must be imposed on it. Thus, in antiquity, the aesthetic was assigned its place in the framework of philosophico-ethical standardizations, and even in the Christian Occident aesthetics remained under the thumb of ethics until and within the modern age.

Modernity then construed the opposition of the two disciplines differently, namely as being one of two equiponderant spheres which were to be kept separated. Autonomy, the modern watchword of aesthetics, originally meant keeping aesthetics free of ethical stipulations. Conversely, aesthetic viewpoints have had no role to play for modern ethics since Kant.

But the traditional model of an ethical preponderation over the aesthetic and the modern model of an autonomous neutrality between the two spheres have been disburdened in the last few years by a new attentiveness to entanglements between the ethical and the aesthetic. Neoaristotelian and poststructuralist ethics (Nussbaum, Foucault) assign aesthetics a key role for ethics, and sociological and ecological aesthetic theories (Bourdieu, Böhme) afford ethical aspects validity as fundamental viewpoints of the aesthetic.[2]

Generally we are today recognizing that the different realms and disciplines – as opposed to the way imagined by the modern differentiation theorem and separation precept – are determined by entanglement. This requires the transition from a separative to an entangled form of thought. Disciplinary purism and separatism have become obsolete strategies. Transdisciplinary and transversal analyses are taking their place.[3]

It's from a perspective of this sort that I want to ask in the following to what extent ethical determinations are inherent in aesthetics as such. I will try to explore the ethical potential of the aesthetic itself and point to some ethical consequences which result from this. The neologism 'aesthet/hics' – formed by the contraction of 'aesthetics' and 'ethics' – is meant to designate those parts of aesthetics which *of themselves* contain ethical elements.

The question concerning such an aesthet/hics – which, since it is new, can only be handled here as a first draft – is to be secured against one misunderstanding straight away. Sounding out the possibilities of such an aesthet/hics does not mean wanting to replace ethics by aesthetics. If I demonstrate ethical implications and consequences of aesthetics, I by no means want to claim that an ethics *sui generis* would become superfluous on their account. An aesthet/hics of this sort could, however, complement the usual ethics or be of help to it – it could close gaps in reasoning, improve arguments, clarify aims and help further at problematic points.[4]

I want to talk about two versions of such an aesthet/hics. Firstly, about a long-familiar ethical imperative in the midst of the aesthetic (sections I and II), and secondly about a newer option which became necessary to oppose this (sections III and IV). The first perspective is concerned with the imperative to step above the immediately-sensible to a higher-sensible; the second perspective concerns the maxim to do justice to the varying demands of sensibility – for instance the immediately-sensible just as the higher-sensible ones. In both cases – as I want to show – versions of an aesthet/hics are involved.

I. An ethics inherent in the aesthetic realm

1. Elementary aesthetics

The first, traditional type of an aesthet/hics already arises in the midst of elementary aesthetics. By 'elementary aesthetics' I understand an aesthetics which – in contrast to those referring to art – relates to *aisthesis*, to *perception*. Indeed the name 'aesthetics' is derived from *aisthesis* too.

As is well known, *aisthesis* has a double meaning. On the one hand, *aisthesis* means *perception*, on the other hand, *sensation*. This double sense was already present in Greek and is to be found in most other languages. It stems from the phenomenon. As *perception*, *aisthesis* addresses genuine sensuous qualities such as colours, sounds, tastes and smells. It serves their *cognition*. As *sensation*, on the other hand, it follows an emotive perspective. It evaluates the sensible on a scale of *pleasure and displeasure*.

The first stage of *aisthesis* is represented by the *sensation*. It complies with vital interests. The pleasure or displeasure by which it evaluates its objects is nothing other than an index of the benefit or detriment for the human's vital needs. In this, however, there is already an indication of the potential relevance of the functional difference between short- and long-range senses. Unlike the short-range senses, the long-range senses are not dependent upon immediate contact with the object, but rather make their observations at a distance. This was to become the point of departure for a subsequent dissociation of perception from sensation, since the vital relevance, as registered by sensation, always results ultimately from direct contact (even a tiger is unable to maul us from afar). Thus the contact-bound short-range senses are, as a matter of principle, fixed more strongly to sensation than are the long-range senses. The latter is afforded by its constitution the chance to absolve itself from the proximity of sensation. To begin with, however, *aisthesis* as a whole moves on the intentional horizon of sensation. It's just that the long-range senses already distinguish themselves functionally – if not yet intentionally too – from the immediate mode of sensation that remains binding for the short-range senses.

The step towards the dissociation of perception from sensation is made as soon as *aisthesis* directs itself to an object's appearance as such – independently of its sensational characteristics. In doing so it assumes an objective orientation in place of the previous subjective orientation. This occurs more easily for the long-range senses because, as I've said, their functional distinction from sensation (their operation at spatial distance) simultaneously countenances an intentional distancing. To this extent the long-range senses act as protagonists of the higher, perception-like form of *aisthesis*. This now addresses itelf to objective qualities, no longer to the sensation-bound aspect of objects. This cognition-like orientation of *aisthesis* can then consecutively be transferred to the short-range senses.

A new type of *aisthesis* is thereby established, the type of actual *perceiving*. It targets the genuine sensuous qualities of objects, that is, colours, tones, tastes, smells and tactile qualities, and this in their objective characteristic – independently of their subjectively vital sensational aspects. This 'pure' perceiving represents the kind of perceiving which has always been treated and esteemed by tradition. It is no longer in the service of vital interests, but is given over completely to the ideal of *cognition*. It has freed itself from the first stage, from sensation-bound *aisthesis* and from the horizon of sensation altogether. Perceiving has become autonomous. With the step to cognizing it has left the sensationally determined level of *aisthesis* behind and below itself.

However, in consequence of this step towards pure perceiving, sensation does not remain quite as it was. Corresponding to the initial solidarity of perception and sensation, the constitution of a higher, purer type of act now comes about analogously in the case of sensation too. This is still in accordance with aspects of pleasure – but no longer those of primary, vital pleasure. Rather another storey is added, so to speak, to the edifice of pleasure: the *piano nobile* of a new kind of pleasure now raises itself above the ground floor of vital-sensuous pleasure: the pleasure of a purely reflective delight or discontentment.[5] It's precisely this which is the birthplace of the specifically aesthetic sense: that of *taste*. This evaluates its objects no longer, as did the primary sensation, according to vital criteria, that is, as, say, alluring, pleasant-tasting or nauseous, but rather according to reflexive criteria, that is, for instance, as beautiful, delightful and harmonic, or as repulsive, ugly and disturbed. The architecture of sensation and pleasure comprehends two levels from here on: the ground floor of the taste of sense and the upper storey of the taste of reflection – as Kant called this distinction.[6]

2.   The aesthetic or elevatory imperative

To what extent – as I want to contend – does the basis of an *aisthesis*-immanent ethics lie in this architecture of *aisthesis*?

The two-storey nature is evidently linked with an *aesthetic imperative*, which, at the same time, is of significance as an aesthet/hic imperative insofar as it indicates how we are to deal with sensibility. This imperative is concerned, first of all, with the perceptive feats of *aisthesis*. Here it states: in perceiving, keep yourself free of sensuous sensation, disregard it, rise above it! Moreover, this imperative applies in relation to sensation too, and there it states: don't just heed primary vital pleasures, but also exercise the higher, peculiarly aesthetic pleasure of a reflective delight! In both versions this aesthet/hic imperative demands that we step above primary-sensible determination. Hence I want to designate it the *elevatory imperative*.

3.   The vital imperative

However this elevatory imperative is obviously not the first imperative in the aesthetic sphere. Rather it is preceded by another, a *vital imperative*. For to begin with, as I've said, *aisthesis*, as sensation, served vital interests alone. It served life, keeping yourself alive, and survival (*zen, soteria*) – but not yet the good life (*eu zen*). It aimed to identify what was useful or harmful, beneficial or detrimental, and effected the corresponding subsistential act of directing or averting one's attention. To this extent a first and elementary connection of aesthetics and ethics is already found on this vital level. These initial aesthetic acts already directly served one, at least rudimentarily, ethical goal: that of sustaining life. The imperative, linked with *aisthesis*, which requires compliance with its observations is extremely conducive to life. This vital imperative is the first aesthet/hic imperative.

4.   *The anthropological difference*

But the following is now revealing: usually we consider the primary constitution of aisthesis just outlined as being distinctive of animal, not human, life, which is supposed rather to distinguish itself precisely in its overcoming being vitally determined in this way.

Aristotle, for example, described it thus: animals only know what's useful and harmful, and pleasure and pain are sufficient and dependable indicators of this. Humans, however, also know of higher predicates like good and bad, just and unjust, and these require more than sensible determination; they demand the ability to reflect and to communicate.[7]

So the elevatory imperative – the call to climb above immediately sensible determination in favour of a pure perceiving, on the one side, and of a higher delight, on the other – is directly linked with the anthropological difference, with humans' Being as humans. Insofar as we are living creatures, the vital imperative is our first aesthet/hic imperative too and the elevatory imperative just the second. But, insofar as we are *humans*, the elevatory imperative is our constitutive and decisive imperative. In human terms it is the categorical imperative *par excellence*.

In the following I concentrate on this second, elevatory imperative. It represents not merely an elementary axiom of our culture, according to which success in life is to be gained only by an ascent of this type; rather, it's this elevatory imperative which is also brought to bear in the philosophical discipline by the name of aesthetics.

But first I want to note one more thing: the elevatory imperative is a genuine ethical imperative growing on aesthetic terrain, that is, an *aesthet/hic* imperative in the precise sense. Here it's not an ethical precept from the outside intruding in the realm of aesthetics; rather this imperative grows within the aesthetic sphere itself. We are faced with the starting point for an ethics in the midst of aesthetics.

II.   Traditional aesthetics and its tendency to absolutize the aesthetico-elevatory imperative

In this section I want to show the way in which traditional aesthetics became a cultural authority for the elevatory imperative's assertion. In addition I would like to point out a highly problematic and almost paradoxical trait of this aesthetics: its tendency to hostility towards the senses.

1. Baumgarten, Meier

In order to create chances of cultural acceptance for their new project of aesthetics, the aestheticians of the eighteenth century had first of all to show that their intentions did not conflict with, but rather corresponded to, the standard ethical demands of established culture, even that it was suited in some particular way to securing these demands' validity in the recalcitrant sphere of the sensible.

With this in mind, Baumgarten, the founder of aesthetics, replied to the objection that his aesthetics amounted to a reinforcement of sensibility, whereas by rights this should be combated and not strengthened, with the assurance that aesthetics would assist us towards the desired mastery over the senses.[8] Baumgarten's student Meier conformed still more vehemently with the cultural precept of control over sensibility.[9] He underlines that 'with the whole amelioration of the lower forces of desire [. . .] one must attend well [. . .] that they don't yet become too strong. Else we shall decline to the beastly state and to moral slavery.'[10] Meier describes 'the sensible powers of cognition' – which actually represent the capital in aesthetics – as being 'the dregs of the soul',[11] and he decrees that 'By rights, the senses ought to be the slaves of reason.'[12] – From such premises, one can understand how aesthetics was able to become an undertaking to discipline the senses.[13]

Utterances of this sort might well have been largely strategical declarations with Baumgarten – in reality he brought many of the sensible's own claims to bear in strong measure. But subsequent and very prominent concepts of aesthetics, for all their apparent affinity with the senses, have in truth thought and argued decidedly anti-sensibly. My example – as surprising as it might seem at first – is Schiller.

2. Schiller

In *On the Aesthetic Education of Man in a Series of Letters* Schiller hopes for everything salutary from the aesthetic education of humanity, or, more accurately, from the 'training of the sensibility'.[14] At the end of the letters, however, he demands that 'the power of perception [be] already broken within its own boundaries'.[15] Sensibility he now considers a 'dreadful foe' which is to be 'fought' against; one must 'play at being at war with matter within the boundaries of matter'.[16] 'The real artistic secret of the master' consists precisely in 'his *annihilating the material by means of the form*'.[17] It is in such combating and extirpation of the originary-sensible that Schiller sees the primary task for 'aesthetic culture'.[18] – Just how can one explain this perversion of an intended affinity towards the senses – as one generally ascribes to aesthetics and as one initially finds formulated with Schiller too – into a programme hostile to the senses, into a war strategy against the senses?

Schiller's original intention aimed for an equilibrium and reconciliation of sensibility and reason. It was concerned with reconciling 'the laws of reason [. . .] with the interest of the senses'.[19] The discrepancy between this intention of affinity towards the senses and the project's execution, with its hostility towards the senses, results from the fact that Schiller makes no concessions in adhering to the elevatory imperative and, in so doing, goes on to give this an absolutist form.

Schiller, as I've said, puts his trust in a 'training of the sensibility'.[20] He calls this 'ennobling'.[21] But since he also thinks of the development of our sensitive capacity in terms of an absolutized aesthetic imperative, which demands the complete departure from the immediately sensible, a martial project is what becomes of this planned cultivation. Schiller calls for nothing less than 'a total revolution' of our 'whole mode of perception'.[22] We are to depart from primary-sensibility *in toto*, are in future to behave not at all sensuously, but solely aesthetically. We should climb above the 'physical condition' not just here and there, but should make the transition 'to the aesthetic [condition]'.[23] The primary-sensible and the higher-sensible conditions are to stand not alongside, or above one another, rather the first is to be abolished fully in favour of the second. – The genteel Schiller is a rigorous executor of the aesthetic imperative. He demands totalizing compliance with it.

As paradoxical as it might seem, the extirpation of the primary-sensible constitutes the basic responsibility of aesthetic education for Schiller. This comes to light repeatedly, occasioned by diverse considerations. Thus, for instance, Schiller praises the mechanical and fine artist alike as 'he does not hesitate to do [. . .] violence' to matter.[24] The annulment of the primary-sensible becomes the basic feat of aesthetics.

This is by no means just Schiller's view – which I cite here with the intention of exemplifying and not attributing particular blame – but it is the view of traditional aesthetics as a whole, so far as it conforms with the elevatory imperative. Schiller epitomizes the basic axiom of traditional aesthetics. Similarly, for instance, Hegel was to explain 'that the sensible must of course be present in the work of art, but may only appear as surface and *semblance* of the sensible'.[25] Art brings forth 'from the sensible side, intentionally, only a shadow world of shapes, tones and intuitions'.[26]

3.   Three absolutisms

An anti-sensible absolutism is built into aesthetic theories of this type – that is, into most traditional aesthetic theories. It is a consequence of the rigorous and absolutist understanding of the aesthetic imperative. This in fact only says that you should go about things not *merely* sensuously, but aesthetically *as well*. But this is rendered as: *nowhere* should you go about things sensuously, rather *everywhere* solely aesthetically. In this way aesthetics becomes – instead of an undertaking to extend and unfold the sensible – an undertaking for its regimentation. Whereas it is commonly believed that aesthetics brings to bear the rights of the sensible, it is in truth turned against the sensible by this form of thought, has the 'war against matter' as its maxim. – It's just this which must change if aesthetics is really to become an aesthetics one day.

In addition to this first absolutism, which obliterates sensibility, comes a second absolutism, one which obliterates the world. Schiller's account is once again significant. With him aesthetics becomes a hermetic game for the subject. Schiller requires that one should 'give form to everything external',[27] that is, accept nothing as it is, but through formation change everything into a human consistency and thereby appropriate it. 'Instead of abandoning [one]self to the world',[28] one should 'eradicate everything in [one]self that is merely world'.[29] In this way aesthetics becomes a form of fulfilment for absolute subjectivity.[30] No predetermination, no externality, no resistiveness, no alterity, is recognized, respected or retained. For aesthetic theories of this type things such as *mimesis*, abandonment to the material, experience of being changed, breaking open the armour of subjectivity, are excluded from their outset.[31] – This legacy too will have to be discarded by a modern aesthetics.

If the first absolutism eliminates the primary-sensuous within aesthetics, then this second alienates everything which is really different, strange, contrasting in relation to the world – basically, that is, almost the very possibility of aesthetic experience. Only aesthetic productivity and the aesthetic brought in by the subject itself remain.

Finally a third absolutism arises. Aesthetics claims to be the only verit-able instance of orientation. The competing modern authorities – science and morality – are systematically degraded by it. Thus Schiller dismisses the orientational claims of enlightenment and science by pointing out their one-sidedness and inadequacy;[32] what's more he claims that only aesthetics can meet the objectives of the 'art of living' (*Lebenskunst*) as well as solving the 'political problem' which caused the French revolution to fail.[33] Thus the one thesis lays claim to the aesthetic's surpassing the cognitive, the other to the aesthetic ursurpation of moral orientation. – As is well known, this programme of aesthetic precedence then made its most grandiose entry in 'The "Oldest System-Programme" of German Idealism', which begins with an ethics project so as to end with the aesthetic absorption of the ethical just as the cognitive.[34]

On the whole the aesthetic imperative's absolutization – which is here inferred from Schiller, but which is deeply engraved within traditional aesthetics as a whole – leads, instead of to aesthetic reconciliation, to a threefold aesthetic absolutism: towards primary-sensibility, towards the world, and towards competing means of orientation. Herein lies the threefold malaise of traditional aesthetics.

The systematic error which underlies this consists, as I've said, in the misunderstanding of the aesthetic imperative. The command to *step above* the immediately sensuous is taken as a call for its *negation* and *extinction*.

That's why aesthetic theories of this type develop not strategies of recognition and emancipation of the sensible, but strategies for its domination, banishment and regimentation. This is the innermost paradox of traditional aesthetics. Insofar as aesthetics was originally intended as an undertaking for the rehabilitation of the senses, this displacement more or less amounts to a perversion of the project.

III.   Modern aesthetics: 'Justice to the heterogeneous' (Adorno)

Although this traditional type of aesthetics is still found in the twentieth century, with reference to Adorno I would like to show how its inner contradiction can be uncovered, hence enabling the attainment of a different concept of aesthetics.

1.   The recurrence of traditional topoi

As is well known, Adorno's basic thesis regarding the relationship between aesthetics and ethics reads: the work of art has, on the level of content and statements, no direct moral, ethical or social relevance whatsoever – and nor should it want to possess such.[35] On the other hand, works are due – that is, indirectly, analogously – the highest moral relevance through their formation. The more immanently accomplished a work is, the more it *ipso facto* takes exception to a society in which nothing possesses value for itself, but everything has value only for something else. – How is this meant?

According to Adorno, art makes the step from raw sensibility to intellectual self-determination through its formative work. 'The raw, subjective core of evil is *a priori* negated by art, from which the ideal of being thoroughly formed is inalienable.'[36] With this Adorno is obviously repeating the old elevatory schema of aesthetics: the raw is the evil against which art sets form. The high-aesthetic defeats the low-aesthetic as Gabriel does Lucifer.

On this overcoming of the raw sensible through formation, Adorno now continues: '[. . .] this, not the announcement of moral theses or the attaining of moral influence, is its [that is, art's] share in morality and links it with a decent society'.[37] The work of art's crystal character is thus to be synonymous with its objection to social conditions; the thoroughly formed work of art is to hold up the mirror of something better to the society of alienation and exchange. There is 'nothing pure, fashioned according to its immanent law, which wouldn't exert silent criticism, denounce the abasement through a condition nearing the total exchange-society: in this everything exists merely for something else. The antisocial in art is the certain negation of a certain society.'[38] The societal utility, in which each thing exists merely for something else, is opposed by the freedom of a work of art, in which everything is itself. In brief: the autonomy of the artistic work criticizes the heteronomy of society.

Some of Adorno's diagnoses might sound spectacular, but basically until this point what's concerned is merely a recurrence of classical topoi in aesthetics. The first diagnosis, that of a step from the raw to the thoroughly formed, corresponds to the traditional aesthetic elevatory imperative, the precept requiring a step above the rough-sensible in favour of the reflective-sensible. The second diagnosis too, the linking of this rise with the freedom predicate, has long been familiar. Traditionally, the step from crude sensuousness to sublime aesthetics was already considered to be the ascent from the empire of utility and heteronomy into the sphere of freedom and autonomy. – Adorno articulates the classic elevatory aesthetic imperative with a contemporary twist.[39]

2.   Inner contradictions and reverse effects

That means, however, that Adorno's contemporary call for an artistic negation of the raw is just as dubious as the traditional one. Firstly – this was already my objection to Schiller – it doesn't preserve the aesthetic difference, but extinguishes it through the elimination of what contrasts with it, the primary-sensible, which is sweepingly discriminated against as raw by Adorno. Secondly, in this way the salvational ideal named autonomy also loses its innocence – running contrary to its being employed by Adorno. Autonomy is to embody freedom. It is to demonstrate the possibility of self-being in contrast to the factual societal condition in which 'everything exists merely for something else'. But it's just this which it doesn't do under the form premiss. For the elements of the work in no way assemble themselves to constitute the work's entirety, but must be forced together to this unity through the formation – in just the same way as are individuals in society.[40] Autonomy might apply for the work, but not for its elements. They have value only through their contribution to the whole, and it's this for which they are prepared.

Negation of the immediately-sensible and form as coercion, these are the two shadowy sides of the traditional approach – irrespective of whether this is articulated in the eighteenth or twentieth century.[41] Adorno, as I've said, helped himself to such traditional ideas to an astonishing extent. Whereas Schiller spoke of 'ennobling', Adorno talks, just as euphemistically, of 'intellectualization'. – In truth, however, what had long since been of importance was to discover the coercive character of such formation.

3.   Criticism of the primacy of form

On the other hand, it's precisely Adorno who recognized what's dubious and dominative about crystalline formation. Tersely he notes: 'Pointed against the sensual element, intellectualization turns blindly against its own differentiation in many ways, something intellectual itself [. . .].'[42] With this Adorno firstly diagnoses the anti-sensible affect of such formation, and secondly he objects that the sensible is not recognized in this; for the sensible's tendency to differentiate – traditionally registered as its manifold character, which is to be overcome through the synthetic activity of form or of the intellect[43] – is in truth to be recognized and esteemed as something intellectual in itself. The objective contradiction of classical aesthetics lay in its practising violence against the sensible, because it mistook the demands of the latter for being raw, instead of comprehending and respecting sensible diversity itself as being intellectual.

4.   Justice to the heterogeneous

At the same time this provides an indication of the direction to be taken in the future: the elements in a work must not be forced together to form a whole, instead their peculiarity must be indulged in. It would be a matter of picking up the diverging impulses of the material so that the design 'follows them where they themselves want to go'.[44] Aesthetic work, instead of exercising dominion, has to follow the 'singular impulses' and attempt to do them justice.[45] It would have to pursue an ideal not of unity through formation, but of doing justice to the heterogeneous. With this in mind Adorno says: 'Aesthetic unity' – and by this he now means true aesthetic unity – 'receives its dignity through the manifold itself. It allows justice to befall the heterogeneous.'[46]

This transformation in the guiding aesthetic idea from committed formation, which compresses the manifold, to the ideal of doing justice to the heterogeneous seems to me to be of great importance.[47] The new guiding idea provides freedom from traditional errors: from the negation of the primary-sensible and from the inability to indulge in the sensible altogether, and thus really to go about things aesthetically. Recognition and justice take the place of domination and oppression; a mimetic interaction becomes possible where previously only an instrumental one had been propagandized.

5.   Aesthet/hic consequences

This aesthetics too – aesthetics in the sense of doing justice to the hetero- geneous – has the structure of an aesthet/hics. An art which adheres to the new ideal will also be able to possess an ethical-moral radiance. It's just that it would no longer advocate an ethics of subjection, but one of justice.

There are two aspects to the ethical relevance of this new aesthetic conception which Adorno detailed. Firstly, the new aesthetic ideal has an exemplary character for a new type of subject. This was characterized by Adorno to the extent that a subject of this type would take satisfaction no longer in imperialism towards the other, but rather in finding that 'in familiar proximity [the other] remains something distant and different, beyond the heterogeneous just as the own.'[48] Subjects of this type would – and, as a matter of fact, the formula at the heart of the new aesthetics recurs in this as a subjective maxim – realize the 'state of distinction without domination [. . .] in which things distinct share in each other'.[49]

Secondly, the concept of aesthetic justice implies a sharp critique of the politico-judicial version of justice. Adorno advocates the view that it's only in aesthetics that justice can be spoken of at all, not in the policies for realization of the idea of justice. Political justice, being based on the 'principle of formal equivalence',[50] causes differences to disappear,[51] exercises 'real power'[52] over them. Aesthetic justice, on the other hand, acknowledges the differences. Hence aesthetic justice – as 'justice to the heterogeneous' – relates to political justice – as 'equality in which the differences submerge' – as does justice to injustice. Whereas political justice remains imprisoned by the machinery of domination, to which the conventional aesthetic guiding idea of formation had also belonged without being rumbled, it is aesthetic justice alone which is able to lead the way out.

IV. Ethical implications and consequences of contemporary aesthetic awareness

To conclude I want to outline how this concept of an aesthetics of justice might be further developed in today's conditions.

1. Plurality

What's needed is a step beyond the work-internal heterogeneity which Adorno had in mind, outwards to work-external heterogeneity, to the recognition not only of varying material tendencies in a single work, but also of the divergence in artistic paradigms between different works and in the sphere of art on the whole.

Basically such recognition of heterogeneity (at least in a moderate form) has long been an essential part of the artistic sphere. It is built in more to this sphere than it is others. Since antiquity it has been known that there can be no unitary canon for the diverse genres, rather that diverse genres and styles are to be valued and respected in their specifity. Thus Cicero said that 'there are almost countless genres and styles of speech, all different in their peculiarity, but praiseworthy as a genre'.[53] Homogeneity and the law of chronology might apply elsewhere, but to art belongs the coexistence of the heterogeneous. Whilst Cronos eats his children, the daughters of art remain alive.

Plurality has become more and more the basic condition following modernity's production of an unsurveyable multitude of work forms and perspectives. What is concerned are no longer differences on a common

basis, but basic differences. Works generate or represent different paradigms and require different sets of criteria for their judgement; they no
longer allow themselves to be tarred with the same brush. The observer –
unless completely insensitive or an incarnate Beckmesser – no longer gets
by with a single model of art. What is diagnosed as the resistivity, the
enigma, or the difficulty in the understanding of modern works is an
indication that they don't comply with one general canon, rather that they
develop their own; it's only when one catches on to this that works unveil
themselves. At the same time they entice you to seek this out and find out
their code.

Thus two things are self-evident for aesthetic awareness from the modern
stance: that one must discover the idiolect in a singular work; and that one
must be aware of the fundamental plurality of paradigms in regard to art
as a whole.[54]

2.   Aesthetics and anaesthetics

In addition to this first elementary aesthetic precept – plurality – comes a
second. It can be characterized by the double figure of aesthetics and
anaesthetics.

All perceiving is specific. By this is meant not the trivial finding that in
perceiving one object you are unable to perceive another, but the fact that
each and every perceiving exhibits a certain typicality and that this
typicality, whilst making some things perceptible, constitutively excludes
other things. To see something is always to overlook something else as well.
There is no vision without a blind-spot. Every perceptual typicality has a
transcendental – and that means a revelatory as well as an exclusive –
function. This already becomes apparent between the individual senses:
what's disclosed to the eye remains hidden to the ear – and so on
throughout the whole sensory scale. The preference for a certain perceptual
typicality or artistic paradigmatics is thus not just an aesthetic decision, but
an anaesthetic one at the same time: it thrusts aside other perceptual
options.

It's precisely where perceptive forms are culturally pluralizing – as is
happening today – that it is important to be aware of this coupling, and of
the dialectic of aesthetics and anaesthetics. Reflected aesthetics sensitizes
not only for the specifity of aesthetic paradigms, but at the same time for
their respective blindness.

3.   The codex of aesthetic awareness

Plurality on the one side and the dialectic of aesthetics and anaesthetics on
the other comprise elementary axioms of modern aesthetic awareness.
From this starting point a codex of this awareness can be drafted. The list
– without claiming completeness – includes the following:

1 *Awareness of specifity*: It's important to pay attention to the specifity of every aesthetic base. One must pick up its scent, get a grip on, and follow, its logic.

2 *Awareness of partiality*: One must not be allowed to declare the respective paradigm to be the only one possible or solely beatific. This would offend against its factual specifity in concrete terms, and against plurality in general.

3 *Vigilance*: One must not simply ponder the fact that each paradigm is specific, and hence that other paradigms legitimately and almost necessarily exist alongside it; rather one must also be sensitive to the unavoidable exclusions of any paradigm and to the contrariety of paradigms. Alterity is to be reckoned with as a matter of principle.

4 *Attentiveness*: An aesthetics sensitized for conditions of exclusion exhorts us to be attentive – in precisely those places where we perceive and suppose nothing, or where we believe we're faced only by things unworthy or undiscussable. You can never be sure whether or not this impression is founded simply on narrow-mindedness, whether or not the supposed dross might show the lustre of a precious metal in some other perspective. In many ways modern art turned to just those things which were societally devalued. Discoveries are most likely to be made where there's 'nothing'. There is a wonderful 'Lecture on Nothing' from John Cage.[55]

5 *Tendency to acknowledge*: Perception always tends to the directing of attention and, moreover, to acknowledgement – of the unseen, the unheard, the unheard-of. The 'unheard-of' as a whole: in day-to-day language use, 'unheard-of' is largely considered synonymous with 'outrageous'. In an aesthetic perspective, however, the unheard-of is: firstly, such that has not yet been heard, but which should be heard (unheard-of in the sense of unheard); secondly, such that has not yet had a hearing, that has not yet been examined in its claims – practically in its pleading (unheard-of in the sense of unredeemed); thirdly, such that exceeds the usual measure and which finds itself outside the accustomed order (unheard-of in the sense of extraordinary). In each case something latent is involved; and hence in each case a perceptive task is identified. The unheard-of will continue to be naturally disqualified as unseemly and outrageous as long as the corresponding perceptual exertions are not undertaken and the barriers not leapt over. – One shouldn't always only talk of the Hegelian threefold sublation (*Aufhebung*), but for once attend to this three- or fourfold sense of the 'unheard-of'. It articulates the reverse side of the sublatory euphoria.

6 *Tendency to justice*: All these points converge in the perspective of justice. Aesthetics should feel compelled to this, should operate in accordance with it. In modern art, which worked far less on the established than on the overseen and unheard-of, and wanted to assist these into language, expression and recognition, there inheres an impetus of justice.

4. Aesthet/hics: above and beyond aesthetics

The elements named represent aspects of a contemporary aesthet/hics which doesn't draw the line at the borders of art, but which is capable of radiating out to contexts in the life-world. Its perspective targets lead it to what I've elsewhere called a 'blind-spot culture'.[56] This would be a culture which is, as a matter of principle, sensitive to exclusions, rejections and differentness. It would subscribe not to a cult of the visible, evident, resplendent and scintillating, but rather to the repressed, void zones, interspace, alterity. The aesthet/hic valencies of reflected aesthetic awareness are also capable of becoming effective, because of the modern analogy between art and living conditions,[57] in just those problem constellations which arise in the life-world. Moreover, assistance of this sort is desirable because, for many reasons, the structures at issue in the complexities of the life-world are relatively opaque, whereas those in the aesthetic sphere are more transparent, were thus grasped earlier there and could now, so to speak, be borrowed as a model. Aesthetics should acquire bearing in the life-world, not – as is rife today – just as a line in embellishment, but as an authority of aesthet/hics. The rind of aesthetics might find shape as design, its aesthet/hic core, however, aims for justice.

The proof of aesthet/hic valencies in the structure of the aesthetic and in contemporary aesthetic awareness ultimately leads to a challenge for the discipline by the name of aesthetics. It should not curtail aesthetic reflexion – in a manner all too conventional – to the aesthetic's beautiful appearance, but rather go about recognizing the aesthet/hic dimension of the aesthetic and bringing it to bear as a cultural ferment. It's only then that it will serve in the cultural household not just to compensate, but also to correct.

Notes

This essay was originally published as 'Ästhet/hik – Ethische Implikationen und Konsequenzen der Ästhetik', in *Ethik der Äesthetik*, eds Christoph Wulf, Dietmar Kamper and Hans Ulrich Gumbrecht (Berlin: Akademie Verlag 1994), pp. 3–22. It has been revised for this volume. (First English publication.)

1. Cf. the account in the previous essay.

2. Cf. Martha C. Nussbaum, '"Finely Aware and Richly Responsible": Moral Attention and the Moral Task of Language', in *The Journal of Philosophy*, LXXXII, 1985, pp. 516–529; Michel Foucault, *The Use of Pleasure* (New York: Vintage 1985), as well as Foucault, *The History of Sexuality, Vol. 3: The Care of the Self*, trans. R. Hurley (London: Penguin, 1990); Pierre Bourdieu, *Zur Soziologie der symbolischen Formen* (Frankfurt a.M.: Suhrkamp 1970); Gernot Böhme, *Für eine ökologische Naturästhetik* (Frankfurt a.M.: Suhrkamp 1989).

3. See my *Vernunft. Die zeitgenössische Vernunftkritik und das Konzept der transversalen Vernunft* (Frankfurt a.M.: Suhrkamp 1995, 2nd edition stw 1996).

4. I have illustrated aesthetic implications of moral-practical discourse in ibid., pp. 516–525.

5. These relationships had already been meticulously analysed by Aristotle. His analysis forms the background of the preceding account. Cf. my *Aisthesis. Grundzüge und Perspektive der Aristotelischen Sinneslehre* (Stuttgart: Klett-Cotta 1987).

6. Cf. Immanuel Kant, *Critique of Judgment*, trans. Werner S. Pluhar (Indianapolis: Hackett 1987), pp. 57–8 [B 22].

7. Cf. Aristotle, *Politics*, I 2, 1253 a 10–18.

8. Cf. Alexander Gottlieb Baumgarten, *Aesthetica* (Frankfurt a.d. Oder 1750; reprint Hildesheim: Olms 1970), § 12, p. 5.

9. Cf. Georg Friedrich Meier, *Anfangsgründe aller schönen Wissenschaften* (Halle a.d. Saale 1748–50; reprint Hildesheim: Olms 1976), 3 vols, here vol. 1, § 22, p. 36.

10. Ibid., vol. 2, § 540, p. 654.

11. Ibid., vol. 1, § 219, p. 516.

12. Ibid., vol. 2, § 341, p. 176.

13. Kant's 'Apologie für die Sinnlichkeit' is still characterized by the paradox that sensibility is described as a 'rabble' in this, its defence (Immanuel Kant, *Anthropologie in pragmatischer Hinsicht*, § 8, A 31 [Eng.: *Anthropology from a Pragmatic Point of View*, trans. Mary J. Gregor, The Hague: Nijhoff 1974]). The defence limits itself to evincing the inability to do without sensibility as an instance for material acquisition in the business of cognition.

14. Cf. Friedrich Schiller, *On the Aesthetic Education of Man in a Series of Letters*, trans. Reginald Snell (Bristol: Thoemmes 1994), here 8th Letter, p. 50.

15. Ibid., 23rd Letter, p. 109.

16. Ibid., 23rd Letter, p. 112.

17. Ibid., 22nd Letter, p. 106.

18. Ibid., 23rd Letter, p. 112.

19. Ibid., 14th Letter, p. 75. It is Schiller's actual intuition (which, however, he doesn't manage to see through) that culture 'owes justice equally to both, and has to uphold not only the rational impulse against the sensuous, but also the latter against the former' (13th Letter, p. 69).

20. Ibid., 8th Letter, p. 50.

21. Cf. ibid. and 23rd Letter, p. 109.

22. Ibid., 27th Letter, p. 132.

23. Ibid., 23rd Letter, p. 109.

24. Ibid., 4th Letter, p. 32.

25. Georg Wilhelm Friedrich Hegel, *Ästhetik*, ed. Friedrich Bassenge, 2 vols (Frankfurt a.M.: Europäische Verlagsanstalt n.d.), vol. 1, p. 48.

26. Ibid., p. 49.

27. Schiller, *On the Aesthetic Education of Man*, 11th Letter, p. 64.

28. Ibid., 13th Letter, p. 69.

29. Ibid., 11th Letter, p. 63.

30. Fichte, that is, Schiller's reading of Fichte, is in the background.

31. This result too is directly contradictory to Schiller's genuine intention. For it is actually his idea that, as an aesthetic person, one should treat everything worldly as if it were an apparition of freedom. But within the framework of the concept he sets out this is only to be possible by a reformation of what's given – instead of through recognition of a freedom already immanent in what's worldly.

32. Cf. Schiller, *On the Aesthetic Education of Man*, 8th Letter, p. 50.

33. Ibid., 15th Letter, p. 80 and 2nd Letter, p. 27.

34. 'Truth and goodness' are to be 'kindred only in beauty' ('The "Oldest System-Programme" of German Idealism', in *Hegel Selections*, ed. M.J. Inwood, London/New York: Macmillan 1989, p. 87).

35. 'Radical modernity preserves the immanence of art, upon penalty of its self-abrogation [. . .]. Nothing societal in art is immediately so, not even where such is art's ambition.' (Theodor W. Adorno, *Ästhetische Theorie*, in Adorno, *Gesammelte Schriften*, Frankfurt a.M.: Suhrkamp, 4th edition, 1984, p. 336.) 'In each [art] which is still possible social critique must be elevated to form, to the fading-out of each and every manifest social content.' (Ibid., p. 371.)

36. Ibid., p. 344.

37. Ibid.

38. Ibid., p. 335.

39. At the same time, the classic concept had long since been energetically criticized by Nietzsche. He protested against the elevatory aesthetic imperative in the name of the primary-sensible and conversely demanded that the primary-sensible be made the criterion for judgement of the higher-sensible. Nietzsche had figured out that aesthetics is 'inseparably bound to [. . .] biological prerequisites' (Friedrich Nietzsche, 'Der Fall Wagner. Ein Musikanten-Problem', in Nietzsche, *Sämtliche Werke. Kritische Studienausgabe in 15 Bändern*, eds Giorgio Colli and Mazzino Montinari, Munich: Deutscher Taschenbuch Verlag 1980, vol. 6, pp. 9–53, here p. 50), indeed that aesthetics is in truth 'nothing but an applied physiology' (Friedrich Nietzsche, 'Nietzsche contra Wagner. Aktenstücke eines Psychologen', ibid., pp. 413–445, here p. 418). Hence he said that all his 'objections to Wagner's music [were] physiological objections' (ibid.). Nietzsche stands the traditional aesthetic scheme on its feet instead of its head: 'My "fact", my "petit fait vrai" is that I no longer breathe calmly when this music begins to affect me; that my foot immediately becomes angry with it and revolts: it has the need to beat, dance, march – not even the young German Kaiser can march to Wagner's Kaiser-marsch – my foot demands, above all, from music the delights which lie in *good* walking, striding, dancing. But doesn't my stomach protest too? my heart? my circulation? are not my bowels afflicted too? [. . .] Wagner makes you ill.' (Ibid., pp. 418f.)

40. Schiller had, after all, revealed this coercive character of artistic formation when he spoke of the violence which the artist does to matter.

41. Both sides are of course interrelated with one another: the on-principle discreditation of the primary-sensible legitimizes preparation through form.

42. Adorno, *Ästhetische Theorie*, p. 143.

43. For example, this terminology occurs all through Schiller's expositions.

44. Adorno, *Ästhetische Theorie*, p. 180.

45. Ibid.

46. Ibid., p. 285. – In part II of the essay 'Experiences at Lulu' from 1968 we read: 'Lulu [. . .] hoists up the suppressed, looks it in the eye, makes it conscious and does justice to it by making herself equal to it; a higher authority, before which the revision of the civilizational process is taking place.' (Theodor W. Adorno, 'Erfahrungen an Lulu', in Adorno, *Gesammelte Schriften*, vol. 13, Frankfurt a.M.: Suhrkamp 1971, pp. 471–490, here p. 486.)

47. This transformation determines Adorno's own development. This can be inferred from his comments on music – of which he said in the *Aesthetic Theory* that it tells tales out of the school of all art (Adorno, *Ästhetische Theorie*, p. 336). In the *Philosophy of New Music*, published in 1949, Adorno pleaded in favour of the sovereign intervention of the composing subject in musical material. He praised in Schönberg the way in which this man – as opposed to Webern – 'composed' with twelve-tone series, that he deals with them sovereignly (Theodor W. Adorno, *Philosophie der neuen Musik*, in Adorno, *Gesammelte Schriften*, vol. 12, Frankfurt a.M.: Suhrkamp 1975, p. 106). On the other hand Adorno saw the specific danger of the twelve-tone technique in that this 'system of mastering nature in music' 'virtually [eradicates] the subject' and his compositional imagination (ibid., pp. 65 and 70 resp.). In the 1961 Kranichstein Lecture 'Towards an Informal Music', however, Adorno strikes a different tone. He now criticizes this compositional method of an autonomously acting subject – Schönberg's composing *with* the tones – as being dominative itself (cf. Theodor W. Adorno, 'Vers une musique informelle', in Adorno, *Gesammelte Schriften*, vol. 16, Frankfurt a.M.: Suhrkamp 1978, pp. 493–540, here p. 507). When he now says of Schönberg, 'Everything in him fought against tones' being able to compose in their own right' (ibid.), this is now meant highly critically. The composing subject should instead become capable of following the movements of the tones. All of a sudden even Cage is declared to be a figure worthy of discussion, an important figure at that: 'In one sense, however, Cage's impulse approaches that of an informal music: as a protest against music's stubborn complicity with the domination of nature' (ibid., p. 534). Adorno's deliberations, which begin here with the self-confession of being attracted by the 'desideratum of musical liberation' (ibid., p. 495), ultimately end up

stating that today the 'form of all artistic utopias' is to 'make things, of which we don't know, what they are' (ibid., p. 540).

48. Theodor W. Adorno, *Negative Dialektik*, in Adorno, *Gesammelte Schriften*, vol. 6 (Frankfurt a.M.: Suhrkamp, 3rd edition, 1984), p. 192.

49. Theodor W. Adorno, 'Zu Subjekt und Objekt', in Adorno, *Gesammelte Schriften*, vol. 10.2 (Frankfurt a.M.: Suhrkamp 1977), pp. 741–758, here p. 743.

50. 'Law is the originary phenomenon of irrational rationality. In it the principle of formal equivalence becomes the norm, it tars everything with the same brush.' (Adorno, *Negative Dialektik*, p. 304.)

51. It's an 'equality in which the differences submerge' (ibid.).

52. 'Legal norms sever what's not covered, every non-preformed experience of the specific for the sake of an uninterrupted systematics and then elevate instrumental rationality to a second reality *sui generis*. [. . .] This enclosure, in itself an ideological one, by means of the sanctions of law as an instance of societal control, exercises real power, all the more so in the administered world' (ibid.).

53. Cicero, *De oratore*, III 34. Similarly: 'There is only one art of painting, and yet Zeuxis, Aglaophon and Apelles were completely different from one another; and none is amongst them, whom one might accuse of deficiency in his art.' (Ibid., III 26.)

54. Cf. for greater detail: Welsch, *Vernunft*, esp. Part Two, Chapter III.

55. John Cage, 'A Lecture on Nothing', in Cage, *Silence* (Middletown, Conn.: Wesleyan University Press 1961; London: Marion Boyars 1973).

56. Cf. the essay 'Aestheticization Processes: Phenomena, Distinctions, and Prospects' in the present volume (section IV.2).

57. Cf. ibid.

4

AESTHETICS BEYOND AESTHETICS
For a New Form to the Discipline

Introduction: Outline of the problems

1. The prevailing understanding: aesthetics centred on art

What is aesthetics? The answer given by the encyclopedias is clear. The *Academic American Encyclopedia* says: 'Aesthetics is the branch of philosophy that aims to establish the general principles of art and beauty.'[1] Correspondingly, the Italian *Enciclopedia Filosofica* determines aesthetics as the 'philosophical discipline which has beauty and art as its object'.[2] The French *Vocabulaire d'Esthétique* defines aesthetics as 'reflective study of the beautiful' and 'philosophy and science of art' respectively.[3] And the German *Historisches Wörterbuch der Philosophie* explains: 'The word "aesthetics" has established itself as the name of the branch of philosophy in which the arts and the beautiful are addressed.'[4] In short, aesthetics is considered as artistics, as an explication of the concept of art with particular attention to beauty.

What, then, could 'aesthetics beyond aesthetics' – as suggested in this essay's title – be? In order to be meaningful, the expression would have to point to something beyond this art-bound understanding of aesthetics, to something beyond artistics. But how could this still be a kind of aesthetics? Does the term 'aesthetics' lend itself to a transartistic meaning?

Traditionally this clearly is the case. 'Aesthetics' goes back to the Greek word class αἴσθησις (*aisthesis*), αἰσθάνεσαι (*aisthanesthai*) and αἰσθητός (*aisthetos*) – that is, to expressions which designate sensation and perception in general, prior to any artistic meaning. Current usage of the word is not restricted to art either; in everyday language we use the term 'aesthetic' even more often outside of than within the artistic sphere, when speaking, for instance, of aesthetic behaviour or an aesthetic lifestyle, or of aesthetic peculiarities of media or an increasing aestheticization of the world..

Traditionally, however, the *discipline* of 'aesthetics' hasn't so much thematized sensation and perception, but has concentrated predominantly on art – and more on conceptual than sensuous issues of art. The mainstream of contemporary aesthetics still does so. The academic discipline tends to restrict itself to artistics – no matter how uncertain the notion of art itself may have become in the meantime.

Certainly, there have been exceptions and counter-tendencies to this predominant approach. Remember, for example, that Alexander Gottlieb Baumgarten, the founding father of aesthetics who gave it its name, conceived of the new discipline as primarily cognitive, designed to improve our sensuous capacity for cognition. Among the scope of aesthetics, defined by Baumgarten as the 'science of sensitive cognition', the arts didn't even get a mention.[5]

Shortly thereafter, however – between Kant's *Critique of Judgment* of 1790, 'The "Oldest System-Programme" of German Idealism' from around 1796, and Schelling's *System of Transcendental Idealism* of 1800 – when aesthetics started an unprecedented career promoting it to the summit of philosophy, it began being understood exclusively as the philosophy of the arts. And for centuries this remained the dominant understanding of aesthetics, shared by philosophers as different as Hegel and Heidegger or Ingarden and Adorno.

There were, to be sure, still counter-tendencies. They ranged from Schiller's shift first from artistic to political and then to pedagogical art and finally to the 'art of life' (*Lebenskunst*), through to Marcuse's idea of a new social sensibility; or from Kierkegaard's description of aesthetic existence and Nietzsche's fundamentalization of aesthetic activity through to Dewey's integration of art into life. But these counter-tendencies didn't really manage to change the design of the discipline. To a certain extent they even shared the basic presumption of traditional aesthetics that art forms the focus of aesthetics; these reformers also continued to consider art as being the very model of aesthetic practice altogether, as well as the paradigm for the shift to the transartistic understanding of aesthetics which they advocated.

Currently, the discipline of 'aesthetics' still tends to the restriction to artistics. There may be many good reasons for the recognition of an aesthetics beyond aesthetics, but throughout the years in which I have tried to foster this tendency I have found far more interest and support outside the discipline – from cultural institutions or theoreticians in other fields[6] – whereas my efforts predominantly met with resistance within the framework of academically established aesthetics (at least in the German-speaking world). It is still considered self-evident that aesthetics has to be artistics; people are still held captive by this traditional picture. And, continuing this allusion to Wittgenstein, one could say: 'And we cannot get outside it, for it lies in our discipline and this discipline seems to repeat it to us inexorably.'[7]

2. *Overcoming the traditional prejudice*

Singularity of works versus the universal concept of art

But there are very good reasons for trying to escape from the aesthetics–artistics equation or – to quote Wittgenstein again – 'to show the fly the way out of the fly-bottle'.[8] For one of the central problems of traditional aesthetics is that it didn't even fulfil its responsibility. It is incapable of doing justice to the singularity of works of art. The aim of aesthetics was shifted to being the establishment of a universal and everlasting concept of art. Hence aesthetics could be – and was even supposed to be – carried out without orientation through individual works of art or historically different types of art. Schelling, for example, frankly expressed this when he declared that a philosophy of art had to treat only 'art as such' and 'in no way empirical art',[9] and that his own philosophy of art was a mere 'repetition' of his 'system of philosophy' – this time implemented with respect to art, just as on another occasion with respect to nature or society.[10]

As inappropriate as this strategy appears to us today, and has long since appeared to artists – Robert Musil, for example, derided such aesthetics as the attempt to find the universal brick fitting every work of art and being suitable for erecting the whole edifice of aesthetics[11] – Schelling undoubtedly expressed a basic conviction of traditional aesthetics: that there is such a thing as an essential and universal concept of art, and that to expound this concept was the actual task and the whole aim of aesthetics. This was the immanent reason why aestheticians didn't regard a detailed study of singular works of art as necessary, but could make do with just rudimentary knowledge of some works of art. It was to suffice as a starting point for their intuition of the general concept of art.[12]

Of course this traditional strategy is untenable. The practice of art doesn't consist in exemplifying a universal concept of art, but involves the creation of new versions and concepts of art. And the new concept will certainly have some aspects in common with the concept formerly dominant, but differ from it sharply in other, no less important aspects. This is obvious in every shift from one style or paradigm to another. Hence, artistic paradigms are connected by some overlaps from one concept to the next (by 'family resemblances' in the Wittgensteinian sense) but not by a universal pattern common to them all or representing an essential core of all works of art. There is no such thing as an essence of art.

This means the traditional approach is mistaken on principle – even within the narrow scope of an aesthetics referring to art alone. It is based on a fundamental misunderstanding of the concept of art – with this misunderstanding even constituting the very core of the traditional concept of aesthetics. On the other hand, insight into the historical genesis of different concepts of art through art itself, and into the family resemblance (instead of an alleged essential unity) of these concepts, makes the failure of this traditional, globalizing approach of aesthetics obvious and commands the shift to a different, pluralistic type of aesthetics.

In favour of an extended understanding of the discipline

But the reorganization of aesthetics which we currently have to consider must go even further. Thus far I have only discussed the paradigm change due within the classical frame of aesthetics, that is, within artistics: we can no longer be held captive by art's essentialistic picture. But it might furthermore prove necessary to go beyond this whole frame – the traditional equation of aesthetics and artistics. The inner pluralization of artistics – the shift from a monoconceptual analysis of art to the consideration of different types, paradigms and concepts of art – should be supplemented by an outer pluralization of aesthetics – by an expansion of the discipline's field to transartistic questions. – That is what I want to advocate in this essay.

In the first section I will develop some of the main themes for an aesthetics beyond aesthetics. In the second section I attempt to clarify the conceptual admissibility of such an aesthetics and make some suggestions as to how the territory of aesthetics should be reorganized. I will advocate aesthetics' opening out to issues beyond art and the development of a transdisciplinary structure of the discipline. This structure, of course, still includes questions of art, but it encompasses transartistic issues as well, and this, as will have to be shown above all, is of importance for the analysis of art itself. Art can more adequately be dealt with in the perspective of an aesthetics which is not restricted to the analysis of art alone.

I.   Some main themes and the relevance of an aesthetics beyond aesthetics

There are, generally speaking, two groups of reasons for a broadening of aesthetics: the first refers to the contemporary *fashioning of reality*, the second to the contemporary *understanding of reality*.[13]

1.   Aesthetic fashioning of reality: embellishment

Global aestheticization

Today, we are living amidst an aestheticization of the real world formerly unheard of.[14] Embellishment and styling are to be found everywhere. They extend from individuals' appearance to the urban and public spheres, and from economy through to ecology.

Individuals are undergoing a comprehensive styling of body, soul and behaviour. In beauty salons and fitness centres they pursue the aesthetic perfection of their bodies, in meditation courses and New Age seminars they practise the aestheticization of their souls, and etiquette courses train them for aesthetically desirable behaviour. *Homo aestheticus* has become the new role-model. In *urban areas* just about everything has been subjected to a face-lift in recent years – at least in the rich Western countries. The *economy* too profits largely from consumers' tendency not actually to acquire an article, but rather to buy themselves, by its means, into the aesthetic lifestyle with which advertising strategies have linked the article.

Even *ecology* is in aesthetic regards a partner of the economy. It is on the way to being an embellishment sector and favours a styling of the environment in the spirit of aesthetic ideals like complexity or natural beauty. If the rich industrial societies were able to do completely as they wish, they would transform the urban, industrial and natural environment *in toto* into a hyper-aesthetic scenario. *Genetic engineering*, which links individual and ecological styling, is a further piece of evidence. It adapts all sorts of life to our needs and enables us – according to our aesthetic expectations – to provide just the sort of products and children we would wish for. Genetic engineering is a kind of genetic cosmetic surgery.

It is surely not necessary to expand on these tendencies towards embellishment and globalized aestheticization in detail – the phenomena are all too obvious. I want instead to consider the relevance of these developments for aesthetics.

These phenomena do not actually provide grounds for new domains of the aesthetic. Aesthetic activity and orientation have always borne upon the real world – however little, on the other side, the discipline of aesthetics may have taken this into account. What's new today is the extent and the status of these aestheticizing activities. Aestheticization has become a global and primary strategy.

The impact on contemporary aesthetics

This tendency must, I think, influence contemporary as well as traditional aesthetics. The impact on contemporary aesthetics consists in the obligatory reflexion on these phenomena since they not only represent an extension of the aesthetic, but at the same time alter its configuration and valency. Hence aesthetics – as the reflective authority of the aesthetic – must also seek out the state of the aesthetic today in fields such as the life-world and politics, economy and ecology, ethics and science. It must, in short, take account of the new configuration of the aesthetic. This does not mean that the globalization and fundamentalization of the aesthetic is simply to be sanctioned – but that it belongs on today's agenda for every sufficient aesthetic diagnosis and critique.

The relation to traditional aesthetics

The effects on traditional aesthetics become evident when we pursue the question as to whether tradition has ever advocated a globalization of the aesthetic. Clearly this is the case. Some prominent aesthetic programmes of the past have stood up determinedly for a global aestheticization, from which they even promised themselves the definitive fulfilment of all our tasks on earth and the ultimate happiness of mankind. Remember, for example, how 'The "Oldest System-Programme" of German Idealism' swore by the mediating power of the aesthetic: by linking the rational and the sensuous, aesthetics was to cause 'the enlightened and the unenlightened [. . .] [to] join hands', so that 'eternal unity reigns among us', this even being 'the last and greatest work of mankind'.[15] In the same way mediators of aesthetic ideas like the Arts and Crafts Movement or Werkbund and Bauhaus – mediators insofar as they sought to realize in the everyday world aesthetic values propagandized by aesthetics – were convinced that a globalization of the aesthetic would altogether improve the world.

Consequently old aesthetic dreams are being redeemed in the present aestheticization. But the irritating fact which demands explanation is that the results today are quite different from the original expectations. They are, at the very least, disappointing. What was meant to endow our world with beauty ends up in mere prettiness and obtrusiveness, and finally generates indifference or even disgust – at least among aesthetically sensitive people. In any case, nobody would dare to call the present aestheticization straightforward fulfilment. Something must then be wrong with this redemption of old aesthetic dreams. Either the current application of old programmes is inadequate, or these venerable programmes themselves already contained a flaw, one which has just remained hidden so far, and which is now being revealed. Sometimes redemptions can equate to revelations. This, I think, is the case with the current aestheticization.

Some flaws in the globalized aestheticization

What are the reasons for the disappointment with the present aestheticization? What are the critical points to be highlighted by an aesthetic reflexion on these processes? I want to mention three points.

Firstly, fashioning everything as beautiful destroys the quality of the beautiful. Ubiquitous beauty loses its distinguished character and decays into mere prettiness or becomes simply meaningless. You can't make what's exceptional a standard without changing its quality.

Secondly, the strategy of globalized aestheticization falls victim to itself. It ends in anaestheticization. The globalized aesthetic is experienced as annoying and even as terror. Aesthetic indifference then becomes a sensible and almost unavoidable attitude in order to escape the importunity of this ubiquitous aesthetic. Anaestheticization – our refusal to continue to perceive the divinely embellished environment – becomes a survival strategy.[16]

Thirdly, instead of this a need for the non-aesthetic arises – a desire for interruptions and disruptions, for breaking through embellishment. If there's still a task for art in public space today, then it consists not in introducing ever more beauty into the already over-embellished environment, but in stopping this aestheticization-machinery by creating aesthetic fallow areas and deserts in the midst of the hyperaesthetic.[17]

Repercussions for traditional aesthetics

These critical experiences with the contemporary redemption of the old aesthetic dreams of the world's enhancement must conversely have repercussions for our assessment of traditional aesthetics.

Aesthetics has usually praised beauty and beautification, and believed it had good reasons for doing so. But it never considered the consequences of the globalized beautification which it advocated and which we are today experiencing. It never even conceived that globalized embellishment might disfigure the world – instead of perfecting, or even redeeming, it. Moreover, the acclamation of beauty championed by traditional aesthetics has repeatedly served as rhetorical support for the current aestheticization processes. The traditional passion for beauty kept us from considering the negative effects of aestheticization, even when these had long since become obvious. The supportive, legitimating and idolizing power of traditional aesthetics is at least partly responsible for the modern tendency toward aestheticization, as well as for the blindness towards its negative effects.

Hence a threefold criticism of traditional aesthetics is called for. Firstly, objection is due to the wholesale praise of beauty. To do this one can either distinguish between more mediocre and greater beauty – whereby the former is in fact so close to mere prettiness that it could be viewed as a good common to both 'the enlightened and the unenlightened', and be believed implemented by the current strategies of embellishment; but only the latter is an exceptional and moving phenomenon – such as Rilke described when he said of beauty that it is 'the beginning of what's frightening'.[18] Or, one can consider that beauty represents a value only in opposition to standard non-beauty, one, however, which loses its distinctiveness by its very propagation.

Secondly, one of the flaws of traditional aesthetics was to promote beauty alone (or predominantly) and to neglect other aesthetic values. In other words, it forgot the discovery, which was aesthetics' own, that *variatio delectat* – and not a single aesthetic quality alone. This flaw becomes painfully clear in the present embellishment. Aesthetics – possibly the actual discipline of plurality – had falsely singularized itself and failed to recognize that homogenization is systematically wrong in aesthetic respects too.

Thirdly, the efficacy of traditional aesthetics in the domain of our cultural beliefs and desires needs to be critically questioned. It is a matter of breaking open old aesthetic dogmas. Aesthetics has every reason to become self-critical.

To sum up this point: the current aestheticization not only brings with it new problems and tasks for contemporary aesthetics, but also has critical repercussions for traditional aesthetics insofar as this was partly responsible for, and broadly supportive of, flaws in aestheticization processes. Therefore, the issues of an aesthetics beyond aesthetics not only concern those who are already willing to broaden the reach of aesthetics, but likewise represent an obligatory subject for those who still adhere to aesthetics' traditional framework. The aesthetics outside of aesthetics cannot today be ignored, even if you only want to develop a valid version of aesthetics within aesthetics.

2. *Aesthetic apprehension of reality*

A second group of arguments in favour of the turn to an aesthetics beyond aesthetics refers to the current apprehension of reality. This has, as I want to demonstrate, become more and more aesthetic.

An obvious predominance of images and aesthetic patterns exists today, not only in the current shaping of reality, but in the current mediation of reality as well. This dominance stretches from the presentation of single objects or subjects and the nature of our daily news, through to our basic understanding of reality. Think, say, of the pictorial dominance in advertising and in the self-presentation of companies, or of our own visual appearance in the World Wide Web. Or think of the pictorial demands of television which not only selectively determine what might count as news at all, but have recently also tinted the presentation of news outside television in, say, the printed media. Finally, think of change in our apprehension of reality. In earlier times, to count as being real, something had to be calculable; today it has to be aesthetically presentable. Aesthetics has become the new leading currency in the reality trade.

Again, I don't want to go into these phenomena in detail. They are far too familiar and have often been analysed. Instead, I will consider the effects of these developments on aesthetics and point out some of the new tasks for aesthetics in the face of these developments.

I concentrate on just one point – on what I call the 'derealization of reality' – and two of its consequences – the reconfiguration of *aisthesis*, and the revalidation of experiences outside electronic media.[19]

Derealization of reality

By 'derealization of reality' I mean the fact that reality – as nowadays primarily conveyed by the media – is deeply affected by this type of mediation.[20] Reality is tending to lose its gravity, to shift from compulsoriness to playfulness, it is undergoing constant processes of weight loss.

This is due to the peculiarities of media aesthetics, which generally favours the free mobility and weightlessness of bodies and images. Everything is an object for possible electronic manipulation, and within the media 'manipulation' is no longer a normative, but practically just a descriptive term. Whatever enters the realm of television steps into a realm of transformability instead of constancy. If there is a 'lightness of being' anywhere, then it is in the electronic realm.

Furthermore, we not only recognize and know that everything is manipulable, but we also have knowledge of factual manipulations. Think, say, of the Gulf War reports which sometimes deluded us with technological simulations, whereas the reality of victims was never shown; or take the example of pixel technology. Ultimately you never know whether you are witnessing a playback of reality or a simulation, and this, of course, colours our belief in the alleged reality. Of course it's true that 'What You

See Is What You Get', but you won't ever get what you shouldn't see, and you can never be sure whether what you get is reality's gift or just the channel's.

Experiences of this kind first of all effect a softening of our belief in media-reality. The difference between the representation and the simulation of reality is becoming less and less evident and tending to lose significance. Accordingly, the media themselves increasingly present their pictures in modes of virtuality and playfulness.[21]

On the other hand this doesn't make us turn away from the media. Although we know that pictures might lie we still stay tuned. We obviously prefer another consequence, that of changing our comprehension of reality and following the road of derealization.

Secondly, this attitude towards media-reality is extending more and more to everyday reality too. This comes about because everyday reality is being increasingly formed, presented and perceived according to media patterns. In that television is the main bestower and the role-model for reality, derealization leaves its mark everywhere. The real is tending to lose its insistency, compulsiveness and gravity; it seems to be becoming ever lighter, less oppressive and less obligating. Already the importunity of media's presentation of reality no longer creates affliction, but rather its opposite: indifference. If you see the same images – however impressively they may be arranged or intended – on different channels on the same evening or repeatedly over several days, then their impact is reduced: sensation plus repetition creates indifference. In the wake of such mechanisms our attitude towards reality – inside and outside the media – becomes more and more as if it were simulation altogether. We no longer take reality quite so seriously, or as being quite as real. And amidst this suspension of reality we judge and act differently too. Our behavioural patterns are becoming increasingly simulatory and interchangeable. Many of the disturbing phenomena in today's everyday world have to do with this ongoing softening of our comprehension of reality – but so too are some steps towards freedom, a point I would like to retain.

Because the processes named are occasioned by peculiarities of media aesthetics their consideration is an obligatory agenda for every contemporary aesthetic theory which intends not to ignore, but to analyse the present state of the aesthetic and hence to do justice to its responsibility.

Reconfiguration of *aisthesis*

Furthermore, a reconfiguration of *aisthesis* can today be observed. For instance, one of the consequences of media dominance is the challenging of the primacy of vision which has shaped occidental culture since the Greeks, and which culminates in the television age. Contemporary critique of ocularcentrism has other reasons too, but the experience of media constitutes an important factor.

Vision was traditionally favoured because of its hallmarks of distance, precision and universality, because of its capacity for determination and its proximity to cognition. From Heraclitus via Leonardo da Vinci through to Merleau-Ponty, vision was considered our most excellent and noble sense.

In the meantime, however, the patterns underlying this privilege – dominative patterns of perception and cognition – have been subjected to critique by authors like Heidegger, Wittgenstein, Foucault, Derrida and Irigaray.[22] What's more we are currently experiencing that vision is in fact no longer the reliable sense for contact with reality that it was once held to be – this no longer holds in a world in which physics has become indemonstrable, and just as little in the world of media.

At the same time, other senses have attracted new attention. Hearing, for example, is being appreciated anew because of its anti-metaphysical proximity to the event instead of to permanent being, because of its essentially social character in contrast to the individualistic execution of vision, and because of its link with emotional elements in opposition to the emotionless mastery of phenomena through vision.[23] Touch has found its advocates in the same way, due both to new developments in media technology as analysed by Marshall McLuhan and Derrick de Kerckhove,[24] and to its emphatically corporal character – this again in contrast to the 'pure', uninvolved character of vision.

In the wake of such developments an increasing departure arises from the traditional hierarchy of the senses – with vision on top, followed by hearing through to smell. The cards of sensibility are being reshuffled. Instead of a firmly established hierarchy one tends either to an equitable assessment of all senses, or (which I would prefer) to different, purpose-specific hierarchies.

This reorganization of *aisthesis* is, at the same time, linked with a significant change in cultural patterns and demands. Aesthetics should make these new states of *aisthesis* and the accompanying transformation of cultural patterns the object of its analyses. By doing so it could presumably also help us carry out these transformation processes in a clearer and more reliable way. Besides, therein lies a chance for aesthetics to change from a rather dusty old discipline to being an interesting field of contemporary analysis and discussion again.

Revalidation of non-electronic experiences

Another consequence of media experience and the derealization tendency consists in the revalidation of experiences outside electronic media. The general scheme is the following: in contrast to the peculiarities of media-reality (or media-derealization) a new appreciation of non-electronic reality and modes of experience arises, one in which particular emphasis is put on those traits which are neither imitable nor substitutable for by media-experience. The highly developed electronic world doesn't simply overcome or absorb traditional forms of experience – as some media enthusiasts would have us believe – rather, a revalidation of ordinary experience complementing media-experience can be observed. This point has received too little attention in the discussions of recent years.

Thus we are today learning to value anew the resistibility and unchangeability of the natural as opposed to the universal mobility and changeability of media-worlds, and in the same way the persistence of the concrete as opposed to the free play of information, the massivity of matter as opposed to the levitation of imagery. In contrast to arbitrary repeatability, uniqueness gains value afresh. The electronic omnipresence awakens the yearning for another presence: for the unrepeatable presence of *hic et nunc*, for the singular event. As opposed to the mutual social electronic imaginary, we are again beginning to evaluate more highly our own imagination, one unavailable to others. And in the same way, we are discovering anew the body's sovereignty and intransigence. – Think, say, of Nadolny's 'discovery of slowness',[25] or of Handke's praise of weariness.[26]

In order not to be misunderstood: of course I understand these tendencies not as a simple counter-programme to the artificial paradises of electronic worlds, but rather as a programme complementary to them. These counter-elements do not deny the fascination of electronic worlds; nor is it simply a matter of returning to sensuous experience, such as this might have been in pre-electronic times. Rather the revalidations are also tinted by the experience of electronic media. And there are obvious links between electronic and non-electronic experience. Sometimes natural experience is just the thing lovers of virtuality are after too. My favourite example are the electronics freaks of Silicon Valley, who in the evening drive to the coast to watch those truly incomparable Californian sunsets before returning to their home computers and diving into the artificial paradises of the Internet.[27]

In accordance with the prevalent media-tendency, on the one hand, and the revalidation of non-electronic experience, on the other, our *aisthesis* is becoming twofold. It pursues both media-fascination and non-media goals. There is nothing wrong in this duality. On the contrary, we have here an interesting example of the widespread turn to plurality which is emerging in the present day. We are becoming capable of wandering to and fro between different types of reality and experience. Contemporary *aisthesis* is perhaps the domain where this is already happening the most naturally and successfully.

Résumé

Having, in my introductory remarks, voted that the discipline of aesthetics should transcend the traditional equation of aesthetics and art, I have weighed up in this first section of my account the influence of the current aestheticization processes on contemporary as well as on traditional aesthetics, and in the meantime pointed out three specific fields of an aesthetics beyond aesthetics. The derealization of reality, the reconfiguration of *aisthesis* and the revalidation of accustomed forms of experience are important issues for any contemporary aesthetics which wants to do justice to its name. Aesthetics would criminally hurt itself if it left the discussion of these issues solely to sociologists and psychologists or the feuilletons.

II. Towards the new form of the discipline

In the second section of my considerations I want to discuss three remaining questions relating to my suggestion to reorganize the territory of aesthetics by expanding it to issues beyond traditional aesthetics. Firstly, why is it conceptually correct to demand of the discipline that it should comprehend all dimensions and meanings of the aesthetic? Secondly, to what extent does the expansion of aesthetics bring with it advantages for the discipline – even with regard to its narrower goal of art analysis? And thirdly, what would the disciplinary structure of such an aesthetics beyond aesthetics look like?

1. Conceptual clarifications

Polyvalency and family resemblance

Some colleagues object to the possibility of an aesthetics beyond aesthetics that the difference in the meanings of the term 'aesthetic' inside and outside aesthetics would make a discipline trying to cover all of them hopelessly ambiguous and a victim of mere equivocation.[28]

Certainly the expression 'aesthetic' exhibits a considerable variety of different meanings. The term can refer to art and beauty in particular, or to *aisthesis* in general, it may mean a type of unobligating existence, or designate an ontology of virtuality, fictionality and suspension. But does this polyvalent grammar of an expression really condemn it to unusability?

The problem of the semantic ambiguity of the aesthetic is as old as the discipline itself. The definitions of aesthetics by Baumgarten, Hegel, Fiedler, Ingarden or Adorno cannot be reduced to a common denominator. But, on the other hand, this ambiguity has never led aestheticians to despair of the usability of the expression and the sense of a discipline devoted to it.

And they had no cause to. Wittgenstein pointed to a way out of this alleged conceptual difficulty, by demonstrating that an expression's coherence need not be due to a unitary essence, but can come about in a different way: through overlap between one usage and the next. The differing meanings are then linked by 'family resemblances'. It is in precisely this way that the term 'aesthetic' functions – family resemblances determine its grammar.

Comprehensiveness of the discipline

This has significant consequences. First of all, a coherence in the discipline of aesthetics is quite possible based on the family resemblances between the different meanings of the expression 'aesthetic'. Of course, one has to differentiate sufficiently between the different usages, but if you do this you can reap great benefit from this manifoldness by pursuing the overlaps connecting them and, from there on, become capable of developing an aesthetics which manages to cover the full range of the expression 'aesthetic'.

Secondly, aesthetics should make use of this opportunity. There are no good reasons for it to restrict itself to artistics. One may, of course, do this in one's own research – just as other aestheticians may primarily refer to non-artistic aspects. But *as a discipline* aesthetics should comprehend the *full* range of such endeavours.

Incidentally, the polyvalency of the expression 'aesthetic' is an indication of fruitfulness rather than of the term's unusability. It is precisely polyvalent concepts which are often of particular importance, and demands for non-ambiguity have never applied with respect to such concepts. How else, for example, could there have been an ontology when the expression '*to on*' is all but hopelessly ambiguous – just as Aristotle himself showed before nonetheless being the first to develop an explicit concept of ontology?[29] Or should one have abstained from developing a logic on account of the different meanings of logos – 'language', 'relationship', 'reason'?[30] The polyvalency of an expression can be no reason for hindrance of the development of a discipline pertaining to all its variants.

Hence, a genuinely comprehensive aesthetics – whose development I advocate – is conceptually possible. We should then face up to this task and not decretorially constrain the discipline to the track of a narrow-gauge aesthetics. To carry out reductionisms and conceptual bulldozing because one doesn't feel up to the complexity of the phenomena and concepts means failing one's duty – in both philosophy and aesthetics.

2.   *Advantages of expanding the discipline*

Being both conceptually possible and factually requisite, to what extent will expanding aesthetics beyond its traditional borders bring advantages for the discipline itself?

Interdisciplinary and institutional advantages

In becoming more complex, aesthetics may – admittedly – become more difficult too. But in no longer being restricted to a narrow set of questions, it can achieve more intense contact and interchange with other disciplines, and gain new fields of research. This would bring an advantage not only with regard to the breadth of its issues, but on the institutional level as well.

The type of aesthetics I advocate will meet with greater interest, both for the breadth of its spectrum and for its contributions to contemporary problems, and it is likely to meet with greater support – including more financial support for its research activities.

Advantages with respect to art analysis

Ultimately an expansion of aesthetics to issues beyond art will also prove advantageous to art analysis itself. I now want to set this out in detail. Art itself always reaches out beyond art, refers simultaneously to transartistic phenomena and states of the aesthetic. Therefore transcending the aesthetics–artistics equation in favour of an aesthetics beyond aesthetics is obligatory even with a view to the traditional nucleus of aesthetics, for the analysis of art. – In which ways does art transcend itself, that is, every overly restricted concept thereof?

Art transcends the borders of traditional aesthetics

Reference to the state of the aesthetic outside art   Even when apparently autonomous, art has always and quite consciously reacted to states of the aesthetic in the world surrounding it. Formerly, in a world more aesthetically sparing, it demonstrated the Elysium of beauty; when in the modern world sensibility has been under threat, art – heedful of its old bond with the sensuous – has understood itself as the harbinger and rescuer of the sensuous (as with Matisse and Dubuffet); where embellishment is rife, as it is nowadays, art can see its responsibility in countering this and behaving decidedly demurely (as in *arte povera* and conceptual art).

Contemporary art reacts to the dominance of media images in particular. It can oppose their importunity, emulate it, or operate with the frictions between traditional artistic patterns and current media perception. Whatever the relationship might be in detail, such works of art require attention to their reference to other modes of design and perception and an understanding of their specific intervention in the artistic as well as transartistic states of the aesthetic. Options for contemplation too are etched by the media and transartistic situation of the aesthetic. There is no sufficient description of art which would not have to incorporate aspects of an aesthetics beyond artistics.

Views of the world   Moreover, the energy of works always transcends their frame, the museum's threshold or the moment of their observation. The works open up perspectives on the world – not only in the manner of their representation, but above all by generating new views of the world. Among the key experiences with art (and conversely, the tests as to whether someone actually confers efficacy upon art or would like to banish it in eulogizing about its autonomy) belongs the fact that, upon leaving an exhibition, one is suddenly able to perceive the world with the eyes of the artist, through the optics of his or her works, in the light of the aesthetics they exemplify.[31]

This is pretty much natural and undistorted behaviour: to engage art's perceptive form in the perception of reality too, not to shut oneself off from the efficacy of artistic optics, but to operate and experiment with them. The elementary aesthetic experience is not that art is something closed, but rather that it is able to open one's eyes to ways of viewing the world.[32] Works of art are often, above all, tools for an extended or intensified perception of reality.

Entanglements between art and reality   Consider further how forms of perception which today appear natural and self-evident originated historically in processes in which art played a pioneering role – romantic art for example had a key role in the perception of the world of mountains. Several parts of our everyday perception are a sediment of generations of art experience. Something similar applies to some behavioural patterns.[33]

Beyond this production of forms of perception and behavioural repertoires, works of art can also provide models for ways of living. This already belonged to the normative demands of classical art and carries on in modernity – subsequent to the dissolution of general norms – in the generation of potentials for individual life planning. Rilke's contemplation of the archaic torso of Apollo, which concludes with the line 'You must change your life', provides an impressive description of this phenomenon.[34]

Certainly, the border between art and reality outside of art should not simply be broken down, but the entanglements and transitions between the two are to be ignored even less. An aesthetics of art always has to consider the dual character of artistics, on the one hand, and of an aesthetics beyond aesthetics, on the other. That is why Adorno, who – as almost no other – knew of and defended the significance of autonomy, all the same opposed the separation of art from reality and the reduction to mere autonomy.

> How deeply [the] innervations of art are rooted in its position in reality could be felt in the bomb-shattered German cities during the first years after the war. Faced by the material chaos, the optical order, which the aesthetic sensorium had long since repudiated, abruptly allured once again as blessed.[35]

Even when, for aesthetic experience, order had long since revealed itself to be a synonym for purposive rationality, an order destroyed (even when this destruction was itself due to such purposive rationality) could still rouse the aesthetic yearning for order. The seemingly purely aesthetic perception – this Adorno makes clear – is blatantly determined by contrast.[36] Aesthetic experience would be systematically misrecognized if it were stripped of its references to reality.

The complexity of aesthetic perception

Following the thematization of art's specific reference to the state of the aesthetic in the world surrounding it and the entanglements between art and reality, which reach from ways of perceiving the world, via models of existence, through to specific interactions, I now want to show that such transartistic references are not introduced to art from the outside in some way, but are internal to it, inhere within the singular work of art. To begin with I want to use some examples to expand on this. This can only take place in abbreviated form here, but the indications should suffice to allow the scope to become clear.[37]

Examples from the visual arts Let's first of all choose Goya's *The Shootings of 3 May 1808* painted in 1815.[38] This picture cannot simply be received in an aesthetically contemplative manner. It offers not just an exciting colour dynamics and compositional innovations, but simultaneously carries out the interpretation of a historical event, and its aesthetic impulse aims for a certain understanding of what's portrayed and serves to awaken a new form of attitude to phenomena of the type shown. Obviously several perceptive modes intersect in the perception of the work: the observational manner of the picture and its artistico-aesthetic arrangement, the expressive manner of its dynamics, the historical manner of the events of 3 May 1808, the narrational manner of a shocking model plot, and the appellative manner of future intervention and prohibition. The explosion in the picture aims for the end of such deeds and simultaneously detonates the process of merely 'aesthetic' representation and reception. The picture cannot be considered simply as an aesthetically contemplative structure, but rather triggers a multitude of perceptive feats. It pierces the contemplation-cocoon in favour of a multidimensional perception, transcends it towards contexts of communication and life. The picture thus becomes a beacon: things such as this shooting are no longer to occur, this pattern of events is to be breached.[39]

A general finding can be derived from this: the perception of art is not restricted to a single aesthetic feat. Rather, a multitude of feats, diverse types of act from the palette of aesthetic perceptive modes, can belong to the perception of a work. The singular work is then characterized by a specific selection and combination from this range of aesthetic feats. It stipulates a specific array of perceptive modes, functioning, so to speak, as their point of intersection.

A traditionalist aesthetician might object: of course several ways of perceiving are in play in Goya's picture, but only one of these is the specifically aesthetic one, and it is this which is to be dealt with exclusively *in aestheticis*. This argument, however, comes close to an oath of disclosure. One would be admitting that in this 'aesthetic' constriction not even art, but at best one element thereof, can be understood. An aesthetics which limits itself to an 'aesthetic' of this sort would render itself recognizable as a narrow-gauge aesthetics.

A further perceptive dimension which is often important for aesthetic consideration becomes clear when one moves on to Manet's picture *The Shooting of Maximilian* of 1868, which obviously has Goya's work as a foil.[40] Perception of the picture by Manet includes that of Goya's precedent. The perception here has to be intericonic, otherwise it would simply be deficient, would fail to recognize the complexity of Manet's picture. In addition to the palette of perceptive modes previously named, perceptive feats involving the history of painting, that is, intericonic awareness, are necessary here.

Let's take Marcel Duchamp's Mona Lisa parody L.H.O.O.Q. of 1919 as a further example.[41] Its intericonic structure is evident. In addition a semantic dimension is to be included: the sequence of letters in the title is to be read as 'elle a chaud au cul' – 'her ass is hot'. How ridiculous the retreat to mere aesthetic contemplation would be in this case! In order to understand a work such as this you must not only see, but also know, suspect, make inferences. Things here are not settled by orientation towards self-referentiality alone. Reflexion is more important than contemplation.[42]

In summary: works of art transcend the merely contemplative dimension. Historical perceptive dimensions belong to them in the same way as semantic and allegorical, societal, everyday or political dimensions – and, of course, emotional and imaginative processes too. Not that the whole palette of these and further perceptive modes must be at play in every picture, but a number of, even several of, these perceptive modes always take part. The works intervene in our communications inventory and organize the field of aesthetic feats, each in their own way.

Musical examples Something similar can be seen with music. You can practically hear the salvation in some of Bach's fugues. The inner-musical prerequisite for this can easily be stated: every resolution of dissonant tension offers the chance of being developed through to salvation. Do we want to object reprovingly – wherever music not merely thematizes salvation, but allows it to become real – that music has drifted into the trans-aesthetic and must be pruned back to the phantom of a pure-aesthetic as a countermove? Petty-mindedness of this type would go too far for everyone. Bach wanted to create music, and not just comply with a reductionist aesthetic theory.

Passages repeatedly occur in Mozart's *Marriage of Figaro* in which the music offers the utmost contrast to the all-too human pettiness and jealousy. In no way does it enter into this human lowliness, but passes over with it a near celestial superiority. In doing this it makes clear the contrast: society is an ensemble of swindlers and the swindled; truth, dignity and humanity, however, lie in music alone. But this radiant sovereignty can only be heard completely when perceived against the backdrop of the scenic events. The music intangibly criticizes that of which it is intangible. It's this double perception – and not merely a 'musically' contemplative hearing of the music – which is needed to perceive this, the music's, superiority and purity.

Adorno once highlighted art's inalienable double structure with reference to Beethoven in the following way:

That someone is so little conversant with a Beethoven symphony unless they understand the so-called purely musical events in it – in just the same way as someone who doesn't perceive in it the echo of the French Revolution; and how both elements mediate themselves in the phenomenon counts among the [. . .] inalienable themes of philosophical aesthetics.[43]

This led Adorno to the observation that 'aesthetic experience [. . .] [must] transcend itself'.[44] This characterizes *in nuce* what I want to point out here on the whole: the aesthetic has need too of the transaesthetic, and what's decisive for the single work is how the two are brought together in it.

Modern art   What has been said previously holds for all traditional art – and even more so for modern art. For this distinguishes itself by testing, questioning and altering its boundary conditions in a particular way. It doesn't simply rinse off an apparently well-defined programme named 'art', but raises anew the question of what art is in each of its works and provides novel answers accordingly. Works of art are able to alter their short- and long-range conditions, can make unaccustomed criteria requisite, or do away with the boundaries of art. In this way Duchamp questioned the dictate of visibility, Joyce the form of the book, Pollock the limit of painting, Cage the status of music.[45]

Highly varying perceptive modes can become relevant according to artistic type. One work of art can require perceptive feats which for another are completely irrelevant. For some of Malewitsch's works it is not enough to observe what's factually given, rather the perception must extend into the cosmic (and Malewitsch helps you in this, for instance through the way he uses black). You actually haven't seen Munch's painting *The Scream* until you've *heard* a scream – the visual perception must proceed through to an acoustic one. With Duchamp, however, the activity of the senses is insufficient altogether; without bringing in reflexion you would recognize only banal nonsense. Pollock can only be apprehended kinaesthetically. But woe betide whoever wants to insist on this with Mondrian. Sol LeWitt demands an analytic construction of vision. And On Kawara can only be really perceived along with the horrific vision of Hiroshima.

Each time a specific reconfiguration of the perceptive field thus takes place. The palette of conventional perceptive modes is overturned or constellated anew, traditional hierarchies are deposed and new ones established. Precisely the perception of something unapparent or unheard – even of something imperceptible in the traditional sense – can slip into first place. Art intransigently determines for itself the field of perceptive types relevant to it.

Art-perception: polyaesthetic   So different perceptive modes always participate in the perception of art. The perception of art is on principle polyaesthetic, not monoaesthetic. Without the introduction of everyday perceptual competence you wouldn't even be able to recognize the objects in pictures; beyond this, it is advantageous to have perception honed by experience of art at your disposal; it can't hurt if you know what a complementary contrast is, or wherein the artificiality of the seemingly natural central perspective lies – its only this which lets you see, for example, the measures which Masaccio had to adopt so as to produce suspenseful pictures in spite of isocephaly. Put another way: you must know the established codes in order to recognize deviations and new emphases; the *pictor doctus* also calls for a *receptor doctus*.

The recipient's perceptive faculty must therefore probe varying forms of perception and discover the specific constellation stimulated by the work. Aesthetic experience as a whole distinguishes itself through a combination of contemplation, imagination and reflexion. Even contemplation is not simply observational, but processual and reflexive. And, moreover, fundamentally so: even the apprehension of linear convergence and divergence or of colour contrasts alone implies feats of sensible reflexion. What is respectively seen is not *factum brutum*, but is preceded by the interpretation process and dependent on subsequent viewing. And in these acts of interpretation pictorial experience as well as life experience come in. The perception that a gesture is reaching out and yet at the same time shies from taking its grasp would not be possible without a certain maturity and sensitivity on the perceiver's behalf. And Caravaggio's attack on the sovereignty of pictures can first be seen correctly against the background of his predecessors and contemporaries. References to the life-world thus belong to the picture process in the same way as intericonic allusions.

Furthermore, experiencing art requires a particular openness to the alteration of familiar categories, sectorial divisions and distinctions. For art assumes the freedom to divide the world up in unaccustomed ways or to show up correspondences, analogies, transitions between sectors considered separate. Morandi's still lifes for instance are not straightforward still lifes of objects, but are sociograms at the same time. The arrangement of objects is to be read just as that of families. You recognize hierarchies, contacts, fears, self-assertions, evasive manoeuvres, dismissals, linkages. As an artist Morandi practises microsociology – just as Mondrian practised macrosociology: his pondering art concerned not only pictorial elements, but represented a model for the balancing of life's burdens at the same time, just as must be achieved in every individual life and is analogously of importance for social cultivation. These silent, seemingly unpretentious works are first fully perceived when their grasping of practical dimensions is recognized. Mondrian himself also understood them as paradigms for the equation of social forces which characterizes democratic societies. – Again it can be seen that the experiencing of art can be compelled to include seemingly alien horizons. Only when complex does it succeed.

Résumé Once again: in the experiencing of art different perceptive modes can be relevant: contemplative, historical, everyday, semantic, intericonic allegorical, utopian, and so on. The field of aesthetic perception is polymorphous.

Single works of art, then, are characterized by a specific selection from this totality of aesthetic perceptive modes. They each activate a subset of such modes and combine these elements in their own way. In doing so they obstinately fix the rank of singular perceptive modes and the hierarchy of these. The same perceptive attitude can have a quite different status in different works of art.[46] The perception of an individual work of art is thus to be practised and apprehended as a specific nexus of differing perceptive modes.

Art brings several types of perception into play, suggesting a specific constellation of these and, often, an unaccustomed organization of the perceptive field on the whole. It is the very fact that neither the range nor the relationship of perceptive dimensions is fixed once and for all, but is always at stake, which distinguishes aesthetic perception.

Then of course it is only an on-principle polyaesthetic attitude, one attentive of singular constellations, which is able to do justice to works. A disposition to general aesthetic contemplation or a restriction to formal analysis would, on the other hand, systematically diminish and misrecognize works' potential to grasp outwards. If one wanted to deny aesthetic perception's polyvalency and lateral holds – because contemplation alone is alleged to be relevant and demands the dismissal of all everyday, societal, semantic, and so on, perceptive dimensions – then the danger exists that august contemplation tends to approach mere gawping. The difference between gawping and really seeing was inimitably expressed by Brecht in the *Life of Galileo*: when the young lad, Andrea, claims: 'But I can see with my own eyes that the sun goes down in a different place from where it rises. So how can it stay still?' Galileo answers, 'You can see, indeed! What can you see? Nothing at all. You just gawp. Gawping isn't seeing.'[47]

The benefits to art analysis of a comprehensive aesthetics

What results from this? If art constantly brings into play a whole palette of sorts of perception and affords each a certain organization, then aesthetics too, as the reflexive authority of the aesthetic, obviously has to be in a position to take account of diverse sorts of perception and differing constellations, and to do justice to them. Put another way, the experiencing of art itself demands an aesthetics which looks both the inner polyaesthetics of art and its transartistic entanglements in the eye, and which is capable of considering *all* dimensions of *aisthesis*. Aesthetics must extend over the whole breadth of the aesthetic.

Incidentally, an aesthetics of this type would not only prove fruitful for the purposes of understanding and interpreting art – that is, not only for observers – but could ultimately be of specific interest for the creation of art too – that is, for artists themselves. It opens up a new perspective on what art is all about. Once an artist (following, say, Schiller's example) has discovered art's ability to develop models for what Schiller called the 'art of life' (*Lebenskunst*), then he may proceed quite differently from the traditional search for the perfection of a work of art in itself – Beuys would be an example of this. Or when an artist (following, say, Nietzsche) has recognized the constitutive role of aesthetic features in cognition, then she might suddenly think, 'Hey, my actual task might consist not in creating art for the sake of art, but rather in developing and exemplifying possible views and ways of perceiving, alternative divergent patterns of perceiving and apprehending' – Eva Hesse is an example of this. In such ways, the type of transaesthetics I advocate can encourage new steps for art itself. It is a type of aesthetics which is of significance to artists themselves who – for good reasons – are so dissatisfied with traditional aesthetics.

To summarize this: an expansion of aesthetics beyond aesthetics to the full extent of *aisthesis* is necessary not only for the sake of a full grasp of the aesthetic, but in particular for the sake of an adequate understanding of art too. This ought ultimately to be the penetrating argument for an extension of aesthetics.[48]

The artistically restricted aesthetics, on the other hand, is not even capable of being an aesthetics of art. Rather it constrains and misrecognizes the art which it purports to serve. It locks art within the golden cage of autonomy – one which neither traditional nor, by any means, modern art wants to accept. Whilst seemingly talking in an art-friendly manner, an aesthetic-theoretical ghettoization is once again practised. If art is not treated from the perspective of an aesthetics which includes viewpoints from beyond aesthetics, then it is unavoidably aesthetically distorted.

3.   Reorganization of the discipline

Transdisciplinary design of the discipline

Finally, what will the structure of the discipline of aesthetics be in the wake of such an expansion? My answer is surely not surprising: its structure will be transdisciplinary. I imagine aesthetics being a field of research which comprehends all questions concerning *aisthesis* – with the inclusion of contributions from philosophy, sociology, art history, psychology, anthropology, neurosciences, and so on. *Aisthesis* forms the framework of the discipline. And art is one – but, as important as it might be, only one – of its subjects.

The following could sound more surprising: I imagine the parts of the discipline referring to *aisthesis* as being effective branches of the discipline of aesthetics. They would be integrated in its institutional structure. Aesthetics ought to be interdisciplinary or transdisciplinary in itself – instead of displaying interdisciplinarity only when occasioned by meetings with other disciplines. In an aesthetics department, as I envisage it, all the branches mentioned ought to be taught; and the individual aestheticians themselves ought to have considerable knowledge of them, and be in a position to teach at least some of these branches themselves – and not just, say, an ontology of art or the history of taste.

Transdisciplinarity in general

Perhaps this suggestion of a transdisciplinary structure of the discipline seems too unaccustomed, but I think that a structure of this type is necessary in almost every discipline today. This derives from insights which have effected a fundamental change in our understanding of the structure of rationalities and which, consistently, demand an altered design to research fields and research objects.

In modernity a differentiation and separation of rationality types was advocated – and these rationality types were held to be clearly outlined and different in their core. More recent analyses, however, have shown that this is at best superficially correct, but is basically wrong. The diverse rationalities cannot be delimited from one another in a watertight manner, but exhibit in their core entanglements and transitions which undercut the traditional departmentalization. Such entanglements, transitions and penetrations have become the contemporary agenda.[49]

Outlook

I cannot expand further on this point here. But if one were to find this perspective perhaps interesting, but not be convinced of the necessity to apply it to every realm – then with regard to aesthetics, at least so I hope, one will find plausible the suggestion of a transdisciplinary design to the discipline. Already in its history aesthetics has experienced significant paradigm shifts. Certainly, such shifts don't happen every day, but one day – for good reasons – they might take place. For a coming generation the transdisciplinary structure of an aesthetics beyond aesthetics could be fairly self-evident. Outside of the discipline this already seems to be the case.

Notes

This essay was originally presented at the XIIIth International Congress of Aesthetics, Lahti, Finland (1–5 August 1995). It has been revised for this volume. (First English publication.)

1. *Academic American Encyclopedia* (Danbury, Conn.: Grolier Inc. 1993), vol. 1, p. 130.
2. *Enciclopedia Filosofica* (Florence: G.C. Sansoni Editore 1967), vol. 2, col. 1054.
3. *Vocabulaire d'Esthétique* (Paris: PUF 1990), pp. 691 and 692 resp.
4. *Historisches Wörterbuch der Philosophie*, ed. Joachim Ritter (Basel: Schwabe & Co. 1971), vol. 1, col. 555.
5. Baumgarten certainly used examples from the arts, especially from poetry, but only to illustrate what aesthetic perfection – as the perfection of sensuous knowledge – could be.
6. Cf. *Die Aktualität des Ästhetischen*, ed. Wolfgang Welsch (Munich: Fink 1993). The volume documents a congress which took place under the same title in Hanover in September 1992. It assembled experts from various fields: philosophy, sociology, political science,

feminism, media studies, design, neurophysiology, philosophy of science, art practice and art history. With a couple of thousand participants it found broad resonance.

7. Wittgenstein said: '*A picture* held us captive. And we could not get outside it, for it lay in our language and language seemed to repeat it to us inexorably.' (Ludwig Wittgenstein, *Philosophical Investigations*, trans. G.E.M. Anscombe, New York: Macmillan 1968, p. 48^e [115].)

8. Ibid., p. 103^e [309]. – This was how Wittgenstein answered the question as to what his 'aim in philosophy' was (ibid.).

9. Letter to August Wilhelm Schlegel, 3 September 1802, quoted from: *Aus Schellings Leben. In Briefen*, vol. 1, ed. G.L. Plitt (Leipzig: Hirzel 1869), pp. 390–399, here p. 397. In his *Philosophy of Art* Schelling explained: 'None of what the more vulgar sense calls art can occupy the philosopher: Art is, to him, a necessary apparition flowing out directly from the absolute, and only insofar as it can be evinced and measured as such does it have reality for him.' (Friedrich Wilhelm Joseph Schelling, *Philosophie der Kunst* [lecture Jena, winter semester 1802–3], reprint of the 1859 edition, Darmstadt: Wissenschaftliche Buchgesellschaft 1976, p. 384.)

10. Schelling, *Philosophie der Kunst*, pp. 7 and 124 resp.

11. 'Die wissenschaftliche Ästhetik sucht nach dem Universalziegel, aus dem sich das Gebäude der Ästhetik errichten ließe.' (Robert Musil, *Tagebücher*, ed. Adolf Frisé, Reinbek bei Hamburg: Rowohlt 1976, p. 449) – This note originates from around 1920.

12. The result of this approach is that a philosophy of this type knows no way of saying anything about real art. When Schelling became Secretary General of the Munich Akademie der bildenden Künste he was obliged through this office to give lectures about the philosophy of art. But he remained silent. He lectured not once throughout his fifteen years in office. If it comes to the verdict, to the confrontation with art, the philosophy of art remains speechless. The hour of reckoning becomes the oath of disclosure for this type of aesthetics. – I have discussed the problems of traditional aesthetics generally in: 'Traditionelle und moderne Ästhetik in ihrem Verhältnis zur Praxis der Kunst' (*Zeitschrift für Ästhetik und Allgemeine Kunstwissenschaft*, XXVIII, 1983, pp. 264-286). My counter-concept was first developed in my *Ästhetisches Denken* (Stuttgart: Reclam 1990, 4th edition, 1995; Eng.: *Aesthetic Thinking*, trans. John Bailiff, Atlantic Highlands, NJ: Humanities Press 1998).

13. I have more broadly developed these thoughts in 'Aestheticization Processes: Phenomena, Distinctions and Prospects' (this volume), and will partly rely on this essay.

14. 'Aestheticization' means that the unaesthetic is made, or understood to be, aesthetic.

15. 'The "Oldest System-Programme" of German Idealism', in *Hegel Selections*, ed. M.J. Inwood (London/New York: Macmillan 1989), pp. 86–87.

16. I discussed this for the first time in 'Ästhetik und Anästhetik' (in *Ästhetisches Denken*, Stuttgart: Reclam 1990, pp. 9-40). (Forthcoming in English as 'Aesthetics and Anaesthetics', in *Aesthetic Thinking*.)

17. Cf. the essay 'Contemporary Art in Public Space: A Feast for the Eyes or an Annoyance?' in the present volume.

18. Rainer Maria Rilke, *Duineser Elegien*, in Rilke, *Sämtliche Werke*, 6 vols (Frankfurt a.M.: Insel 1955–66), vol. 1, p. 685 (first elegy).

19. For derealization and revalidation see the essay 'Artificial Paradises?: Considering the World of Electronic Media – and Other Worlds' in the present volume.

20. By 'media' I will – in the following – always refer to electronic media, without suggesting that there might be any kind of experience independent of media of *some kind or other*.

21. For the viewers the desire for media-entertainment is gaining the upper hand in the same measure as the former belief in the reality of what's transmitted is disappearing. – I am referring here primarily to television, although this is somehow an old-fashioned medium in today's electronic world. It is, however, the one which everybody knows and uses. And the effects of the more advanced technologies are not qualitatively different, but intensify the derealization tendency.

22. Cf. Martin Jay's survey *Downcast Eyes: The Denigration of Vision in Twentieth-Century French Thought* (Berkeley: University of California Press 1994).

23. Cf. for more details the essay 'On the Way to an Auditive Culture?' in the present volume.

24. Cf. Derrick de Kerckhove, 'Touch versus Vision: Ästhetik neuer Technologien', in *Die Aktualität des Ästhetischen*, pp. 137–168.

25. Sten Nadolny, *Die Entdeckung der Langsamkeit* (Munich: Hanser 1983).

26. Peter Handke, *Versuch über die Müdigkeit* (Frankfurt a.M.: Suhrkamp 1989).

27. Cf. the essay 'Information Superhighway or Highway One?' in the present volume.

28. Cf. my more detailed discussion of this point in section II of 'Aestheticization Processes: Phenomena, Distinctions and Prospects'.

29. Aristotle points out in the fundamental chapter *Metaphysics* IV.2 that the manifold uses of *to on* point only to a weak unitariness: not the strict one of a *kath' hen legomenon*, but merely the looser one of *pros hen legomena* – the categorical senses of being are used not *corresponding* to a primary meaning, but merely *with reference* to such (namely *ousia*). The manifoldness reaches still further when one additionally includes the transcategorical senses of being, that is, 'in itself' and 'accidental', 'true' and 'false', 'possible' and 'real' (cf. *Met.* V.7). Aristotle's point, however, is precisely that such a weak unitariness is completely adequate for the realization of a science of being referring to all the senses of being.

30. Or do we not want to consider, say, Hegelian logic – which in this respect is almost exemplarily complete – to be a logic at all? With what right?

31. Goethe had already described and paid tribute to this. Upon entering a cobbler's workshop, he believed suddenly he could see a picture by Ostade before him, 'so perfect that one ought only really to have hung it in the gallery. [. . .] It was the first time that I came to notice in such high degree that gift, which I subsequently exercised with greater awareness, namely to see nature with the eyes of this or that artist to whose works I had just dedicated a particular attentiveness. This ability has accorded me much enjoyment.' (Johann Wolfgang von Goethe, *Aus meimem Leben: Dichtung und Wahrheit*, Part II, Book 8, Zurich/Stuttgart: Artemis 1948, p. 353.) In the *Italian Journey* he speaks of his 'old gift, that of seeing the world with the eyes of that artist whose pictures have just impressed me' (*Goethes Werke*, vol. XI, Munich: Beck, 8th edition, 1974, pp. 7–349, here p. 86; 8 October 1786).

32. This is not at all astonishing, since the artistic perceptions were themselves developed in contact, and in the coming-to-grips with environmental as well as other artistic perception. Therefore, they are also able to intervene in the realm of our experience and to reconfigure our world's aesthetic nexus. Works of art do this in a mysterious way. They are, so to speak, intensified structures which generate a magnetic field through their inner crystallization and can bring about wondrous effects in their human – mental as well as emotional – vicinity.

33. George Steiner has pointed out how much our amorous behaviour and rhetoric have been formed by generations of artistic models: 'The words, phrases, tropes, gestures of spirit and body with which we seek to communicate the birth, ripening, withering of love in our being, with which we seek to convey these elemental experiences both to our own perception and to "the other", whose otherness is, at this very point, most critical to us, are taken very largely, whether consciously or not, from the repertoire of the great sayers, painters, music-makers before us. [. . .] According to the levels of our verbal and literate holdings, we experience and signify love as did Jack and Jill, as did Romeo and Juliet or Tolstoy's Natasha before us. Our jealousies ape Othello's. [. . .] The broken syllables which generations whispered or panted in the rhetoric of seduction and of intercourse were out of Petrarch's phrase book.' (George Steiner, *Real Presences: Is There Anything in What We Say?*, London: Faber and Faber, 1989, p. 194.)

34. Rainer Maria Rilke, 'Archäischer Torso Apollos', in Rilke, *Sämtliche Werke*, vol. 1, p. 557. George Steiner considers this appeal common to 'any poem, novel, play, painting, musical composition worth meeting.' (Steiner, *Real Presences*, p. 142.)

35. Theodor W. Adorno, *Ästhetische Theorie*, in Adorno, *Gesammelte Schriften*, vol. 7 (Frankfurt a.M.: Suhrkamp, 4th edition, 1984), pp. 237f.

36. Klee had, already in 1915, noted a connection of this type in another way: 'The more shocking this world (just as today), the more abstract the art, whereas a happy world produces a worldly art.' (Paul Klee, *Tagebücher*, Cologne: DuMont 1957, p. 323.)

37. I first presented the following arguments in the essay 'Erweiterungen der Ästhetik – eine Replik' (in *Bild und Reflexion*, eds Birgit Recki and Lambert Wiesing, Munich: Fink 1997, pp. 37–67).

38. Francesco Goya, *The Shootings of 3 May 1808 in the Manzanares Valley*, 1815, Madrid, Prado.

39. Anti-fascist demonstrators in Paris in the 1930s carried with them placards on which the picture had been copied. Its transgression of the museum's threshold was not just metaphorical.

40. Edouard Manet, *The Shooting of Maximilian*, 1868, Kunsthalle Mannheim.

41. Marcel Duchamp, *L.H.O.O.Q.*, 1919, Philadelphia Museum of Art, collection of Louise and Walter Arensberg.

42. Conversely one can already sense here the danger which threatens when, in view of such works, someone clings to contemplation as the sole legitimate aesthetic outlook and seeks to make it the general criterion. It's then that petty-mindedness is close, and censorship not far distant. Whatever doesn't reveal itself to the merely contemplative approach is then faulted, denounced and dispensed with: 'That's no longer art', people will say, or that it's just 'a marginal effect at most' which is 'unworthy of attention'.

43. Adorno, *Ästhetische Theorie*, p. 519.

44. Ibid.

45. It was precisely the project of the avant-garde to transcend the confined status of an artistics and to open itself to an aesthetics beyond aesthetics. It would be an anachronism to want to ignore or annul this through an aesthetic-theoretical restriction.

46. To give an example: it is well known that Edouard Manet's *Déjeuner sur l'herbe* is intericonically structured. It relates, via Riamondi, back to Raphael and ancient representations of river gods. But this is merely a silent subtext to the picture; the historical perceptive dimension must remain in the background here. If one were to shift it into the foreground (and this was paradoxically attempted, so as to make the picture presentable for a bourgeois taste, which certainly values Raphael and antiquity), then one would thereby sacrifice the point and provocative gesture of the picture, which is indeed strong because it visually slaps the bourgeois in the face. Giulio Paolini's sculpture groups (e.g. the *Mimesis*) are a quite different matter. They too are intericonically structured, refer back to ancient representations. But the historical perception must assume first place here. For the androgynous beauty, the emotion and also the irony of Paolini's figures – characteristic features of these works – result entirely in this dimension. Thus, historical perception belongs to both works – but their ranking is highly variant.

47. Bertolt Brecht, *Life of Galileo*, trans. John Willett (London: Methuen 1986 [1938/9]), p. 9 (Scene 1).

48. In a similar sense, already with Adorno we read: 'Modified aesthetics [. . .] no longer considers, as did traditional aesthetics, the concept of art to be its obvious correlate. Aesthetic thinking today, in conceiving art, would have to go beyond it [. . .]' (Theodor W. Adorno, 'Funktionalismus heute', in Adorno, *Gesammelte Schriften*, vol. 10.1, Frankfurt a.M.: Suhrkamp 1977, pp. 375–395, here p. 395.)

49. Cf. my *Vernunft. Die zeitgenössische Vernunftkritik und das Konzept der transversalen Vernunft* (Frankfurt a.M.: Suhrkamp 1995, stw 1996).

II   DIAGNOSES AND PROSPECTS

5

HOW MODERN WAS MODERN ARCHITECTURE?

There exists between philosophy and architecture an old congeniality or family resemblance. Not only did Vitruvius, architectural theory's classic author, recommend architects to 'have followed the philosophers with attention',[1] but classic philosophers, like Aristotle, Descartes or Kant, and more recent ones like Nietzsche and Wittgenstein, have also made use of architectural images and concepts in important passages.[2] Postmodern thinking too repeatedly links its questioning of traditional philosophizing with reflections on the architectural implications thereof and with suggestions for a different architecture of thinking as well as construction – think, say, of Lyotard or Derrida. To speak out on architecture from the side of philosophy is thus not all that uncommon. It is perhaps, where the concept of modernity is concerned, particularly appropriate.

I.   Modernity *per se* does not exist

I want to start out from an observation: in some metropolises today you find galleries with the designation 'gallery of modern and contemporary art'. Obviously 'modern' is no longer synonymous with 'contemporary'. Modernity has become old.

But the title of my essay is not meant in the same way as these door-plates. I don't want to suggest that modern architecture today is no longer modern. I want to imply something far more incisive: that even in its own time it was not modern.

Of course in a statement such as this 'modern' must be being used with two different meanings. In a certain sense modern architecture was certainly highly modern; in another, more important sense, however, it was not at all.

This isn't just a play on words. For the concept 'modernity' is not only multifaceted but in effect plurivocal. Contrary conceptions are recommended under this label. 'Modernity' is actually just a pseudonym which gives rise to the false appearance of unitariness for these different versions.

Modernity *per se* – such is my first thesis – does not exist. What do exist are varying concepts of modernity, and their relationship to one another is only partially one of continuation, but partially too one of reaction, and these concepts are often at war with, and practically exclude, one another. One should, hence, only ever talk of 'modernity' specifically, stating the *type* of modernity which one has in mind. This should be registered by dedicated defenders of modernity as well as by the apologists of a post-modernity. Much would resolve itself in the dispute between modernity and postmodernity if one were to state exactly which modernity one actually wants to defend, and from which type of modernity one wishes to set oneself aside.

Much would be gained too for architectual debate if clarity were to exist as to which *type of modernity* the so-called modern architecture corre-sponds to and which other contemporary type it misses. Not only the stimuli and successes of modern architecture, but also its troubles and its necessitation could then be better understood. Furthermore the deficiencies could then be responded to more appropriately. – My attempt to determine the modernity-type of modern architecture is located in the context of such considerations.[3]

II.   Types of modernity

To begin with I want to quote some examples from the rich catalogue of modernity concepts. The list is in no way complete. It merely has the aim of making the diversity of such concepts familiar through a few cases and of awakening the inclination to speak in future of 'modernity' no longer in wholesale terms, but specifically.

There is, first of all, 'modernity' in the sense of *temps modernes,* as the French say, or *Neuzeit* in German, which in English corresponds to the modern age. And these *'temps modernes'*, despite sounding the same, are a quite different matter from the English 'modern times' of someone like Charlie Chaplin; whereas Chaplin refers to the 1920s, the *'temps modernes'* of the French designate a programme developed in the *seventeenth century*, a programme typical for the modern age, one of a new, universal science by the name of *mathesis universalis.*

With the 'modernity' of the *eighteenth century* it is already a different matter. It is now the project of the Enlightenment which is meant by 'modernity'. It is about human rights and the programme of social emanci-pation. Habermas, for example, refers to this programme of Enlightenment when he talks of modernity as being an incomplete project. 'Project of Enlightenment' and 'project of modernity' are synonymous for him.

The term 'modernity' in the *nineteenth century* stands for yet another programme. Modernization is now meant in the sense of industrialization. Others, however, meant the exact counter-programme to this – such as

Baudelaire in his concept of *modernité*. Instead of increasing industrialization and the erection of what Max Weber was later to call 'the steely
housing of modernity', for Baudelaire modernity consisted in subtle
exaltation through the ephemeral, the transient. Hence, two completely
contrary modernity concepts exist here alongside one another.

Finally, in the twentieth century the most variant of modernity concepts
continually oppose one another: the modernism of the avant-gardes, the
modernization concepts of totalitarianisms, the modernity of the eternal
recurrence of the same. One and the same author can (even in the same
text) take up arms against modernity – 'To hell with this modern world!',
declares Breton in the First Manifesto of Surrealism[4] – and then, a few
pages later, praise the surrealist mental attitude itself as being 'specifically
modern'.[5]

In view of such disparities in the concept of modernity some contemporaries are inclined to abandon the expression generally. But, equally,
little would be gained by doing this. All that remains is to develop a
differentiated way of dealing with this concept.[6]

III.   The modern-age type of modernity

Of these modernity types I would like to characterize two more closely in
the following. First of all I shall expand on the specifically *modern-age*
type, the project of *mathesis universalis* as was founded in the seventeenth
century and permeated subsequent centuries. It is still alive in our present
day in various forms – for example in the concept of a 'technological age'.
– What is this modern-age programme all about? I begin with Descartes,
the most important of its founders.

1.   The modern age ideal: uniformity

Proceeding from the surprising discovery of analytic geometry, that is, from
the representability of spatial relationships (phenomena of external perception) with the purer – since wholly unsensuous, solely intellectual – means
of the number and calculation, Descartes believed that *all* spheres of reality
could be apprehended and structured with this one mathematical method.
This was the spirit of his programmatic foundational text of 1637 entitled
Discourse on Method.

This conception is still fascinating today – although in the meantime this
fascination must be admixed with terror. Descartes believed that from then
on everything, from the world of natural events just as that of human
phenomena, could be comprehended uniformly. Admittedly his method
was, to begin with, only successful in the natural scientific realm and in
questions of theoretical philosophy. Descartes did not have in hand the
solution for practical philosophy, for ethical and political questions – but a

Spinoza was to come along and carry out the *more geometrico* ethics, and a Hobbes would apply it to politics. And Descartes himself already spoke of the revolutionary achievements which were to await medicine: it would not only find a cure to all possible illnesses, but would in the end even invent a remedy against death. In the same way one would be able to structure and institutionalize the oppressively impure sphere of emotion, of corporality and of dubious sexuality according to the maxims of clarity and lucidity. With this method people were to be able to cognize everything, put everything to rights, arrange everything according to the intellect. – On the whole you sense in the texts of this early modern age an urge to transform the whole world into one of light and universal transparency. There were to be no more people, but just intelligences, that is, angels. A rebuilding of the world as a whole was the innermost hope of this modern age.

2. Topoi of the modern age

I want to set out five cornerstones of this concept in somewhat greater detail: the radicality of the new beginning, universality, quantification, technical character and uniformization.

1 The *radicality of the break* with tradition was of a scale previously unknown. The Renaissance, for instance, had also effected a break with what it called the 'dark ages'. But in so doing it reverted back to another past, to antiquity. Furthermore, it 'rescued' more parts of history than just antiquity: for example, many things from the middle ages, because they were viewed as being ancient or passed themselves off as being ancient – such as the Florentine Baptisterium, for example, an eleventh-century construction. The modern age, however, executes a radical break with *everything* preceding it. Descartes allows nothing of the old science to retain validity – not even that which is right; for it bears the proof of its correctness not on its brow, but is first to be inferred from agreement with what the new science teaches.

Not even logic remains unaffected by this revision. Bacon, one of Descartes's companions in foundation, thought it necessary to write a *Novum Organum*: the classic logic texts of Aristotle (they bore the name *Organon*) were considered to be insufficient. The old could not be improved, rather everything had to be created anew starting with its own principles. – Admittedly, another modern-age philosopher – Hegel – was later to praise the Aristotelian logic. According to Hegel, Aristotle's views on concept, judgement and inference had remained valid through to his day; not a single step had been made beyond Aristotle.[7] From this it can be recognized that the modern-age rejection of tradition of course had boastful features too, and was to a good extent mere rhetoric.

2 *Universality* is simply the other side of the same coin. If one breaks with everything, then *everything* must be built up anew, and one must view one's own principle as being universal.

3   The decisive new principle – the new method – consists in the transfer of all qualitative predicates into *quantitative* determinations. This begins with sensuous qualities, for example the colours. Red, yellow or blue – according to the modern age – don't actually exist at all; objectively there exist only size, shape and motion. And this elimination of qualities is continued with throughout the whole world. Thus for the new science there are no more actual disciplinary distinctions. Ethical questions were considered not to be different in their structure from those of mathematics – the opposite was supposed merely to have been the mistake of such traditional and unreliable minds as Aristotle. In truth there was to be only a single real rationality, the mathematical one, and this was to be capable of solving all problems. It was to be a matter only of fully unfolding this rationality and applying it everywhere.

4   At the same time this science is an undertaking which *shapes the world*. It is *technical* in its approach and spirit. It will not rest before realizing its principle through to the last corner of the earth. Even antipodes such as Heidegger and Adorno were in agreement on this technical character of modern-age thinking: 'Technology is the essence of this knowledge' – a key sentence from *Dialectic of Enlightenment* - might at the same time serve as a résumé of Heidegger's analysis of the technical character of modern-age thought.[8]

5   Of course what's concerned in all of this is a *uniformization* operation. The uniformity of the approach is decisive for the thinking, just as it is for the success of the whole programme. It must lead to a theoretical, as well as a practical, unification of appearances. In the realized modern age the world would look the same all over. This follows straightforwardly from the principle that there is *one* method for *all* problems.

3.   The modern age and modern-age modernity

This form of thought remained definitional throughout the whole modern age. Even where the domination of the mathematical scientific world model became at least superficially questionable, the candidates for replacement or succession reproduced the same monopolistic structure everywhere. They too appeared once again with the claim of possessing *one* model of solution for *all* problems. In terms of content they were indeed very different; in the obsession with totality, however, the same everywhere. Whether Hegel's teleologization of history in the name of the world-spirit (*Weltgeist*), Marx's salvation of humanity through the proletarian revolution, the capitalist programme of the greatest possible riches for all, or the technology euphoria which is fashionable today: the new paradigm was alw supposed to solve *all* problems, to spare *nothing*. In this modern age ä modern-age modernity it was not possible for a truth to appear other tl with the claim to exclusivity. Singularity and universality were its innerm own, plurality and particularity profoundly alien.

This even applies still to the counter-options to this main strand – to the romantic just as much as to the surrealist one, and to the existentialist just as to some esoteric ones, right through to the proclamation of a New Age (which superficially turns vehemently against Descartes, but wholly retains his totalizing form of thought). These counter-conceptions also have uniform models and single-cure utopias in mind. 'One size fits all.'

IV.   The scientific and artistic revolutions of the twentieth century: the break with the modern age

In opposition to this a second type of modernity is now to be presented, one which criticized and abandoned the core of this modern-age modernity. This first occurred in the twentieth century and just where it was perhaps least to be expected, where, however – when it happened – it had to gain the greatest penetrative power: in science, in mathematical natural science, that is, in the guiding medium of the modern age itself. Through the so-called 'foundational crisis' (Einstein's relativity theory, Heisenberg's uncertainty relation, Gödel's incompleteness theorem) science itself recognized and began to teach us that reality is to be apprehended not with totality claims, but with plural models and situation-specific theories. Reality is not homogeneously but heterogeneously, not harmonically but dramatically, not uniformly but diversely structured. It has, so to speak, a postmodern design. The fact that this was shown by *science* made the abandonment of the old obsession with totality obligatory.

The arts in the early decades of this century also played their part. Their splitting of the concept of art into a multitude of most diverse paradigms and undreamt-of experiments productively acted out the plurality which had become obvious and acceptable through the scientific foundational crisis.

Postmodernity is then nothing but the consistent continuation and radicalization of this critique of the modern-age project and its totality obsession which began with the modernity of the twentieth century. Postmodernity is not the invention of dreamers, but a committed sequel to this scientific and artistic revision. One of its most important thinkers, Lyotard, then rightly says that the scientific and artistic avant-gardes from the start of this century had already anticipated postmodernity as he understands it.[9]

Postmodernity's criticism and abandonment thus refers not to modernity in general, but to the modern age alone – the spirit of the modern age as the spirit of great unity concepts. On the other hand postmodernity is congruent with the 'hard' scientific and the 'experimental' artistic modernity of our century. In view of this postmodernity ought in effect to be designated radically modern, and anything but anti-modern. It is at one with *this* modernity, whose achievements it continues. That is why I talk of 'our postmodern modernity' and mean by this that, although we are still living in modernity, we nonetheless realize its present-day form precisely when we take account of the tendencies which one has in the meantime – as unfortunate as it might be – got used to calling 'postmodern'.

V. The modern-age spirit of 'modern' architecture

1. The thesis

Having presented in detail, from the spectrum of historical modernity concepts, first of all the on-principle uniform concept of the modern age, and then the on-principle plural concept of the modernity which achieved the breakthrough against this modern age in the early twentieth century, I now turn to modern architecture.

Stated in advance, my thesis with regard to the modernity of this architecture reads: modern architecture is actually Cartesianism in built form. Perhaps after everything I've set out this isn't completely surprising. All the same I will have to provide detailed evidence for this thesis. I shall attempt first of all to make it plausible by looking at a section of Descartes. It is a passage in which Descartes – I'm exaggerating slightly, if at all – draws up a Bauhaus programme.

2. Descartes the precursor

Descartes makes use of the city metaphor.[10] The old cities which have grown in the course of history, he says, are not good for much. Their construction was ill considered, most things were left to coincidence; much turned out crooked in detail and ill proportioned on the whole. Certainly there are also some fine houses in its midst, but, as a whole, the city is bungled.

Descartes then develops his counter vision: how different it would be, he says, with those cities erected by an engineer, freely designed on free space, where everything can be proportioned according to a uniform measure and perfectly ordered as a whole.

The city metaphor with Descartes stands for the new science. Soon the new science, and some day the whole world, was to become just as this dream city. Merely to convert or to improve things from the past was to make no sense. One had to begin from the start according to one's own order and create everything anew.

In the meantime, however, we have learned, alongside this direct sense of the metaphor, to perceive its implicit sense too, the perturbing converse side of its alluring obverse. Descartes's utopia was indeed visionary – but in a somewhat gruesome sense. In the passage cited, he outlines in advance the spirit and method of dismal satellite towns such as those which later arose

from the Märkische quarter and Neu-Perlach, through to Nanterre, and in
which the troubles of this type of planning euphoria came to light.

To be sure, one could object to my comparison that Descartes's allusion
can be related more directly to planning forms like the French garden or
baroque city layouts such as Karlsruhe. But significantly in Descartes's
description the element is already omitted which essentially distinguished
this planning from the uniformity of later modernity: centrality with all its
symbolic and real connotations. Hence it is justified to detect in Descartes's
words, in a subterranean way, the uniformity of isotropic building which
belongs to the consistency of this mathematical modern-age concept and
which comes to light unadulterated the moment that modern-age thinking
is asserted completely, such as occurs in International Style.

I do indeed think that, in functionalist architecture, which I take here as
the guiding type of modern architecture,[11] all the elements of modern-age
sentiment outlined and the Cartesian ideology do in fact recur. This is now
to be illustrated in detail.

3.   Modern architecture's modern-age topoi

1   First of all there is the *radicality* of the break with everything past and
the will to shape everything according to one's own pattern. Let's hear, as
an example, such a negation of tradition by Le Corbusier:

> A great epoch has begun. There exists a new spirit. [. . .] Architecture has for its
> first duty, in this period of renewal, that of bringing about a revision of values, a
> revision of the constituent elements of the house. [. . .] We must create the mass-
> production spirit. The spirit of constructing mass-production houses. The spirit of
> living in mass-production houses. The spirit of conceiving mass-production
> houses.[12]

Note: The task of the architect is not to build houses. It is also not his task
to create houses for people as they are. His actual task is rather to consist
in creating new people – who would then suit the architectures which one
intends to build.[13]

Walter Gropius made similarly short work of tradition: when in 1938 he
took up his office as dean of the faculty of architecture at Harvard he had
all books about historical architecture removed from the library.[14] The
tradition was null and void; you weren't even supposed to be able still to
study it. A break in epoch, this was the wholly modern-age historical
gesture of this modernity.

Of course all of this was executable only at the level of official rhetoric.
Actually the classics of modernity allowed themselves to be inspired
throughout by earlier forms of architecture too. Mies van der Rohe seems
to me to be the prime example of this. He had studied Schinkel's classicism
thoroughly and reverted back to architecture's absolute classic paradigm –
Greek temple – often enough. That he designated the double-T-pillars
the 'Doric columns' of modern architecture was no coincidence. And

naturally a building such as the Neue Nationalgalerie in Berlin is a prime example of such classicism. This is a temple architecture. And the secret recourse can even be proven in detail. The slight curve upwards in the horizontal roof line for instance – statically just as optically necessary – corresponds to the centimetre to the upwards bend of the architrave at the Parthenon of the Athenian Acropolis.

2   As everyone knows, universality also belongs to the sentiment of this modern architecture. This, however, is practicable only as *uniformization*. It belongs among the innermost paradoxes and most revealing phenomena of this alleged functionalism that in the end – against the programme – it became a superb formalism and alarming uniformism. 'Functionalism' was actually just a pseudonym which concealed something else. Functionalism purported to orient itself according to the diverse functions, to comply with them: 'form follows function'. In truth, however, the opposite came about, a decretorial reduction and fixing of the functions.

The claim was to submit all acts in life to a uniform calculus. Four functions – inhabiting, working, recreation and circulation; nothing more and nothing else – were to comprise the 'keys to urbanism'.[15] So can everything be calculated uniformly – and does someone doubt that humans are all the same?

Yet already in 1930 all necessary criticism had been voiced by Adolf Behne:

> The linear building intends to solve and cure, if possible, everything by means of the apartment, surely in a serious endeavour for people. But in fact it's precisely here that the individual becomes a concept, a figure. The individual is to inhabit and to become healthy by inhabiting, and the exact living diet is prescribed to him in detail. He has – at least with the most consistent architects – to go to bed in the east, to eat and answer mother's letter in the west, and the apartment is organized in such a way that he cannot in fact do anything but this.[16]

Functionalism, I said, leads to uniformism. In the end all functions become *de facto* the same for it. One knows the most famous example for this: the latest purely functionalist building on German soil, the Neue Nationalgalerie in Berlin. With this assignment Mies van der Rohe literally took out of the drawer the blueprint for a building with a different purpose: for the administration building of the Bacardi rum company in Santiago de Cuba. Whether a museum temple or administration building, whether Europe or the Caribbean – what difference does it make? One size fits all – such is the innermost credo of this ostensibly modern, in truth, however – that is, according with its spirit – modern-age, architecture. At the same time this is the reason for all its troubles.[17]

3   Formalism complies with – and this is the third congruence with the spirit of the modern age – a *geometrico-mathematical* matrix. We are familiar with this from Le Corbusier. Simple, primary forms are praised. The talk is of the 'laws of the universe' and 'accord with the world order'. Above all, I think, it is a question of an accord with modern-age thinking. For already with Descartes sensory qualities were eliminated in favour of

pure forms. Still in Linné's (truly Cartesian in spirit) plant classification the plants possessed no colours, not even their flowers were coloured – a biological nonsense, but a significant document of this modern-age ideology. Equally, modern architecture entirely backs the intelligible, the mathematical spirit, the spirit of clarity and lucidity, the *esprit de géometrie*, and forgets the *esprit de finesse* – no, worse still: it discriminates against this, drives it out.

4   That modern architecture is a matter of world design is in need of no further demonstration. This it is more than any preceding architecture. With the International Style it sets about putting up the same buildings worldwide in a functionally neutral manner. With a self-assured gesture it sets itself above all local, regional and cultural peculiarities. It erects signals of modernity. It wants to transform the entire world into the manifestation of its modernity.

5   The final definitional feature of the modern-age spirit, the technical one, is also inscribed into this architecture in the most obvious manner. It is also self-consciously conceded to. The triumvirate of modern architecture – Le Corbusier, Mies van der Rohe and Gropius – is in agreement on this (corresponding to their common origin in Behren's Berlin atelier). 'We claim, in the name of the steamship, of the airplane, and of the motor-car, the right to health, logic, daring, harmony, perfection' – in Le Corbusier's words.[18] Mies van der Rohe said he wanted to create 'architecture for a technological society'. Gropius, finally, pleaded for art and technology as a new unity – as in the famous 1923 lecture which set the course of Bauhaus in the direction of International Style.

The congruency of modern-age thinking and the spirit of modern architecture is evident. Yet it is a matter not of a superficial influence through authors – say, of how much Descartes Mies van der Rohe had read – but of an equality in spirit, which establishes itself via more manifold and subterranean processes than literal reception.

4.   The insight is painful – but necessary

My intention in all of this was in no way to sketch an alarming picture of modern architecture. This architecture meant, at a certain point in time, too much to me and I still value some of its constructions too highly for that. The concern here is with something different. It must be realized that the popular separation of these modern architects' wonderful intentions and their, in part, disastrous results is too convenient and incorrect. A good part of the troubles stems precisely from the point of departure outlined, stems from this architecture's modern-age spirit, is its consequence. This insight might hurt, but it doesn't help at all: people must become aware of the shadowy side of their old love. It's not the building industry's functionalism and individual errors, but this architecture's modern-agedness which is to blame for the troubles. And only full clarity on this point can protect against a repetition of the same mistake – even if it be among quite different forms.

6. The retardedness of modern architecture and its postmodern sucession

At the same time, following everything set out here, it must be said that this modern-age status of modern architecture is – considered in a temporal comparison – astonishing and strange. Indeed it means that this architecture was typologically retarded and almost retrograde. Whilst in the sciences the spirit of the modern age had been broken, and whilst the other arts acted out this break, the spirit of the modern age asserted itself in modern architecture as never before. One almost has the impression that the moment it was driven from its original sphere, from science, this spirit sought a different riverbed and found this in architecture.

Moreover, this asynchronicity is rich in consequence. From this something can be explained which would otherwise be difficult to understand: the fact that the break from modernity to postmodernity took place nowhere as spectacularly as in architecture. This was a consequence of the retardedness of modern architecture. Whereas the other arts had long since pursued a modernity of plurality, which involved itself in the hetero-geneous, so-called 'modern' architecture picked up once again the most antiquated, that is, the modern-age, uniform strain of modernity.[19] Hence the break here was less avoidable than elsewhere and fell more drastically than in other spheres. In this way architecture – at least for public con-sciousness – was able to become the show sector of postmodernity.

VI. Postmodernity

1. From modern-age to postmodern modernity

I shall round up this tableau by showing how postmodern architecture can in fact be understood as an attempt to get away from the *modern-age* dictate of modern architecture and to create an equivalent to the modernity of the *twentieth century* in architecture as well.

This can be recognized straight away with Robert Venturi. He pleaded in 1966, in *Complexity and Contradiction in Architecture*, for 'a complex and contradictory architecture based on the richness and ambiguity of modern experience',[20] and significantly in doing so he appealed to modern science and art – in contrast to modern architecture. 'Everywhere, except in architecture, complexity and contradiction have been acknowledged.'[21] – This corresponds exactly to the distinction between a modern-age type of modernity and one characteristic of the twentieth century.

Similarly Charles Jencks's criterion of double or multiple coding,[22] as well as Heinrich Klotz's postmodern formula 'Fiction as well as function!',[23] testifies that postmodern architecture wants to overcome just this modern age bound of modern architecture. – A different question, however, is to what extent one is able to redeem these postmodern intentions in the architectural realization.

As much as scepticism is called for here, a word of criticism is also in order against a fashion which is today taking hold. You currently get the impression – in monographs, at exhibitions, in opening speeches – that in truth modern architecture had long contained and redeemed everything that some people had expected of, or hoped for with postmodern architecture. That is a crude retrospective illusion. Ever since our consciousness became postmodernly sensitized, modernity has retrospectively been being given postmodern contours. I would like to denote this the geiger counter method: one traces the tracks of the postmodern with a highly sensitive instrument – and in so doing forgets the megatons of dead stone which comprise the bulk of modernity. – Incidentally, the procedure reached its ironic peak when in 1989 a collected discussion of recent monographs on the architecture of modernity appeared under the title 'Complexity and Contradiction'. Does one not remember the cries of protest which were triggered by Robert Venturi's 1966 manifesto of the same title? Didn't this then count as the betrayal of modernity? In the meantime, however, the lovers of modernity have cunningly discovered the formula which they once perceived as provocation as being the formula at the heart of what was itself under attack. This is the scheme: within a few years history is rewritten, and then it is explained to the one-time provocateurs that their challenge was in fact nothing of the sort; the forebears (and contemporaries) were always to have been as clever as they are. – A switch of labels which is far too obvious.

2. Against the mathematical obsession

To conclude I want to broach upon another thought which can summarize what's been said and which seems particularly important.

There is an incommensurability between life and mathematics. An obsession with wanting to grasp everything mathematically has, however, long since belonged to the Occident. We meet this obsession already with Plato. And the Aristotelian criticism thereof – as pertinent and unsparing as it was – did little good. Aristotle demonstrated that the mathematical type of rationality is just not relevant for questions of ethics, that is, for questions of good living. For mathematics knows the singular only as a case of the general; for ethics, however, it is precisely the particular which matters, that is, that singular which is not merely a case of the general. Hence the implementation of ethics in a mathematical spirit must systematically fail the task of ethics. This applies analogously for architecture, since this too is related primarily to living processes. Hence it may not orientate itself one-sidedly through mathematics.

3.   Wittgenstein

The disparity between mathematics and life can be exemplified with the help of Wittgenstein. His *Tractatus logico-philosophicus* was a consummative book of the modern age which sought to grasp everything through mathematical rationality and to arrange everything according to this. Wittgenstein then believed that he had, in his work, solved all philosophical problems. For the point of the text for Wittgenstein lay in the following insight: if, as he had done in this book, one completely surveys the island of scientific problems, then it can be seen that the problems soluble there have nothing in common with those questions which really motivate us. It is precisely when one clearly determines the contours of what can be said that one notices the ocean of life's questions which lies beyond, the questions which are not at home and are not to be solved on this island, which thus do not fall within the competence of science, but are only to be straightened out in another way: through life itself.[24] – With this conception the contrast between mathematics and life is apprehended and the modern-age attempt to mathematicize life is superseded.

The named problem presents itself with Wittgenstein once more in relation to architecture. For, as is well known, at one time in his life Wittgenstein was active as an architect. Together with Paul Engelmann he erected one of the most consistent of modernity's constructions: 19 Kundmanngasse in Vienna. This building was a crystal, one of the purest constructions of modernity – completely in the mathematical spirit. Revealingly, however, Wittgenstein himself later – having undertaken his philosophical turn, which led him away from the mathematical ideal of the *Tractatus* towards the life-world concept of the *Philosophical Investigations* – harshly criticized this house: the building was to lack just that which distinguishes not only accomplished architecture, but all great art: 'Within all great art there is a WILD animal: *tamed*.'[25] His house, however, unfortunately possessed only 'good manners'; the 'primordial life, wild life striving to erupt into the open' – this was lacking.[26] Nothing could be sensed of the dynamics of life, no element of chaos, nor of the animal which should have been noticeable – albeit as one tamed.

4.   A balance between chaos and order

A piece of guidance might be taken from this: that we have every cause to free ourselves in matters of life as well as architecture from the mathematical obsession.[27] What matters is not the establishment of perfect order, but finding a balance between chaos and order. – Certainly it is right to create footholds of order within life's disorder. But it is not right to derive from this the project of a complete throughgoing planning, of an entire construction, of the conversion of life into mathematics.

Finding a balance between chaos and order will certainly be difficult, and it will look and turn out differently in different circumstances. But difficulty of this type must be a stimulus, rather than being allowed to be the reason for rejection of such an intention. – Architecture – like life – should move between chaos and order, it should be a double project, binocular and with a sense of proportion.

Notes

This essay was originally published as 'Wie modern war die moderne Architektur?', in *Nachdenken über Städtebau. Stadtbaupolitik, Baukultur, Archiktekturkritik*, eds Klaus Novy and Felix Zwoch (Brunswick: Vieweg 1991), pp. 55–73. It has been revised for this volume. (First English publication.)

1. Vitruvius, *The Ten Books on Architecture*, I 3.
2. For more details see the essay 'Cities of the Future: Aspects from Architectural Theory and Cultural Philosophy' in the present volume.
3. In doing so – with regard to the 'modern age', 'modernity' and 'postmodernity' – I shall draw upon expositions in my book *Unsere postmoderne Moderne* (Weinheim: VCH 1987; Berlin: Akademie, 5th edition, 1997).
4. André Breton, *Die Manifeste des Surrealismus* (Reinbek bei Hamburg: Rowohlt 1968), p. 42 (Eng.: *Manifestoes of Surrealism*, trans. Richard Seaver and Helen Lane, Ann Arbor: University of Michigan Press 1972).
5. Ibid., p. 47.
6. Also the popular sneer that modernity need not be taken seriously because tomorrow something else will be modern – that you thus need only wait quietly and then the whole modernity furore will pass by of its own accord – is based on a misestimation. There exist concepts whose structure is such that a change of occupation does not invalidate, but confirms them. You would not consider an expression such as 'guest' senseless just because the guest tomorrow is somebody different to today. The term 'modernity' ought to be dealt with in a similarly sober manner.
7. Cf. Georg Wilhelm Friedrich Hegel, *Lectures on the History of Philosophy*, vol. 2, trans. E.S. Haldane and Frances H. Simson (New York: Humanities Press 1974 [repr. of 1894 edition]), p. 210.
8. Max Horkheimer and Theodor W. Adorno, *Dialectic of Enlightenment*, trans. John Cumming (New York: Continuum 1994), p. 4.
9. Cf. Jean-François Lyotard, Jacques Derrida, F. Burkhardt, G. Daghini and B. Blistène, *Immaterialität und Postmoderne* (Berlin: Merve 1985), p. 38.
10. René Descartes, *Discourse on Method*, in *The Philosophical Writings of Descartes*, vol. 1, trans. J. Cottingham, R. Stoothoff and D. Murdoch (Cambridge: Cambridge University Press 1985), pp. 111–151, here pp. 116–117.
11. To begin with, the spectrum of modern architecture was certainly broader – it encompassed at least expressionism and constructivism as well; but expressionism was driven out already in Bauhaus, and ultimately, in the International Style, functionalism alone remained and became the guiding architecture worldwide.
12. Le Corbusier, *Towards a New Architecture* (Oxford: Butterworth 1987), p. 6. (*Vers une architecture*, 1922.)
13. Of course Le Corbusier's plan to tear down old Paris and replace it with a new one is also evidence of such ruthless negation of tradition and modern-age gigantism.
14. Cf. Heinrich Klotz, 'Vision der Moderne', in *Vision der Moderne. Das Prinzip Konstruktion*, ed. Heinrich Klotz (Munich: Prestel 1986), pp. 9–26, here p. 11. (Until now the occurrence has nowhere been convincingly denied.)

15. Le Corbusier, *The Athens Charter*, trans. Anthony Eardley (New York: Grossman 1973), p. 95 [§ 77].

16. Adolf Behne, 'Dammerstock', in *Die Form* 6, Book 6, 1930 (quoted from: *Tendenzen der Zwanziger Jahre*, Exhibition Catalogue Berlin 1977, part 2, pp. 125 and 126).

17. As a building celebrating itself, as a temple, the Neue Nationalgalerie is a jewel; functionally however, as a museum building, it borders on catastrophe.

18. Le Corbusier, *Towards a New Architecture*, p. 19. Note: Not in the name of people, but in the name of these technical implements; consistently then the house is defined as a 'house machine' (ibid., p. 7).

19. Where, for example, is a cubist architecture or a collage architecture to be found which might compare with the simultaneous experiments of the cubists or dadaists? – In 1941 Sigfried Giedion wanted to have us believe that modern architects, in the knowledge of the scientific and artistic discoveries of around 1910 (particularly relativity theory and cubism), attempted to create an architectural equivalent to these discoveries. This was to apply especially to 'the generation of Le Corbusier, Gropius, and Mies van der Rohe' (Sigfried Giedion, *Space, Time and Architecture: The Growth of a New Tradition*, Cambridge, Mass.: Harvard University Press 1949, p. 428). Sokratis Georgiadis has shown how untenable this construction is. For example, Le Corbusier, Giedion's principal witness, had together with Ozenfant in 1918 drawn up a pointed polemic against cubism under the title *Après le cubisme*. The cubist attempt to transfer a fourth dimension to painting was described as a straightforward absurdity, a 'hypothesis beyond all plastic reality' without 'material contact to the real world', the likes of which could in no way come into question for architecture. (Cf. Sokratis Georgiadis, 'Von der Malerei zur Architektur. Sigfried Giedions "Raum-Zeit-Konzeption"', in *Sigfried Giedion 1888-1968. Der Entwurf einer modernen Tradition*, eds Verena Rentsch, Jos Bosman and Sigfried Giedion, Zurich: Museum für Gestaltung 1989, pp. 105–117, here pp. 106–109).

20. Robert Venturi, *Complexity and Contradiction in Modern Architecture* (New York: Museum of Modern Art 1966), p. 22.

21. Ibid.

22. 'It is the discontinuity of taste cultures which generates both the theoretical basis and the "double-coding" of postmodernity.' 'A postmodern building, so as to give a brief definition, addresses at least two different levels of the population simultaneously: architects and a dedicated minority who concern themselves with specifically architectural problems, as well as the broad public or the local residents who are concerned with matters of comfort, of traditional building and their way of living.' 'Hence double-coding, an architecture which addresses the elite and the man on the street.' (Charles Jencks, *Die Sprache der postmodernen Architektur. Die Entstehung einer alternativen Tradition*, Stuttgart, 2nd edition, 1980, pp. 6 and 8 [Eng.: *The Language of Post-Modern Architecture*, London: Academy, 3rd edition, 1980]; quoted from *Wege aus der Moderne. Schlüsseltexte der Postmoderne-Diskussion*, ed. Wolfgang Welsch, Weinheim: Acta Humaniora 1988, pp. 85–94, here pp. 85 and 88.)

23. Heinrich Klotz, *The History of Postmodern Architecture* (Cambridge, Mass./London: MIT Press 1988), p. 421.

24. Wittgenstein's friend (and architectural partner) Paul Engelmann put this in the following way: Wittgenstein, who '*is so imbued with the idea that all that matters for human life is that whereof, in his opinion, one must remain silent*', nonetheless in the *Tractatus* directs 'his tremendous efforts' to 'circumscribe' this 'unimportant thing', namely the realm of what can be said scientifically; but not because for him 'the coastline of this island, but rather the bounds of the ocean was scrupulously to be observed' (Paul Engelmann, *Ludwig Wittgenstein. Briefe und Begegnungen*, ed. Brian F. McGuiness, Vienna: Oldenbourg 1970, p. 77).

25. Ludwig Wittgenstein, *Culture and Value*, ed. G.H. von Wright, trans. Peter Winch (Chicago: University of Chicago Press 1984), p. 37^e.

26. Ibid.

27. Walter Lippman coined a golden phrase for this: 'To every human problem there is a solution that is simple, neat, and *wrong*.' (Quoted from: Stephen Toulmin, *Cosmopolis. The Hidden Agenda of Modernity*, Chicago: University of Chicago Press 1990, p. 201.)

6

CONTEMPORARY ART IN PUBLIC SPACE

A Feast for the Eyes or an Annoyance?

'Art in public space' is a subject filled with problems. Do we still have public spaces at all? Are the spaces which we so describe really spaces for a public? What is meant today still by 'public'?

What is commonly called 'public space' is no longer, as was once intended, a democratic public's space, but is rather a shopping zone, traffic domain or authorities' area. Publicness exists, if at all still, not there, but more in the media. Public space is public space still only according to the wording, no longer according with fact.

Some people have not noticed this change, this demise in the preconditions of the notion of 'art in public space'. They still follow the old patterns, criteria and rules of decision, although the context has long since become a different one. – There is a French film in which a singer steps on to the stage every night, although for years there has no longer been an audience. Elsewhere I have experienced how an old man regularly prayed in the church of his youth, although it had long since been redeveloped into a leisure centre. It is similar with the talk of art in public space today. For all the inside dealings the subject's aficionados obviously haven't picked up on the demise of a decisive external precondition, an incisive change in the boundary conditions of 'art in public space'.

I. Public space: a hyperaesthetic arrangement

The conventional framework of thought with regard to 'art in public space' states: to begin with there is public space which, as such, is without art; art steps into it, comes on top of it. But this figure no longer applies today. Public space today – this is my thesis – is as such already hyperaesthetic, even before art comes into it.[1]

Think, for example, of the aesthetic staging of our inner cities. For years they have been subjected to a pseudo-postmodern face-lift. Shopping areas are being fashioned to be elegant, chic and animating. The urban environment on the whole is being highly polished, embellished and beautified. This is called 'aestheticization'. Nothing in our public space – no paving-stone, no door-handle and certainly no public square – has been spared this aestheticization-boom. 'Live more beautifully' was yesterday's motto; today it runs 'live, shop, communicate and sleep more beautifully'.

Aesthetics has also become indispensable for the economy's self-representation. It is banks which are currently erecting the most spectacular pieces of architecture – spectacular too in the sense that you no longer recognize straight away that it is a bank. The staging of a play, of a spectacle, is being carried out. If, until recently, it was museum buildings which were present as monographs on the book market at the same time as their completion, then today it is bank buildings. Equally pregnant with aesthetics are the catchwords of 'corporate identity' and the sponsoring of art and culture which every self-respecting firm today practises.

It would, admittedly, be wrong to make economic interests or political processes solely responsible for the global aestheticization of our age. We ourselves are cooperating strongly in this aestheticization through our individual styling. It is no longer the saints (as at one time) and not researchers or intellectuals (as perhaps until recently), but the 'beautiful people' who are the contemporary paragons in life. In beauty farms and fitness centres we are practising a merciless beautification of our bodies; and genetic technology – this new branch of aestheticization – promises us a world full of perfectly styled mannequins.

The aestheticization wave – this I wanted to emphasize first of all – is breaking everywhere. It has long since conquered and washed over public space. Everything in this space is styled through and through. And the beauty which is thus engendered is full of gloss; even apparent irritations are calculated. This is the finding from which one must today set out when speaking about public space: public space has become hyperaesthetic.

II.   Art in a hyperaesthetic public space?

What does there remain for art to do in such a hyperaesthetic space? What more can it do? And how can it differentiate itself?

1.   Beautiful art is superfluous

Doing more is obviously no longer necessary. Already everything has been done. Already everything is beautiful. Indeed, by no means all of the aesthetic stagings are bad. There are exquisite feats among them, and incidentally not least because many artists have taken the path to being beautifiers of the everyday or designer architects. Some did it consciously, such as Roy Lichtenstein, David Hockney, Sam Francis, Norman Foster and Michael Graves, who designed attractive patterns for a carpet factory after this had suffered strong falls in turnover – with immediate success. Others changed terrain almost without noticing. Jean Tinguely, for instance, who was once an offensive artist, increasingly became an affirmative one. One of his later works, the *Luminator*, adorns the arrivals hall of the central station in Basle.

The former functions of art have sprung up widely in the aestheticization of the day-to-day. Michael Schirner, the Düsseldorf-based advertising expert, rightly says: 'Advertising has today taken over the function which art previously had: the mediation of aesthetic contents into everyday life.'[2] In an everyday world which is hyperaestheticized in such a way art is no longer needed to bring beauty into the world. This has been done by designers and town planners with the greatest success.

The new conditions were first described by Jean Baudrillard. He called our reality the hyperreal which 'effaces the contradiction of the real and the imaginary'.[3] His conclusion reads: 'So art is everywhere, since artifice lies at the heart of reality. So art is dead, since [. . .] reality itself, entirely impregnated by an aesthetic [. . .], has become inseparable from its own image.'[4] In order to understand completely this fact, that art has become superfluous, you must formulate it more or less positively: art has become superfluous because it has triumphed. The old aestheticization programmes have been redeemed more comprehensively than their former apologists had ever dreamt. Everything has become beautiful.

Winning all along the line is one way of becoming superfluous. This seems to be the fate of these aestheticization programmes, and of their advocation of beautiful art and beautiful design. It is just that one must then finally take note of this, instead of still repeating the old run-dry adjurations. Far too many experts, however, when talking about contemporary art in public space, basically still think of 'street furniture'. To supplement the designer furniture in interiors they want to see art furniture erected in public space.[5]

2.   *Beautiful art would be indistinguishable*

Obviously then beautiful art, introduced into public space, would, in any case, today scarcely be distinguishable from the beautiful design already existing, that is, from the design of our public space. One might, in an intermediary phase, believe that the works of art themselves would manage to set themselves apart from the aestheticization of the everyday. But too many artists have themselves changed sector and adapted to the animatory staging needs for this; they now – successfully and lucratively – cooperate in the embellishment of public space. Besides which, the absorptive power of the context should never be underestimated: works which deviate only a little will be integrated straightforwardly in the functional circulation of aestheticization. The certain strangeness that they exhibit works more as an incrementation of the everyday aestheticization. Artistic ingredients complete the aesthetic daily menu. And it's only under this condition that they are desired, that they get the contract.

But the times in which a work of art could cause us to stare in wonder by demonstrating to us an unknown beautiful world (in contrast to the trivial, ugly, day-to-day one) are over with – this pattern no longer works. If art in public space is still to have any sense, then it cannot be that of a continual aesthetic beautification. It will have to lie elsewhere.

III. Art in public space: interruption of aestheticization

Do these reflections amount to the end of art, to the end of the meaningful possibility of art in public space? Yes and no.

On the one side, in public space we really no longer need an art which caters only for beautification; these tasks have, as I've said, long since been being fulfilled in other ways. But, on the other side, art remains an alternative: it can come into effect as an authority of strangeness, of irritation, of unwieldiness. Today it must – in public space – take this path. Art ought to take steps against beauteous astheticization and its amalgam, to interrupt these. Public art which is worthy of its name will have to intervene against rampant aestheticization.

And this is itself an aesthetic task. For our perception (*aisthesis*) also needs zones of interruption, of alterity and quiet. Every psychologist of perception knows this. Where everything is beautiful, nothing is beautiful any more, continued excitement leads to indifference.[6] In the midst of the hyperaesthetics of public space aesthetically fallow areas are necessary.

Thus the actual task of art in public space today would be: to set itself against beauteous aestheticization instead of adapting itself to it. Art should not impact accommodatingly as an article, but rather strike like a meteor.

Different methods for this are conceivable. For instance, hermetic structures of high self-logic and unwieldiness, comparable with a crystal, could create places of autonomy and quiet amidst the pepped-up aestheticization scenarios. Equally works of art could make their entry in a manner explicitly resistant, hurtful, difficult or impossible to understand, could represent a disruption and afford annoyance. Of course, less controversial interventions also come into question, but they must always contain an element of the unusual. I am thinking, for example, of the reinterpretation of existing situations, of irritating interferences which turn against building layouts, road systems or the optics of advertisements. With all of this works must exhibit traits which make them inappropriable.

Referring to the alternative 'a feast for the eyes or an annoyance',[7] this means that art should offer no feast for eyes, as everyday aestheticization already does so successfully; rather it must be prepared to be an annoyance and to cause offence. If works today cause no stir, then this is mostly an indication that they are superfluous. Even when works behave unspectacularly, the element of the unusual and of resistiveness must be strong.

Only in this way can they set themselves against the danger of being requisitioned by everyday aestheticization. Richard Serra's works are an example of this. They are so resistant that they cannot be absorbed, but are rather either tolerated or torn down.

Thus resistance to the rampant aestheticization of public space seems to me to be the *conditio sine qua non,* and strangeness, disruption, interruption and alterity appear to me to be mandatory categories for art in public space today. Only an art of this type is worth the effort.

Notes

This essay was originally published as 'Gegenwartskunst im öffentlichen Raum – Augenweide oder Ärgernis?', in *Kunstforum International,* 118, 1992, pp. 318–320. It has been revised for this volume. (First English publication.)

1. For more details on the aestheticization diagnosis see the essay 'Aestheticization Processes: Phenomena, Distinctions and Prospects' in the present volume, especially section I.

2. Michael Schirner, *Werbung ist Kunst* (Munich: Klinkhardt & Biermann 1991), p. 12.

3. Jean Baudrillard, *Symbolic Exchange and Death,* trans. I.H. Grant (London: Sage 1993), p. 72.

4. Ibid., p. 75.

5. Incidentally the concept of art in public space is characterized by drastic and highly problematic selections. If this were not so, then the architecture which shapes public space would have to occupy first place. But this is not what one thinks of under this label at all. An almost self-evident constriction to sculpture dominates. Even painting, which still belonged within the conventional context of 'art in the building', is today almost completely eclipsed. The restriction is not innocent but scandalous. It keeps alive the wrong basic scheme, according to which public space is without art and given, and into which art makes its entry.

6. I have set this out more closely under the title 'Ästhetik und Anästhetik' in *Ästhetisches Denken* (Stuttgart: Reclam 1990), pp. 9–40. (Forthcoming in English as 'Aesthetics and Anaesthetics', in *Aesthetic Thinking,* trans. John Bailiff, Atlantic Highlands, NJ: Humanities Press 1998.)

7. This alternative was the motto of the event at which I delivered these theses as an introductory statement (Münster University, 13 November 1991).

7

ON THE HERMENEUTIC
CONSTITUTION OF ART

Introductory explanations. Philosophy and art: congruency or opposition?

1. The reciprocal relationship between philosophical hermeneutics and art

It is well known that affinities exist between philosophical hermeneutics and art. Gadamer's *Truth and Method* is one piece of evidence of this. The 'question of truth' emerges there 'in the experience of art'.[1] Already according to Gadamer's teacher, Heidegger, art was to represent a distinguished authority of truth.

On the other hand, the relationship between the philosophical and artistico-aesthetic sphere is one filled with tension. Gadamer's *Truth and Method* can serve as proof of this too. The question concerning the truth of art must be regained as a countermove against aesthetic awareness. On this point even Gadamer's adversary Derrida is in agreement with him – he too thinks that traditional aesthetic awareness has failed what is peculiar to art.

Both positions – that of congruency and that of opposition – were linked to one another by another twentieth-century great: Theodor W. Adorno. On the one hand, he explained: the 'truth of the work in itself is commensurable with philosophical interpretation'.[2] On the other hand, he pointed out the tense relationship between philosophy and art: 'works of art are not to be comprehended by aesthetics as hermeneutic objects; what ought to be comprehended, in the present-day state, is their incomprehensibility'.[3]

2. The traditional competition between philosophy and art

Philosophy and art have forever been in competition with one another. This could be an indication of their equality. The opposing condemnations always contain a piece of recognition. Plato and Leonardo da Vinci provide examples of this. When Plato reproves poetry firstly because it binds us to the apparent instead of directing us to being, and secondly because it arouses the passions instead of controlling them and asserting the voice of reason alone, then he obviously held art to be genuinely dangerous – hence his exiling of the poets, including Homer. And when Leonardo da Vinci says that painting's standing is higher than that of philosophy, since painting targets the surface of natural things, whilst philosophy attempts to get inside them, whereas, however, the truth of natural things reveals itself precisely at the surface and is in no way hidden in their inners, then you sense how great Leonardo's efforts were to assert his restricted truth against an outsized and respected opponent.[4]

3. The hermeneutic relationship of philosophy and art

But it is not a *competition* between philosophy and art which is to be the subject here, but a possible *cooperation* between the two, as is found in the philosophical hermeneutic understanding of art. Do the examples cited teach us anything about this?

The traditional contest between philosophy and poetry or between painting and philosophy could be settled under several aspects – from an anthropological point of view with Plato, from a veridical point of view with Leonardo, and other distinguishing points of view can be found variously, say those of societal nobility, or of prospective ability, or of prognostic power. But never in this history were *questions of interpretation* taken as cause for dismissal.

There are two reasons for this. Firstly, interpretation fundamentally demands congruency. If art is to be an object of philosophical interpretation, then art and philosophy must basically be commensurable – otherwise there would exist no *possibility* of interpretation; a difference, however, must exist secondarily – otherwise there would exist no *assignment* for interpretation.[5] So much for the first reason why problems of hermeneutics didn't traditionally appear among the dismissive schemata between philosophy and art: hermeneutics must insinuate compatibility, not incompatibility.

The second reason is hence obvious. A hermeneutic determination of the relationship between philosophy and art is a special case. Viewed historically something of this type first appeared relatively late. Around 1800 art became primarily an object of interpretation for philosophy – whereas it had previously been considered a competitor, or a paragon, or as a comparatively insignificant embellishment of being. This new relationship is most clearly demonstrated in Hegel's lectures on aesthetics.

In the following I want to discuss three approaches altogether: firstly, the traditional approach, epitomized by Hegel, of a philosophical hermeneutics of art which sets out from a fundamental *commensurability* between art and philosophy; secondly, the modern approach, which, as a counter-move, asserts incommensurability between art and philosophy as a matter of principle; finally, a third approach, surpassing both one-sidednesses, one which takes the *hermeneutic constitution of works of art themselves* as its point of departure – this is the approach which I suggest.

I. The traditional commensurability thesis and the claim of a philosophical apprehension of art

1. Hegel: from art to the philosophy of art

Hegel brings art within the grasp of philosophy, within the dictate of philosophical apprehension. This claim might sound surprising at first since in the course of time Hegel, not least in matters of art, had become critical of subjugation. Even though in his early years he himself had collaborated in an aesthetic subjugation – 'The "Oldest System-Programme" of German Idealism' indeed advocated an obvious aesthetic subjugation in wanting to allow 'truth and goodness [to] become kindred only in beauty' and declaring the 'highest act of reason' an 'aesthetic act' and 'the philosophy of the spirit' an 'aesthetic philosophy'[6] –, in his Berlin lectures on aesthetics Hegel then turned sharply against another subjugation, against that of the aesthetic by moral viewpoints. To the attempt to compel art to the goal of 'moral betterment'[7] he objected that, although 'a good moral may be drawn' 'from every genuine work of art',[8] the work of art cannot be viewed in its core 'as a useful tool for realizing this end which is independently valid on its own account outside the sphere of art'.[9] The case is rather that art has 'its end and aim in itself'.[10]

It's just that this thesis with Hegel then becomes the starting point for another subjugation – this time a philosophical subjugation of art. For in what does the final aim of art lie for Hegel? It lies in that art 'is to unveil the *truth* in the form of sensuous artistic configuration'.[11] Thus art is attributed with truth, but it is to contain this truth merely in a sensuous, not yet its true, intellectual form. The binding to the sensuous marks the limit of art. Art indeed 'spring[s] from and [is] created by the spirit', and thereby represents 'a development of the Concept out of itself' – but only in the manner of a 'shift [. . .] from its own ground to that of sense'.[12] Yet it is precisely this shift which is to be done away with; art's sensuous limitation is to be overcome. This takes place through the 'power of the thinking spirit', which in directing itself to the work of art 'changes into thoughts what has been estranged and so reverts to itself'.[13] And according to Hegel, the work of art 'stands open throughout in every respect to conceptual thinking', so long as that thinking is really equipped 'with the power of the Concept'.[14] Art in effect invites us to intellectual consideration[15] so as only here to experience 'its real ratification' – and that means its actual verification.[16] In brief: the final aim of art, to unveil truth, is not already fulfilled within art, but only in the intellectual comprehension thereof.[17]

With this concept Hegel legitimizes a self-perception for the philosophy of art as the actual redeeming authority of art. Art might well achieve its end in this – but in the sense of its perfection, the liberation of its truth, the definitive redemption of its 'end and aim'. Through the release of art from its sensuous dress by the philosophical concept, that which art actually wanted to say – but as art was unable to say – finally appears unveiled. The artistic residue falls away, leaving behind the pure concept. Thus the end of art and the ascent of the philosophy of art belong together.[18]

2.   *Traditional philosophical aesthetics:* ad maiorem philosophiae gloriam

Hegel is no exception; rather he epitomizes one of traditional aesthetics' construction principles. Soon after its foundation aesthetics became an undertaking to usurp art philosophically. It aimed not for an understanding of art, but for a betterment of philosophy.[19] And it was convinced as a matter of principle of the commensurability of art and philosophy.[20]

The fact that this traditional aesthetics was concerned more with philosophy than with an understanding of art (which is why it is unserviceable for a real hermeneutics of art) can be most clearly inferred from Schelling. In 1800 Schelling had – seemingly commendingly – called art 'the only true and eternal organ [. . .] of philosophy' because it 'opens to [the philosopher], as it were, the holy of holies' in realizing the unconscious and its original identity with consciousness, beyond whose identity philosophy must think, but which – in consequence of its own reflexivity – it is incapable of genuinely conceiving.[21] Of course this view is tantamout to a philosophical functionalization of art – indeed 'organ' means 'tool'. Schelling himself says of his *Philosophy of Art* that it is nothing but another application of his 'system of philosophy', namely 'the general philosophy', carried out now 'in the potency of art'.[22]

It is precisely because this aesthetics proceeds from an on-principle commensurability of art and philosophy that, firstly, it is able to requisition art straightforwardly for philosophical purposes; and that, secondly, it has no need to allow itself to be told anything by real art, the art of works of art.[23] Admittedly, it would also have nothing to say about this either. When Schelling became Secretary General of the Munich Akademie der bildenden Künste and was required by this office to lecture on art, he lectured not once about art throughout his fifteen years in office. The hour of reckoning becomes the oath of disclosure for aesthetics.[24]

3.   *The unserviceability of this aesthetics for a hermeneutics of art*

This traditional type of aesthetics is altogether unfit for the purposes of a hermeneutics of art. Its apprehension of art intends not an understanding of art, but art's appropriation, its translation into philosophy, its philosophical substitution.

Two premises are decisive in this. And if, in future, the hermeneutics of art is not to be such a business of appropriation, then these premises must be abandoned: firstly, the claim that the truth of art is basically *of the same type* as, is *commensurable* with, philosophical truth; and, secondly, the thesis that the truth in art is found first of all only in a form restricted to sensuousness and must be freed from this estrangement through *translation into the philosophical concept*. Both these axioms of traditional aesthetics were expounded by Hegel in full clarity – just as their consequence was: the downfall of art.

II. The modern incommensurability theorem

1. *Adorno*

Criticism of traditional aesthetics

How can this desperate state of affairs be escaped from? Adorno characterized traditional aesthetics' deficiency in the following way:

> That the same spirit was at work in philosophy and art allowed philosophy [. . .] to deal with art without yielding to the works. Of course it failed regularly in the requisite attempt, motivated by the non-identity of art with its universal definitions, to conceive of art's specifications: it is then that the most embarrassing of misjudgements resulted for speculative idealists.[25]

Does the way out lie then in switching to the interpretation of single works? To what extent did Adorno himself take this route? What is it that changed with him – and thus with one of the most influential aesthetic theories of recent decades – compared with the traditional approach?

Adorno's traditional motives

Adorno did indeed try to seek out what is particular to singular works. But he wasn't content with doing this. Philosophical analysis must, according to him, be more than merely work-immanent analysis; it must get through to the truth content; and this first discloses itself where one grasps out into the whole, where the position of the work is apprehended in the societal context.[26]

Adorno thus sticks to the truth motive – and not only to this, but also to the thesis of a congruency, or commensurability, between philosophical and artistic truth. 'Philosophy and art', he says, 'converge in their truth content: the progressively unfolding truth of the work of art is none other than that of the philosophical concept.'[27]

Finally, Adorno also adopts the thesis that in effect art awaits its philosophical interpretation: 'The works, above all those of uppermost dignity, await their interpretation.'[28] And: 'genuine aesthetic experience must become philosophy otherwise it doesn't exist at all'.[29]

Art, then, is still – as already with Hegel – to present itself to intellectual consideration; only through philosophical interpretation is it finally to experience its ratification and verification. To this extent Adorno – to adopt the words of Herbert Schnädelbach – 'remained with Hegel in spite of all criticism of Hegel'.[30] Adorno had retained precisely those assumptions of traditional aesthetics which were problematic – the commensurability and redemption theses.

Adorno and the modern position

On the other hand, statements can be found in Adorno which transcend this traditional framework and which are characteristic of the modern approach. For instance, he says: 'The task of a philosophy of art is not so much to explain away the moment of the inscrutable, as speculation almost unavoidably attempted to do, but rather to understand the inscrutability itself. [. . .] this alone keeps the philosophy of art from acts of violence against this [namely art].'[31] Ultimately Adorno's hermeneutic – or almost anti-hermeneutic – maxim reads: 'works of art are not to be comprehended by aesthetics as hermeneutic objects; what ought to be comprehended, in the present-day state, is their incomprehensibility.'[32] – Adorno here is no longer a partisan of the *furor hermeneuticus*.

2.   Modern hermeneutics of art: the recognition of incommensurability

From the standpoint of modernity the emphasizing of incommensurability has become obligatory for a hermeneutics of art. Incommensurability is to be understood here in two ways: firstly, as an incommensurability existing in the works of art themselves (say of heterogeneous materials or forms or times), and, secondly, as general incommensurability between art and philosophy.

Nietzsche the forerunner

Incommensurability as a precondition of a hermeneutics of art – this is a thought which was first formulated by Nietzsche. In the *Birth of Tragedy* he apprehended art fundamentally as the authority of the incommensurable – ever since Attic tragedy had arisen from the Dionysos cult. Philosophy, however, he considered to be an exemplary commensuration exercise – ever since Socrates initiated the triumphal march of reason through elimination of everything incommensurable.[33] From then on, art – as the prototypical sphere of the incommensurable – and philosophy – as the exemplary exercise in commensuration – themselves stood incommensurably in opposition to one another.

Lyotard and others

In more recent times incommensurability has been underlined above all by Lyotard. For him it in effect forms the focus of modern art. Duchamp, for instance, is to have done nothing other than deliver 'material, tools, and weapons for a policy of the incommensurable'.[34] 'All the research of the avant-gardes [. . .] for a hundred years has gone in this direction, toward discovering the incommensurability between linguistic regimes.'[35]

In view of this incommensurability on the object side, and in view of the incommensurability between philosophy and art, a modern hermeneutics of art can no longer aim for translation, substitution, comprehension or verification of art, but must conversely make it its task to give voice to its untranslatability. That's why Lyotard says that 'philosophers enter the stage of "criticism"' wherever 'the work escapes being converted into meaning'.[36] Today's philosophy – ever since Nietzsche, Adorno, Lyotard and equally with Derrida, Kofman and others – is concerned not with a comprehension of works of art as hermeneutic objects, but with a safe-guarding of their incomprehensibility. It is not a matter of interpretive work, but of the dismantlement of the hermeneutic overkill arsenals, of resistance against the *furor hermeneuticus*.[37,38]

III.   The hermeneutics of art today

1.   The question

But hasn't the hermeneutics of art drifted into an awkward situation through this modern step? Doesn't the incommensurability amount to philosophy and art's now being incapable of saying anything to one another? And isn't art thus locked within the ghetto of the artistic sphere and robbed of its potential for further-reaching communication? Isn't philosophy silenced here, and art muted?

These questions demand a cautious discussion – and perhaps a change of perspective too. If philosophy is incommensurable with art then it must at least also be possible and meaningful, for once, to consider art for its own sake alone – without philosophy, that is, disregarding both its claims to possession and more recent interests in alterity.

Hence my question in the following considerations reads: is art hermeneutically constituted in its own right? How can art's genuine mode of communication be described?

2.   The hermeneutic structure of works of art themselves

It is important to come to terms with a double finding: art must be understood in its own right – but it never speaks from itself alone. The work of art speaks in its own way, but its speaking results in connection with existing symbol systems, through a specific intervention in the midst of available means of communication. A work only comes to express itself in contact with something else.

No semantic space exists without surroundings – neither does that of a work of art. However, these surroundings do not have to represent a stable precondition. Works of art in particular can alter their surrounding's coordinates, can modify their short- and long-range conditions. Modern works especially distinguish themselves in that they thematize and displace the definitional markers of 'art'.

Every gesture of art refers to other gestures, to gestures inside as well as outside of art. The same blue can have very different meanings – according to the other colour values in the picture, in accord with symbolic precepts, on the basis of the economic availability of colours, or in accordance with cultural fashions. Something similar applies for whole forms of composition and works. Inner and outer components always belong to the internal meaning. The inner crystallization of a work, its demarcation from and reconstruction of its surroundings occur simultaneously. Even the autonomous arises only through interaction. Works of art always refer to other works of art, or to the limits of art, or to what lies beyond art. The greater a work is, the more it will do this.

Works take shape in the midst of semantic contexts from the start. They are nourished by them, take up their stance within them. They don't, however, simply adopt these contexts and pass them on unaltered, but intervene in their constellation and amend this – through continuation, reorganization, transcendence, or in whatever other way. Their reference to their surroundings is receptive and productive at the same time. Works are not stationary reserves in preordained frameworks of meaning, but work on and with these. Through their inner constitution of meaning they simultaneously provide the external networks of meaning, to which they refer, with a new form and a point of their own. What is specific in this to *artistic* constitution of meaning lies in that it results from the sensuous and that this work of the senses is imaginitive in high measure and open to reflexion.

This means that works are already *hermeneutically constituted within themselves*. First of all, they refer receptively to preceding semantic contexts – in specific selection and interpretation; secondly, each and every element in their inner structure is an interpretation of the others; and, thirdly, through their internal constitution of meaning, works generate semantic constellations which then emanate out to artistic and living conditions external to the work, and are capable of intervening in the latter.[39] Even the most closed of works of art is hermeneutically structured internally as well as externally. It is a node of understanding in a further-reaching mesh of understanding.[40]

Thus if works already exhibit a hermeneutic *in their own right*, if indeed this in effect comprises their *ratio essendi*, then the interpretation and analysis of art is compelled first and foremost to explicate this hermeneutic structure of works – and what's more in both their internal and external aspects. The interpretation must retrace and uncover the whole hermeneutic architecture of a work to some extent – its reference to given conditions, its inner articulation, and the intervention in exterior semantic contexts which proceeds from this. One must, for example, realize how the Palazzo Farnese takes up the tradition of Italian palace construction, how it articulates Roman against Florentine tradition, how it assumes its position in the city, and with which image of domination it confronts society. – In doing this the works' hermeneutic mesh can prove to be very wide-ranging.

Hermeneutic aspects are in play in four ways altogether. Firstly, in the sense of works' reference to preceding semantic contexts of an artistic and non-artistic nature. Secondly, in the sense of the internally interpretative character of works – the reciprocal hermeneutics of their elements. Thirdly, in the sense of the hermeneutic intervention in the remaining conditions of understanding through the meaning which is constellated in works. And then fourthly, of course, in the sense of the interpretation of works by the observer or interpreter.

These four aspects – contextual hermeneutics, work hermeneutics, interventionary hermeneutics and interpretative hermeneutics – are related just as are precondition, centre, consequence and articulation. Without the preceding semantic contexts works would be able neither to exist nor to speak. But they are not a mute material, which must first be roused to life by interpretation. Rather they are already exegetic or interpretation-like in themselves. The subsequent interpretation of works through perception and reflexion itself finds its lead and its measure in this hermeneutic structure of works.

My relocation of the hermeneutic accent from processes of interpretation back to the structure of works themselves is comparable to the adjustment which Heidegger undertook faced with traditional hermeneutics, when he showed that understanding is not first a subsequent feat of *Dasein*, but that *Dasein* is fundamentally concerned with understanding. 'Hermeneutics' refers in my considerations primarily to the interpretative character of works of art – and from there on, and secondarily to the subsequent understanding. What I am concerned with is the dimension of hermeneutics inherent within the works themselves.

3.   Résumé

Traditional aesthetics aimed for a comprehension of art. The incommensurability objection – from Nietzsche onwards, in Adorno, with Lyotard and in the present day – was directed against this. The intention was, through this, to put a stop to the philosophical usurpation of art.

But perhaps the incommensurability thesis was merely an antithesis to the classical insinuation of commensurability and ultimately no more tenable than its predecessor. To be sure, it was right to take issue with the philosophical possession, but it was as an exaggerated claim, and overlooked above all the fact that a hermeneutic structure is exhibited not first by our processes of understanding, but already by works themselves.

Hence it seems expedient to me to proceed to a third position, beyond the classical commensurability thesis and the modern incommensurability claim, one which shifts the hermeneutic structure of works themselves into the centre. This position is – unlike the simple commensurability thesis – capable of safeguarding the peculiarity of art. Furthermore – in contrast to the plain incommensurability thesis – it doesn't have to proclaim this peculiarity abstractly, but is able to expose it concretely in explicating the hermeneutic structure of singular works step by step.

Notes

This essay was originally given as a paper, 'Zur hermeneutischen Verfassung der Kunst', at the conference 'Interpretazione: Pluralità e Fedeltà' in Rome (21 May 1994). It has been revised for this volume. (First English publication.)

1. Hans-Georg Gadamer, *Truth and Method*, trans. Joel Weinsheimer and Donald G. Marshall (London: Sheed and Ward 1989), p. 1ff.

2. Theodor W. Adorno, *Ästhetische Theorie*, in Adorno, *Gesammelte Schriften*, vol. 7 (Frankfurt a.M.: Suhrkamp, 4th edition, 1984), p. 197.

3. Ibid., p. 179.

4. Cf. my 'Das Zeichen des Spiegels. Platons philosophische Kritik der Kunst und Leonardo da Vincis künstlerische Überholung der Philosophie', in *Philosophisches Jahrbuch*, 90(2), 1983, pp. 230–245.

5. The classic author for the assertion of philosophy and art's commensurability is Aristotle, who, in the *Poetics*, comprehended all art as cognitive practice and even attributed great art the rank of a philosophical type of truth (in contrast, say, to history).

6. 'The "Oldest System-Programme" of German Idealism', in *Hegel Selections*, ed. M.J. Inwood (London/New York: Macmillan 1989), p. 87.

7. Georg Wilhelm Friedrich Hegel, *Aesthetics. Lectures on Fine Art*, vol. 1, trans. T.M. Knox (Oxford: Clarendon Press 1975), p. 51.

8. Ibid., p. 52.

9. Ibid., p. 55.

10. Ibid.

11. Ibid.

12. Ibid., p. 12.

13. Ibid.

14. Ibid., pp. 91f.

15. Cf. ibid., p. 11.

16. Ibid., p. 13.

17. This is the more profound sense of Hegel's thesis of the end of art. From the onset of the age of reflection onwards (cf. ibid., p. 10) we have wanted a philosophy of art instead of mere art. The 'days in which art by itself yielded full satisfaction' are over with. Today we demand 'the *philosophy* of art' (ibid.).

18. Perhaps this also explains the latent and often manifest iconoclasm of the philosophy of art.

19. Kantian aesthetics had obviously already grown not from aesthetic, but from philosophical motives. Kant needed the *Critique of Judgment* to mediate 'the connection of the two parts of philosophy to a whole'. And 'The "Oldest System-Programme" of German Idealism' picked up on this idea of the beautiful as a connecting link between the true and the good, and hoped on this aesthetic path to fulfil once again the old yearnings for unity.

20. On the other hand, the fact that incommensurability loomed was noted by Schlegel: 'In that which one usually calls the philosophy of art one of the two is usually lacking; either philosophy or art.' (Friedrich Schlegel, 'Lyceums-Fragmente', in Schlegel, *Kritische Ausgabe*, ed. Ernst Behler, vol. 2, Munich: Schöningh 1967, pp. 147–163, here p. 148.)

21. Friedrich Wilhelm Joseph Schelling, *System of Transcendental Idealism* (Charlottesville, Va: University Press of Virginia 1978), p. 231 [Part 6, § 3.2].

22. Friedrich Wilhelm Joseph Schelling, *Philosophie der Kunst* [Vorlesung Jena, Wintersemester 1802/3] (reprint of the 1859 edition, Darmstadt: Wissenschaftliche Buchgesellschaft 1976), pp. 7 and 124.

23. Schelling declared that his philosophy of art had to treat only 'art as such' and 'in no way empirical art' (Letter to August Wilhelm Schlegel, 3 September 1802, quoted from: *Aus Schellings Leben. In Briefen*, vol. 1, ed. G.L. Plitt, Leipzig: Hirzel 1869, pp. 390–399, here p. 397).

24. I have discussed the problems of traditional aesthetics in greater detail in 'Traditionelle und moderne Ästhetik in ihrem Verhältnis zur Praxis der Kunst', in *Zeitschrift für Ästhetik und Allgemeine Kunstwissenschaft*, XXVIII, 1983, pp. 264–286.

25. Adorno, *Ästhetische Theorie*, p. 496.

26. 'Philosophical aesthetics, in close contact with the idea of work-immanent analysis, has its place wherever this does not reach. Its second reflection must drive the content matter, which that analysis comes across, beyond itself and through emphatic criticism penetrate through to the truth content.' (Ibid., pp. 517f.) 'The truth content of works is not what they mean, but rather what decides whether the work in itself is true or false [. . .].' (Ibid., p. 197.) Society 'inheres within the truth content' (ibid., p. 198).

27. Ibid., p. 197. The 'truth of the work in itself is commensurable with philosophical interpretation and coincides [. . .] with philosophical truth.' (Ibid.)

28. Ibid., p. 193.

29. Ibid., p. 197. More complex: 'Hence art has need of philosophy, which interprets it [art] in order to say what it [art] cannot say, whereas however it can only be said of art in that art does not say it.' (Ibid., p. 113).

30. Herbert Schnädelbach, 'Dialektik als Vernunftkritik. Zur Konstruktion des Rationalen bei Adorno', in Schnädelbach, *Vernunft und Geschichte. Vorträge und Abhandlungen* (Frankfurt a.M.: Suhrkamp 1987), pp. 179–206, here p. 202.

31. Adorno, *Ästhetische Theorie*, p. 516.

32. Ibid., p. 179.

33. Cf. Friedrich Nietzsche, *The Birth of Tragedy*, in *The Complete Works of Friedrich Nietzsche*, vol. 3, ed. O. Levy (Edinburgh/London: Foulis 1909), here pp. 93f.

34. Jean-François Lyotard, *Die Transformatoren Duchamp* (Stuttgart: Edition Patricia Schwarz 1986), p. 22 [Eng.: *Duchamp: TRANS/formers*, Venice, Cal.: Kapis Press 1990).

35. Jean-François Lyotard, *Tombeau de l'intellectuel et autres papiers* (Paris: Galilée 1984), p. 84.

36. Jean-François Lyotard, 'Philosophy and Painting in the Age of Their Experimentation', in *The Lyotard Reader*, ed. Andrew Benjamin (Oxford: Blackwell 1989), pp. 181–195, here p. 182.

37. The conventional philosophical method of retrieving art by linguistically outdoing it or substituting for it has today migrated into the loquacity of art commentaries and degenerated into the discursive cream cornets of the art scene.

38. Reflected art history too will have to make its mind up. You can hardly want to emphasize the 'je ne sais quoi' on the one side and on the other hand declare that 'aesthetics converges with interpretation' (Gottfried Boehm, 'Der erste Blick. Kunstwerk – Ästhetik – Philosophie', in *Die Aktualität des Ästhetischen*, ed. Wolfgang Welsch, Munich: Fink 1993, pp. 355–369, here pp. 357 and 359).

39. For some examples of this see the essay 'Aesthetics beyond Aesthetics: For a New Form to the Discipline' in the present volume (section II.2, pp. 92–97).

40. Hence the talk of works' own languages and autonomous meaning is only half true. All artistic semantics is constituted in an entangled and interventionary manner. It is only within a semantic network that idiolects can take shape; it is there that specific, unmistakeable and seemingly autonomous positions can first be assumed.

8

CITIES OF THE FUTURE
Aspects from Architectural Theory and Cultural Philosophy

It might seem unusual for a philosopher to speak about architectural issues. But philosophy and architecture are more closely related than is commonly assumed. There is practically an old allegiance between them. Philosophy has made use of architectural concepts and metaphors over and over again. This is still familiar to us through the talk of *foundations* and *fundaments*, which one expects from philosophy and its thinking, or from the talk of *construction* of concepts or *edifices* of thought. In addition, philosophy has linked its self-reflection with thoughts on architecture and urban planning over and over again. In antiquity Aristotle compared the philosopher with an architect[1] – and Goethe later said that Aristotle himself had stood as does a master builder to the world.[2] In the modern age Descartes in his *Discourse on the Method*, which can be considered the foundational text for modern philosophy, repeatedly drew parallels to the building of a house or city.[3] Kant's *Critique of Pure Reason* contains towards the end a chapter headed 'Architectonic of Pure Reason' in which he explains how 'the originative idea of a philosophy of pure reason' was essentially '*architectonic*'.[4] And Nietzsche characterized man as a 'mighty genius of construction' who has succeeded, with the help of metaphors and fictions, in erecting a social and individual edifice of life and thinking 'upon an unstable foundation, and, as it were, on running water'.[5] Besides this, Nietzsche had considered in detail how architecture factually restricts or promotes our opportunities for thought; he said for instance that 'what [. . .] is lacking in our big cities [is] quiet and wide, expansive places for reflection. [. . .] Buildings and sites that would altogether give expression to the sublimity of thoughtfulness and of stepping aside.'[6] We could not be satisfied with traditional buildings because the language they speak 'is far too rhetorical and unfree' – 'we who are godless could not think *our thoughts* in such surroundings. We wish to see *ourselves* translated into stone and plants, we want to take walks *in ourselves* when we stroll around these buildings and gardens.'[7]

Present-day philosophy also repeatedly comes to talk of the architectural traits in thinking. This applies to Lyotard's postmodernity just as it does to Derrida's deconstruction.[8] One of the most important philosophers of the twentieth century, Ludwig Wittgenstein, once even practised as an architect himself: he created (together with Paul Engelmann) one of modernity's purest constructions, the house at 19 Kundmanngasse in Vienna. Moreover, Wittgenstein pointed out the parallels between philosophy and architecture several times: both, for example, he said are 'really more a working on oneself. On one's own interpretation. On one's way of seeing things. (And what one expects of them.)'[9] Architecture, however, was to be more difficult: 'You think philosophy is hard enough, but I can tell you it is nothing to the difficulties involved in architecture.'[10]

Conversely there are countless examples of how architects have allowed themselves to be inspired by philosophers; think of, say, Abbott Suger and the Neoplatonic metaphysics of light, or of Schinkel and Humboldt, or in the present day of Tschumi and Derrida, or Eisenman and Deleuze and – once again – Derrida. Incidentally, Vitruvius, the forefather of all architectural theory, admonished architects at the beginning of his treatise to 'have followed the philosophers with attention.'[11]

I don't, however, mean that philosophical reflections can automatically find their way into architectural deliberations, in a sort of 1:1 relation. But they often contain a potential for self-awareness and stimulation which permits someone to see their own affairs more sharply or something altogether new. The results of the reception might then of course be significantly different from the initial consideration. Along with Proust it could be said that philosophical reflection is like a pair of glasses which you try out, and if you see more sharply with them then you'll keep them on and use them for a while.

In the following I want briefly, in section I, to expand on the prevalent aestheticization tendency as it affects architecture and city planning and, in contrast, to point out architecture's actual responsibility. In section II I want to comment on 'blending', a buzzword in architectural discussions: to what is this concept opposed, and to what extent is it right in being so? Section III underlines the blending aspect by introducing a topical cultural perspective, the perspective of transculturality. Finally, in section IV, I want to outline the possibilities and responsibilities of architecture and city planning in the conditions of transculturality.

I.   An aesthetic look, or attention to living conditions?

1.   Against urban embellishment

West German cities have experienced a gigantic aestheticization in the last few years.[12] The inner cities in particular have undergone a face-lift. Shopping areas have been fashioned to be elegant, chic and animating. Today even the outskirts of cities and country refuges are being affected by this trend.

'Experience' is a central watchword in these processes of embellishment. Gerhard Schulze, with a view to these aestheticization processes, rightly calls our society an 'Experience Society'.[13] The experiences, however, are indeed not experiences. Rather they are stale and dreary. That is why people quickly seek the next experience and hence rush from one disappointment to the next. Beautiful ensembles drift into prettiness, and sublimely intended staging descends into the ridiculous. – This cannot be what architecture ought to be achieving.

2.   *Architecture and living conditions*

Architects should not – as is occurring amidst this prevalent aestheticization – build for glossy brochures and architectural journals, but for people and users. Architecture must be first and foremost the architecture of living spaces. Architecture moulds, steers and encourages or hinders living processes. These, however, are not of a merely aesthetic nature. Hence, although architecture which attends only to its aesthetic components might trigger euphoria in a society hooked on experience, this enthusiasm won't last long; rather it will soon become stale, when it becomes clear that you're being aesthetically euphorized alone, but left out in the cold with regard to all other dimensions of architecture. After all, aesthetics is not everything; architecture fares badly and it even does aesthetics no good if the latter is given precedence. An objection such as this is necessary against many tendencies of neomodern and postmodern architecture. It is only when architects think beyond the aesthetic from the outset, when they are not content with simply putting up showpieces and organizing shows of their work, but rather bear in mind primarily the living procedures prepared for, encouraged or hindered by their measures, that they can adequately fulfil the responsibility of architecture.[14]

II.   On the concept of 'blending'

What is one turning against when one appeals for blending – for example, for the 'blending of living and working'[15] – as is today becoming the custom? One is opposing the modern programme of function separation. This programme was propagated by the Athens Charter. 'The keys to urbanism', it was there explained, 'are to be found in the four functions: inhabiting, working, recreation (in leisure time), and circulation.'[16] A city was to be planned, and life organized, according to these four functions. This could be done most easily when these functions were separated. – The mistake in this, however, was twofold: the rigorous and reductive fixing of the functions, on the one hand, and their separation, on the other.

The architecture critic Adolf Behne had already said everything necessary relating to the first point in 1930:

> The linear building intends to solve and cure, if possible, everything by means of the apartment, surely in a serious endeavour for people. But in fact it's precisely here that the individual becomes a concept, a figure. The individual is to inhabit

and become healthy by inhabiting, and the exact living diet is prescribed to him in detail. He has – at least with the most consistent architects – to go to bed in the east, to eat and answer mother's letter in the west, and the apartment is organized in such a way that he cannot in fact do anything but this.[17]

Functions are laid down without paying attention, with the same intensity, to opportunities for variation. And only a single catalogue of functions is reckoned with – as if people and their needs were to be the same universally.

Admittedly this programme isn't executable in any case. A complete catalogue of functions and a perfect throughgoing planning would never be achieved. So the advice that Mies van der Rohe gave his colleague Hugo Häring when the latter didn't know how to proceed with the functional analysis for a factory building was shrewd: instead of a complete functional plan Häring should simply make the 'sheds' large enough, then everything would fit inside and the users would be able to settle in themselves and alter the partitioning again according to change in production processes. On the other hand, of course, Mies's hint and way out was a blatant *démenti* of the functionalist doctrine.

The intention of perfect throughgoing planning is also systematically flawed because things that elude planning belong essentially to life: things unprogrammable, unpredictable, spontaneous. The difference between life and mechanism lies in just this. It is precisely in wanting to pay attention to living functions and to do justice to living conditions that architecture must adjust to openness instead of wanting to be absolutely definitive.

Architecture cannot be allowed to take the mathematical ideal as its paragon.[18] We should break with mathematical compulsions in living matters. The classic modern maxims of functional separation and of purity – both mathematical in spirit – agree badly with life and are not much use for an architecture which is to agree with life. To accept impurity, to promote blending, is the more promising strategy.

III. Transculturality: on the constitution of today's cultures

In addition to this comes a topical viewpoint which is in effect decisive in making an appeal for blending requisite. It results from the altered cultural boundary conditions of contemporary architecture. The constitution of present-day cultures is – in an incisive and positive sense – a constitution of blending.

1. Architecture and cultural context

Architecture refers basically to cultural issues in a deep sense. Not only because it itself represents a cultural activity, but because it deals with cultural conditions and, in doing so, also contributes to the image we obtain of culture. Architecture is effective in real just as in symbolic terms. Whereas, in real terms, buildings furnish living spaces and provide possibilities for actions, on a symbolic level they mould our notions of urbanity, coexistence and society, contribute to work on the inventory of our urban and cultural fantasies, wishes and perceived aims. Conversely, however, architecture also depends on cultural conditions which it does not itself generate, but must consider so as not to operate – in some circumstances for decades – at cross-purposes to cultural reality.

Jean Nouvel recently pointed out how decisive 'taking stock of the cultural and social situation' is for the modernity of architecture.[19] 'Architecture can only arise as very exact reflection on the external conditions, whose influence is increasing and is becoming ever less avoidable.'[20] 'In doing this the architect reverts to notions and concepts from other fields, for example philosophy, and relates them to one another.'[21]

A dramatic change can today be observed in the field of culture. The form of cultures is changing itself fundamentally. Cultures are assuming a novel, transcultural constitution instead of the traditional, monocultural one. To begin with I want to explain the extent to which the conventional, monocultural concept of culture has today become obsolete, in order then to set out why, in its stead, transculturality is the order of the day, and finally what this means for architecture and city planning.

2.   The traditional concept of culture and its problems

Fundamental features

The traditional concept of culture was anything but friendly towards blending. It favoured separations. In the form founded by Herder this concept – which to many among us still seems to be unquestionably valid – is characterized by three definitional elements: by social homogenization, ethnic consolidation and intercultural delimitation.[22] Firstly, a culture is supposed to mould the life of the people concerned, as a whole and in its details, making every act and every object an unmistakable component of precisely *this* culture. The concept is thus strongly *unifying*. Secondly, culture is always to be the culture of one *people*. It represents, as Herder put it, '*the flower*' of a people's existence.[23] Thirdly, a decided *delimitation* towards the outside ensues: every culture is, as the culture of *one* people, to be specifically distinguished and separated from the cultures of *other* peoples.

Objections

With regard to this concept of culture I assert that it no longer applies to today's conditions. Its three definitional elements have become obsolete.

Firstly, modern societies are differentiated within themselves to such a high degree that uniformity is neither still foundational nor altogether attainable for them. In 1948 T.S. Eliot tried to take up the Herderian concept and claimed that culture denotes 'the *whole way of life* of a people, from birth to the grave, from morning to night and even in sleep'.[24] But obviously it has long since failed to apply that we all still spend our lives, our days and even nights in the same way. The culture of a working-class quarter, a well-to-do residential district, and that of the alternative scene hardly exhibit any common denominator. Modern societies have become multicultural within themselves,[25] they encompass a multitude of different forms of life. The traditional concept of culture, however, is structurally incapable of taking account of differentiations of this type.[26] First of all, then, the traditional concept of culture already fails once faced with the inner complexity of modern cultures. It is descriptively wrong.

Secondly, the ethnic consolidation of the classic concept of culture is dubious: Herder envisaged cultures as being like closed spheres or autonomous islands, each coextensive with a people's territorial and linguistic extent.[27] But as we know (not only from the German history of the twentieth century), such people-bound definitions are highly imaginary and fictional and must laboriously be brought to prevail against historical evidence of mixing. What's more, they are politically dangerous, as we are today experiencing almost worldwide.

Thirdly, the concept demands outward delimitation. Herder says: 'Everything which is still the *same* as my nature, which can be *assimilated* therein, I envy, strive towards, make my own; *beyond this*, kind nature has armed me with *insensibility*, *coldness* and *blindness*; it can even become *contempt* and *disgust*.'[28] – It can be seen that Herder *defends* the double figure of concentration on the own and rejection of the foreign. The traditional concept of culture tended, as a consequence of its conceptuality, to cultural racism which states: this culture is different from that one; nothing can be transferred unamended into the other; the cultures must be purely divided and separated; policing is needed inwardly as well as outwardly: inwardly, so as to keep watch over the authenticity of the culture which is not to be diluted through imports or undermined by immigration; outwardly, so as to keep the borders sealed. There is to be no free traffic – not of cultural substance and ultimately perhaps not even of people – between cultures.

To sum this up: the classical model of culture is not only descriptively wrong, but also normatively dangerous and untenable. This old cultural model, however, still seems to be behind some wishes for the separation of milieu and function, and behind the calls for a splitting of cultures and forms of life. The abandonment of this concept is indicated in every respect. What is necessary today is to think of cultures beyond the contraposition of ownness and foreignness – 'beyond both the heterogeneous and the own', as Adorno once put it.[29]

3.   Transition to transculturality

Criticism of the traditional concept of single cultures can be summarized as follows: if today's cultures were in fact still, as this concept insinuates, constituted in the form of islands or spheres, then one could neither rid oneself of, nor solve the problem of, their coexistence and cooperation. However, the description of today's cultures as islands or spheres is factually incorrect and normatively deceptive. Our cultures have, *de facto*, long since not had the form of homogeneity and separateness. Rather they have assumed a novel form, which I call *transcultural* because it *passes through* traditional cultural borders as if it were natural to do so. Cultural conditions today are characterized everywhere by mixing and permeations. The concept of transculturality – which I now want to set out – seeks to bring to light this altered cultural constitution.[30]

Macrolevel: the altered cut of today's cultures

Firstly, the old homogenizing and separating idea of cultures has been surpassed through *cultures' external networking*. Lifestyles today no longer end at the borders of national cultures, but transcend these, are found in the same way in other cultures. These permeations are a consequence of migration processes, worldwide traffic and communications systems as well as of economic dependencies.

As a result of this blending the same basic problems and states of consciousness today appear in cultures alleged to be fundamentally different – think, for example, of human rights discussions, of the feminist movement or of ecological awareness. These form powerful active factors across the board culturally.

Secondly, today's cultures are characterized generally by *hybridization*. For every single culture, all other cultures have tendentially come to be internal elements or satellites. This applies on the levels of population, merchandise and information. Worldwide, in the majority of countries, live members of all other countries of this planet; more and more, the same articles – as exotic as they may once have been – are becoming available the world over; moreover the global networking of communications technology makes all kinds of information identically available from every point.

Hence, strictly speaking, there is no longer anything absolutely foreign. Everything is within internal or external reach. Equally there is no longer anything absolutely own either. Authenticity has become folklore, is ownness simulated for others – to whom the indigene himself has long since belonged.[31]

Microlevel: transcultural formation of individuals

Just as on the macrolevel of society, transculturality is also gaining ground on the microlevel of individuals. Most of us are determined in our cultural formation by *several* cultural origins and connexions. We are cultural crossbreeds. Today's writers, for example, emphasize that they're shaped not by *one* homeland, but by differing reference countries: say by German, English, French, Russian, South or North American literature. For architects it cannot be any different; their cultural formation is transcultural. That of subsequent generations will be even more intensely so. The American political scientist Amy Gutmann emphasizes that today 'most people's identities, not just Western intellectuals or elites, are shaped by more than a single culture. Not only societies, but people are multi-cultural.'[32]

Sociologists have been pointing out since the seventies that modern lives can only be understood 'as a migration through different social worlds and as the successive realization of a number of possible identities',[33] that we all possess 'multiple attachments and identities' – 'cross-cutting identities', as Daniel Bell, the theoretician behind the postindustrial society, put it.[34]

Richard Sennett, with a view to architecture, has drawn attention to the fact that already in the thirties the Chicago sociologists recognized the advantages of such a fragmented self: 'A woman who thinks male/female, a businessman who thinks rich/poor, a Jamaican who thinks black/white, experience low levels of stimulation from the outside, Wirth thought. A fragmented self is more responsive.'[35] It is for precisely those social feats specific to city life – allowing a stranger complete proximity without (as in villages or small communes) having to be interested in his or her life story, and respecting them as a person all the same – that such a plural self offers better preconditions than a monolithic one.

To sum up the diagnosis of transculturality given until now: cultural determinants today, from the macrolevel of society through to the micro-level of individuals, have become transcultural. Every concept of culture which intends to comprehend today's reality, and every cultural activity which doesn't wish to be retrograde, must face up to this transcultural constitution.

Transculturality in history

Incidentally, transculturality is in no way completely new historically. Rather it was – in contrast to the insinuation of cultural homogeneity which spread with the nineteenth century and which today still bewitches many among us – virtually the rule. Carl Zuckmayer described this wonderfully in *The Devil's General*:

> [. . .] just imagine your line of ancestry, from the birth of Christ on. There was a Roman commander, a dark type, brown like a ripe olive, he had taught a blond girl Latin. And then a Jewish spice dealer came into the family, he was a serious person, who became a Christian before his marriage and founded the house's Catholic tradition. – And then came a Greek doctor, or a Celtic legionary, a Grisonian landsknecht, a Swedish horseman, a Napoleonic soldier, a deserted Cossack, a Black Forest miner, a wandering miller's boy from the Alsace, a fat mariner from Holland, a Magyar, a pandour, a Viennese officer, a French actor,

a Bohemian musician – all lived on the Rhine, brawled, boozed, and sang and
begot children there – and – Goethe, he was from the same pot, and Beethoven,
and Gutenberg, and Mathias Grünewald, and – oh, whatever – just look in the
encyclopaedia. They were the best, my dear! The world's best! And why? Because
that's where the peoples intermixed. Intermixed – like the waters from sources,
streams and rivers, so, that they run together to a great, living torrent.[36]

This is a realistic description of a 'people's' historical genesis and constitution. It breaks through the fiction of homogeneity.

For architects who know Europe's architectural history, historical transculturality is evident in any case. Styles reached beyond countries and
nations, and many architects created their best works far from home. The
culture was European and formed a network straight through the states.

Philosophical transculturality: annexability and permeation

The philosopher who provides the greatest help for a transcultural concept
of culture necessary today is Wittgenstein. In his late phase he developed an
on-principle pragmatically based concept of culture, free of ethnic consolidation and unreasonable demands for homogeneity from the outset.
According to Wittgenstein, culture is at hand wherever practices in life are
shared, wherever that is – put casually – we get on with each other. An
understanding of foreign cultures matters less for this than practical interaction with foreignness. And there is always a good chance for such
interactions, because there always exist at least some entanglements, intersections and transitions between the different forms of life.[37]

Continuing along these lines, the concept of transculturality aims for a
multi-meshed and inclusive, not separatist and exclusive, understanding of
culture. The achievements of such a culture and society will lie in blending
– not in preclusion. What's important is to make use of, and develop the
overlaps between, forms of life. By this means the scale of commonalities
can broaden surprisingly and a form of life can come about which also
incorporates reserves which hadn't previously seemed capable of being
linked in. Such extensions and permeations today represent a pressing
assignment for cultural activities.

**Excursus on analogous changes in science, rationality theory and
everyday problems**

Incidentally, it is not only more recent developments in cultural theory, but
equally those in science and rationality theory, as well as everyday
problems, which make an analogous transition to thought forms of mixing
necessary. They call for a shift away from the old preference for clean
separation, division of the world and unilinear analysis and for a transition
to web-like, entangled, networked thought forms.[38] Thus the different
rationalities cannot, as the modern age hoped, in yielding to and carrying
out differentiation, be delimited from one another in a watertight manner;
rather they exhibit entanglements through to and in their core. In reality

too we are finding ourselves confronted more and more with problematic issues which result from networking effects. Even when problems arise locally their effects transcend borders, become global. Our old, separatist thought forms, however, are incapable of reacting to this. For them such transcending of borders is merely an 'undesired side-effect' – which you accept with a shrug of the shoulders and with which you are helplessly confronted. But of course it appears only to be a 'side-effect' because one has thought separatistically from the outset. The causal chains of reality, however, do not stop at these small-minded desires for division. Hence we must shift away from separative thinking and make the transition to thought forms of entanglement in economic, ecological, and all planning issues.

Conclusion

Transculturality, as I wanted to show, will comprise our constitution more and more. My thesis is that assignments of the future will only be solvable through a determined commitment to transculturality. This applies in social and political respects as well as – and this alone is what I now want to talk about – in the realm of architecture and urban planning. Planners and architects should, I believe, take an urgent look at the perspective of transculturality and design cities and living space in its spirit – instead of once again turning the clock back in the direction of musty 'ownness', which always stands at the threshold to intolerance.

IV.   Architecture and urban planning in conditions of transculturality

How can transculturality be expressed or erected in architecture? I want to describe this first of all with regard to individual buildings and then with a view to city development.

1.   Transculturality in singular buildings

For the sake of general comprehensibility I have chosen very well-known building works. My first example is the John Hancock Tower in Boston, built by I.M. Pei and Partners from 1966 to 1976. This is an exemplary piece of transcultural architecture. Pei created a skyscraper, that is, an emblematically American structure (it's even New England's highest skyscraper), but with an obvious Asian declination. The ground plan is formed by a rhomboid which exhibits asymmetrically placed indents on the base and façade, which affects the astonishing slenderness of this 62-storey-high building. To begin with, this tower, which blends two cultural patterns into one another, was highly controversial; today it is a great success. At night I asked a homeless man whether he liked the building. He answered:

'It generates a lot of attention, that's why I like it.' Obviously the building is transcultural not only in the sense previously described, as a link between differing cultural traditions, but also in the social sense: it is valued equally by members of different forms of life – by high and low, establishment and outsiders.

My second example is structurally completely different: Le Corbusier's Carpenter Center for the Visual Arts, built from 1961 to 1964 at the edge of the Harvard campus. Le Corbusier in no way adapted himself to Harvard's standard architecture, but did entirely his own thing: he built a typical Le Corbusier building – so to speak, an even more exhilarating version of the Villa Savoye on the other side of the Atlantic. Cultural mixing results here only in ensemble, in contrast to the surrounding buildings. In this constellation an evidently transcultural impression is made. Harvard on the whole would be a lot more boring and uncontemporary without this strange body.

My counter-example on the same site is James Stirling's Arthur M. Sackler Museum from 1986, just 200 metres away: a building wholly adapted to the Harvard standard, but pepped up with some Stirling insignia – light green railings and ventilation slots, for example. Here the standard-anxiety was victorious, and the result is correspondingly mediocre. Transculturality neither exists in the building (as with Pei) nor does it result in ensemble (as with Le Corbusier). The opportunities of today's architecture are squandered, transculturality is ignored; instead an architect leaves his calling card.[39]

My fourth example is Jean Nouvel's Institut du Monde Arabe in Paris from 1987.[40] Nouvel effects an architectonic encounter of European and Asian culture by operating with forms which can be read as high-tech documents and as Arabian ornamentation in one. The functional and ornamental are coupled in an amazing way; they are, so to speak, blended into one another. This occurs exemplarily in the carrés of the façade. This consists of seemingly Oriental diaphragms, which, like photographic apertures, change their degree of contraction, and hence the import of light to the inner, depending upon variation in daylight; on the inside this linking of technical installation and Arabian filigree attains a nearly unbelievable perfection and value of its own. All in all the high-tech building, finished chiefly in aluminium, is so masterfully tuned in shades of grey that you can simultaneously picture yourself in a seraglio. Nouvel didn't just put together European and Arabic like a patchwork, but invented forms which can be read twofold. Postmodern aesthetics often spoke of double-coding, but seldom was it attained. Nouvel succeeded. He created an exemplary piece of transcultural architecture.

My final example is again from Pei: his Bank of China in Hong Kong erected between 1982 and 1990. At the time of construction it was Hong Kong's highest skyscraper erected on a quadratic ground plan with sophisticated tubular construction and determined in its formal language by diagonal breaks which seem to convey the three-dimensional body more and more into the planar, whereby the angles become smaller with growing height. Some people see in this a Chinese bamboo whose growth knots symbolize intellectual ascent; others regard the building as a hyper-technical skyscraper which with mathematical precision transforms itself into an almost weightless apparition. Of course the building is both. In a manner similar to Nouvel's, two cultural patterns are interwoven with one another. The transculturality goes so far that the two elements can hardly be distinguished at all. – Incidentally I consider it noteworthy that today it is an architect with a Chinese background who leads Western modernity to its best forms.

2. City planning

What, finally, does the perspective of transculturality mean with regard to city design?

Permeability

For cities of the future it will be important to admit possibilities for transition, to contain ambiguity and guarantee permeability. A city should be less a completed pearl than a point of intersection for varying networks. Even in medium-sized cities will live not only people who want to feel absolutely 'at home' there, but also those who can only feel themselves at home if the city is an efficient communications node at the same time, if, that is, it provides good opportunities for variety within the city as well as communications – transport and telecommunications – outside the city. Not everyone who lives in a city should be obliged either to have their entire identity there or to be unhappy. You should also be able to have your identity elsewhere, but want to locate the residential part of your identity here – or the professional part or the recreational part of your identity.

'Home'?

Some people today want once again to present the city as being 'home' in opposition to the 'characterlessness' of modern cities. This is a tricky venture. In the European tradition the city was for centuries associated with connotations of freedom: 'City air liberates.'[41] In past decades, however, this estimation seems to have changed. Even in the early twentieth century conservative cultural criticism had often branded the city a place of estrangement. And recently people have wanted, as a countermove against a supposed threat through internationalization, to associate cities with expectations of home and identity, and with notions of a base providing deep rooting and a firm footing.

This intention threatens to turn out retrograde and musty, amounting to a basic resistance towards contemporary life. Some familiar and widely regarded diagnoses might be critically questioned in this perspective, for instance Mitscherlich's polemics against the 'inhospitality of our cities' from 1965.[42] Is not the host-ideal, which Mitscherlich – in connection with expectations of homeliness – wanted to assert as a 'critical' viewpoint, far too stale? Furthermore is his argumentation not based on an outdated identity-ideal? Mitscherlich polemicizes, for example, against the modern 'momentary personality',[43] one capable of diversity and transition. As if competence with diversity and the ability to make transitions had not become the very conditions for successful subjectivity in modernity.[44] And as if it were not precisely transcultural subjects who would be capable of managing diversity and would want and need an external equivalent to their inner plurality. Compared with the views of the thirties' Chicago sociologists previously mentioned, Mitscherlich's plea indeed makes a hopelessly retrograde show of itself. I'm not saying that Mitscherlich's initial findings were wrong in their time, but his suggested therapy was and is.

With stabilizations of the old type, however, a socially desirable identity will no longer be attainable in a context defined by transculturality. Faced with the expectations of hospitality and homeliness *à la* Mitscherlich, transcultural subjects side more with a phrase from Horkheimer and Adorno: 'Homeland is the state of having escaped.'[45]

To be sure, not only a cosmopolitan, but also a local component belongs to transcultural identity. And it is a responsibility of architecture to enable and to accommodate in part local belonging. But this is not to be achieved by tightening the screws of cultural identity and by enacting a monolithic cultural identity. Instead we need an opening in the direction of other portions and forms of identity. Rather than changing cities or turning to electronic media to find a multitude of facets, these should be found up to a point in one's own city. Cities certainly should have a character – but they should also accommodate the transition to other characters.

Wherever this is guaranteed I have no concerns about the future of the city. Electronic cities cannot replace the real ones. But transversal cities – that is, those which permit the transition between different identities – could advantageously take the place of some conventionally constituted ones.

There are of course still parts of cities and whole cities whose fixed and compelling identity has an effect like a closed asylum. Planners and architects should protect us from these. They should instead make it possible for us to live in an open asylum. A visitor to Vienna once said that the city appeared to her to be like an open asylum, since the most diverse and half-mad characters walk around freely there. – I hope we will also be able to pay this compliment to other cities in greater number in the future.

Notes

This essay was originally published as 'Städte der Zukunft – architekturtheoretische und kulturphilosophische Überlegungen', in *Wohnen und Arbeiten. Städtebauliches Modellprojekt Schwerin-Lankow*, published by the Kulturkreis der deutschen Wirtschaft im Bundesverband der Deutschen Industrie, Heidelberg 1993, pp. 12–18. It has been revised for this volume. (First English publication.)

1. Cf. Aristotle, *Nicomachean Ethics*, VII 12 [1152^{b}1].

2. 'Aristotle [. . .] stood to the world as does a man, a master builder. Now that he is here, he should have effect and create here. He inquires after the soil, but no further than where he finds ground. From there through to the middle of the earth, the rest is immaterial to him. He sets out an enormous base circle for his building, gathers materials here from all sides, orders them, stacks them up and thus climbs into the heights in regular, pyramidical form; whereas Plato seeks an obelisk, indeed a pointed flame equalling the sky.' (Johann Wolfgang von Goethe, *Schriften zur Farbenlehre*, vol. 16 of the *Gedenkausgabe*, Zurich: Artemis, 2nd edition, 1964, pp. 346f.)

3. Descartes compares – negatively – the old cities which have grown in the course of history, in which, although some fine houses may be found, their whole is ill proportioned and disordered, with the equally futile tinkering around with handed-down systems; whereas, on the other hand, he draws a positive parallel between the completely new construction of cities on free space to a unitary design and the new creation of a scientific conception (II 1). He further points out the necessity of possessing a transitional abode during the building period of a new system or house (III 1). Finally he expresses his endeavours towards a science secured in its fundaments thus: 'my whole aim was [. . .] to cast aside the loose earth and sand so as to come upon rock or clay'. (René Descartes, *Discourse on the Method*, in *The Philosophical Writings of Descartes*, vol. 1, trans. J. Cottingham, R. Stoothoff and D. Murdoch, Cambridge: Cambridge University Press 1985, pp. 111–151, here p. 125 [III 6].)

4. Immanuel Kant, *Critique of Pure Reason*, trans. Norman Kemp Smith (New York: St Martin's Press 1965), p. 663 [A 847], cf. p. 655 [A 835].

5. Friedrich Nietzsche, 'On Truth and Lies in a Nonmoral Sense', in *Philosophy and Truth. Selections from Nietzsche's Notebooks of the early 1870's*, trans. and ed. Daniel Breazeale (Atlantic Highlands, NJ: Humanities Press 1979), pp. 79–91, here p. 85.

6. Friedrich Nietzsche, *The Gay Science*, trans. Walter Kaufmann (New York: Vintage Books 1974), p. 226 [280].

7. Ibid., p. 227 [280].

8. Cf. my 'Das weite Feld der Dekonstruktion', in *Schräge Architektur und aufrechter Gang – Dekonstruktion: Bauen in einer Welt ohne Sinn?*, ed. Gert Kähler (Brunswick: Vieweg 1993), pp. 50–63.

9. Ludwig Wittgenstein, *Culture and Value*, ed. G.H. von Wright, trans. Peter Winch (Chicago: University of Chicago Press 1984), p. 16e.

10. This is reported by M.O'C. Drury, in: 'Some Notes on Conversations with Wittgenstein' (*Recollections of Wittgenstein*, ed. Rush Rhees, Oxford/New York: Oxford University Press 1984, pp. 76–96, here p. 76).

11. Vitruvius, *The Ten Books on Architecture*, I 3. Vitruvius even thought that 'philosophy [. . .] makes an architect high-minded and not self-assuming, but rather renders him courteous, just, and honest without avariciousness' (ibid., I 7).

12. For more detail see the essay 'Aestheticization Processes: Phenomena, Distinctions and Prospects' in the present volume.

13. Gerhard Schulze, *Die Erlebnisgesellschaft. Kultursoziologie der Gegenwart* (Frankfurt a.M.: Campus 1992).

14. Cf. my 'Architektur ist nicht alles', in: *Werk, Bauen + Wohnen*, 11, 1988, pp. 18–23.

15. The present essay dates back to a paper given at a seminar 'Living and Working – a Support Project for Archicture Students' on 8 November 1992 in Schwerin, Germany. This was occasioned by a model town-planning project in which aspects of blending were foregrounded.

16. Le Corbusier, *The Athens Charter*, trans. Anthony Eardley (New York: Grossman 1973), p. 95 [§ 77].

17. Adolf Behne, 'Dammerstock', in: *Die Form* 6, Book 6, 1930 (quoted from: *Tendenzen der Zwanziger Jahre*, Exhibition Catalogue Berlin 1977, part 2, pp. 125 and 126).

18. For more detail on this see the essay 'How Modern was Modern Architecture?' in the present volume.

19. Jean Nouvel, 'Design für die Gegenwart', in *Das Internationale Design-Jahrbuch 1995/ 96*, ed. Jean Nouvel (Munich: Bangert 1995), pp. 6–9, here p. 6.

20. Jean Nouvel, interview in *El Croquis*, 1994; quoted from: *Das Internationale Design-Jahrbuch 1995/96*, p. 10.

21. Nouvel, 'Design für die Gegenwart', p. 6.

22. See Johann Gottfried Herder, *Outlines of a Philosophy of the History of Man* (New York: Bergman Publishers 1966). The work appeared in four separate parts, each of five books, in the years 1784, 1785, 1787 and 1791, published by the Hartknoch Press in Riga and Leipzig. For the sake of brevity I shall concentrate on the *typology* of Herder's concept of culture and not take account of details for Herder.

23. Ibid., p. 394 [13, VII].

24. T.S. Eliot, *Notes towards the Definition of Culture* (London: Faber and Faber 1948), p. 31.

25. I am thinking here, under the heading 'multiculturality', primarily of the differentiation of various forms of life linked with the dynamics of modernity, and only secondarily of the ethnic cultural differences which are the result of immigration processes. Ethnic multiculturality (which is spoken of far too exclusively in matters of multiculturality) comprises only a part of modern societies' factual multiculturality.

26. It should be considered too that in modern societies there exist not only vertical differentiations – such as between regionally, socially and functionally different cultures, between higher and lower, leading and alternative, or between scientific, technical, artistic, religious culture, and so on – but that horizontal distinctions also assert themselves: gender differences, for example, cut through ethnic, class or professional cultures; dissimilarities between male and female, heterosexual, lesbian and gay orientation can found incisive differences in cultural patterns and forms of life.

27. 'Every nation', Herder declared, 'has its *centre* of happiness *within itself* just as each sphere its centre of gravity!' (Johann Gottfried Herder, *Auch eine Philosophie der Geschichte zur Bildung der Menschheit* [1774], Frankfurt a.M.: Suhrkamp 1967, pp. 44f.)

28. Ibid., p. 45.

29. Theodor W. Adorno, *Negative Dialektik*, in Adorno, *Gesammelte Schriften*, vol. 6 (Frankfurt a.M.: Suhrkamp, 3rd edition, 1984), p. 192.

30. I have been developing the concept of transculturality since 1991. The first version appeared in an abridged form as 'Transkulturalität – Lebensformen nach der Auflösung der Kulturen', in *Information Philosophie*, 2, 1992, pp. 5–20; and unabridged in *Dialog der Kulturen. Die multikulturelle Gesellschaft und die Medien*, eds Kurt Luger and Rudi Renger (Vienna: Österreichischer Kunst- und Kulturverlag 1994), pp. 147–169 (Italian version: 'Transculturalità. Forme di vita dopo la dissoluzione delle culture', in *Paradigmi. Revista di critica filosofica*, Special Edition 'Dialogo interculturale ed eurocentrismo' X(30), 1992, pp. 665–689). In the meantime more developed renderings have become available: 'Transkulturalität – die veränderte Verfassung heutiger Kulturen', in *Sichtweisen. Die Vielheit in der Einheit* (Weimar: Edition Weimarer Klassik 1994), pp. 83–122; as well as 'Transculturality – The Form of Cultures Today', in *Le Shuttle: Tunnelrealitäten Paris–London–Berlin* (Berlin: Künstlerhaus Bethanien 1996), pp. 15–30.

31. There is indeed still rhetoric of autonomous regional cultures, but when you look carefully, it can be seen that in substance everything is transculturally determined or modified. What's regionally specific is now only décor, superficies, aesthetic enactment. This is, of course, one of the reasons for the eminent spread of the aesthetic noticeable today (cf. *Die Aktualität des Ästhetischen*, ed. Wolfgang Welsch, Munich: Fink 1993).

32. Amy Gutmann, 'The Challenge of Multiculturalism in Political Ethics', in *Philosophy & Public Affairs*, 22(3), 1993, pp. 171–206, here p. 183.

33. Peter L. Berger, Brigitte Berger and Hansfried Kellner, *The Homeless Mind. Modernization and Consciousness* (New York: Random House 1973), p. 77.

34. Daniel Bell, *The Winding Passage. Essays and Sociological Journeys 1960–1980* (Cambridge, Mass.: Abt Books 1980), p. 243.

35. Richard Sennett, *The Conscience of the Eye: The Design and Social Life of Cities* (New York: Norton 1992), p. 127.

36. Carl Zuckmayer, *The Devil's General*, in *Masters of Modern Drama* (New York: Random House 1963), pp. 911–958.

37. Following on from Wittgenstein Peter Winch writes: 'Different aspects of social life do not merely "overlap": they are frequently internally related in such a way that one cannot even be intelligibly conceived as existing in isolation from others.' (Peter Winch, *The Idea of a Social Science and its Relation to Philosophy*, London: Routledge, 2nd edition, 1990, pp. xvf.)

38. I have set this out in more detail in my *Vernunft. Die zeitgenössische Vernunftkritik und das Konzept der transversalen Vernunft* (Frankfurt a.M.: Suhrkamp 1995, stw 1996).

39. This is worthy of mention because Stirling's Neue Staatsgalerie in Stuttgart, completed two years previously (1984), was an exemplary transcultural building which spectacularly and skilfully combined codes of varying architectural origin and social standing (Hellenism, classicism, constructivism, functionalist modernity, pop culture, high-tech) and impressively demonstrated the image of a plural and transcultural society (see my *Unsere postmoderne Moderne*, Weinheim: VCH 1987; Berlin: Akademie Verlag, 5th edition, 1997, pp. 117–120).

40. The institute is supported by the French Government along with nineteen Arab states and is to promote awareness of Arabian culture and civilization among the French public.

41. Cf. Joachim Ritter, 'Die große Stadt' (in Ritter, *Metaphysik und Politik. Studien zu Aristoteles und Hegel*, Frankfurt a.M.: Suhrkamp 1977, pp. 341–354) as well as Sennett's *The Conscience of the Eye*.

42. Alexander Mitscherlich, *Die Unwirtlichkeit unserer Städte. Anstiftung zum Unfrieden* (Frankfurt a.M.: Suhrkamp 1965).

43. Ibid., p. 129.

44. Cf. my 'Subjektsein heute. Zum Zusammenhang von Subjektivität, Pluralität und Transversalität', in *Vernunftnähe, Vernunftferne – La raison, proche et lointaine*, Studia Philosophica 51, 1992, pp. 153–182.

45. Max Horkheimer and Theodor W. Adorno, *Dialectic of Enlightenment*, trans. John Cumming (New York: Continuum 1994), p. 78.

9

ON THE WAY TO AN AUDITIVE CULTURE?

Introduction

1. The grand programme of an auditive cultural revolution

A suspicion is circulating: our culture, which until now has been primarily determined by vision, is in the process of becoming an auditive culture; and that this is both desirable and necessary. Not only for reasons of equal treatment must hearing be emancipated following more than two thousand years of vision's dominance. Moreover, the person who hears is also the better person – one, that is, able to enter into something different and to respect instead of merely dominating it. A continued existence of the human species and the planet earth is to be hoped for only if our culture in future takes hearing as its basic model, since in technicized modernity the old dominance of vision is driving us unavoidably towards a catastrophe, from which only hearing's receptive, communicative, semiotic relationship to the world is able to keep us. Downfall or rescue, catastrophe or salvation – this is the scenario of alternatives with which people are trying to rouse us, to open our ears.

It was Joachim-Ernst Berendt who most insistently pleaded for the transition from a visual to an auditive culture. From the latter he expects the solution to all problems – from relationship crises through to the ecological threat to the planet.[1] Berendt is prophetically certain that an age of hearing will come: 'The old forms of organization were "visual orders", the new ones will be "auditive organisms".'[2]

Berendt is not alone. Heidegger as a philosopher, and Rosenstock-Huessy as a sociologist had pleaded long ago for a transition of our culture from seeing to hearing. In the present day recent French philosophy has, with great commitment, been paying attention to auditive elements in texts: one listens to the tone of a speech, is attentive to the rhythm of a letter, turns towards the 'unheard'. Nietzsche's complaint about the Germans' bad style, due to their lacking 'the third ear' – unfortunately German writers do not 'read aloud, not for the ear but only with the eye' and even have their 'ears put away in a drawer'[3] when composing their texts – would be unnecessary in our neighbouring country. In the meantime in Germany too authors like Dietmar Kamper or Peter Sloterdijk are speaking of the end of the optical age and of a new 'secret prevalence of hearing' or of a 'meta-physics of receptivity' which criticizes modernity.[4] For North American authors such as Marshall McLuhan the transition from a visual to an auditive culture has long been a matter of fact.[5]

The commendations for such an auditive culture sound altogether con-genial and auspicious. An auditive culture would intensify our awareness of other people and nature; it would be capable of learning, rather than merely issuing decrees; entanglements and networks – that is, the thought forms which we will in future need – lie far nearer to it from the start than do the conventional logical incisions; it would on the whole be full of understanding, reserved, symbiotic, receptive, open, tolerant – and what-ever other fine-sounding predicates Berendt might bring forward.[6]

2. Concerns

But isn't there also cause for concern, perhaps even for suspicion? Must one not – precisely when one has become capable of hearing – also hear in the plea for hearing a fatal link with subordination?[7] Is it really so far from the congenial eulogy of hearing to fatal apologias of subordination and obedience?

No one wants to plead in favour of subordination. No one wants to abandon frivolously the gains of the Enlightenment – which had made precisely the end of subordination its programme. Therefore, demarcation criteria are required which detail the limits beyond which hearing is no longer to be complied with. Hearing cannot be everything. Care needs to be taken that – as ever justified – criticism of modernity does not recklessly proclaim a postmodern epoch of hearing, which could in truth reveal itself to be an epoch of premodern subordination.

I want to attempt such demarcations in the following. Apart from this I would like to address the boundary conditions of the subject and to deal with some of the prejudices which hearing also has to combat. Further-more, an examination is needed of the sense in which a predominance of vision has existed in our tradition, and with what reasons we can question this visual primacy and argue for hearing's equality.[8]

3. 'Auditive culture'

The talk of an 'auditive culture' can be understood in a double sense. It can have a large, demanding, metaphysically encompassing sense, that is, aim for a complete adjustment of our culture with hearing as the new base model of our self-conduct and behaviour in the world. Or it can have a smaller, more modest, yet also more pragmatic sense. It then aims first and foremost for a cultivation of the auditive sphere alone, of our civilizational sound sphere. Thus, in one case, one wants to make hearing the medium for a revision of culture, indeed to make it the guiding sense of a new culture; in the other case, one restricts oneself to an improvement of hearing conditions within the existing culture. The latter would still be important enough in view of the factual underprivileging of hearing and an acoustically decayed civilization.

The importance of our senses has always reached beyond their own narrow realm. If it is said of tradition that it was visually dominated, then this does not mean that it decided all issues according to the messages from the sense of sight. What's meant is far more that the *typology* of vision was engraved even in our cognition, our behavioural forms, our entire technical-scientific civilization. The latter, for example, is fundamentally ascertaining – in just the way vision is. Equally on the other side the great plea for hearing does not mean that people in future should only make use of their ears. Rather it is pointed out that already micro-physically the world consists of oscillations, that a hidden acoustics is inscribed into our thinking and our logic, and that our conduct towards other people and to the world on the whole should become more receptive, attentive, accommodating. The purely sensuous meaning of seeing and hearing is always accompanied by farther-reaching dimensions of meaning.

Hence it is not only the great auditive revolution, but already a more modest auditive revision which would be able to radiate through the entire inventory of our culture. Plato for instance – as everyone knows, not a great friend of the senses – had a very exact sense for the fact that the introduction of new musical forms would not leave the forms of communal living and the laws of the state untouched.[9] How we humans deal with our senses affects our remaining self-being and our wordly conduct as a whole.

4. *On my intention*

I want to handle three question areas in more detail: I. Is the Western tradition and present day in fact determined by a visual primacy? And why has this become a problem and hearing the new hope? II. In what does the typological difference between seeing and hearing consist? What are the motives for the traditional preference of vision? How would an auditive culture differ from a visual one? III. With what good reasons can we argue for a transition to, and indeed legitimize, a culture of hearing? And what would the demands and criteria of such an auditive culture be?

Hugo Kükelhaus, the great old man favouring a rehabilitation of our senses, once complained that people affected by the flawed acoustic forms of civilization and technology lack the 'arguments in their defence', having nothing to hand 'but reference to their feelings'. With this, however – with mere reference to feeling – one would be unable to operate effectively when confronted with political decision makers and institutions.[10] I want to attempt to provide arguments of the type Kükelhaus so badly missed.

I. Traditional visual primacy and the contemporary questioning thereof

1. Visual primacy – from the Greeks through to today

Originally, occidental culture was not a culture of vision at all, but one of hearing. It had first to become a culture of vision. Greek society was initially determined by hearing. Egon Friedell has pointed out that 'the receptivity and sensitivity of the Greeks for the power of tones [. . .] [was] almost pathological'.[11] And Nietzsche, from whom Friedell had adopted this view, derived the central invention of classical Greek culture, the tragedy, from the spirit of music. In the Homeric aristocracy hearing was of central importance.[12]

A primacy of vision first came about at the turn of the fifth century before Christ, and, moreover, principally in the fields of philosophy, science and art. Thus Heraclitus declared that the eyes are 'more accurate witnesses than are [the] ears'.[13] He even called Pythagoras, the theoretician of spherical harmony (to which many apologists of an auditive culture today appeal), the 'chief captain of swindlers'.[14] This signals the departure from the primacy of hearing and the transition to the primacy of vision.

With Plato the visual model then prevailed completely. The basic determinations of being are from then on called 'ideas', that is, they become objects of vision right through to the word. The highest human feat now becomes theory, the viewing of these ideas; the human's path is to lead from the darkness of the cave and silhouettes to daylight, so as finally, following long practice, to reach the source of light, the sun as the epitome of pure good. The path is thus visually determined from start to finish. The truth of the cosmos is sought in the grammar of vision, no longer in the structures of hearing. Visual primacy was thus secured for the foreseeable future. It was to determine Neoplatonic and medieval light metaphysics just as it did the Enlightenment's modern-age and modern passion for light.

It is only in an anecdote that an awareness betrays itself of the possibility that the truth of vision might not be the whole truth after all. A few hours before his death Socrates tells his pupils of a dream which had often instructed him to make music; but he had always understood this music to be philosophizing – which must, after all, be the most excellent music. Now, however, faced by death, he was having doubts as to whether music in the usual sense might not have been meant. Hence at the last Socrates wrote a prooemium to Apollo, the god of music, and set some of Aesop's fables to verse. – Nietzsche – the 'master of suspicion' and the precursor of those philosophers who, more than two thousand years after Heraclitus, Plato and Socrates, have begun to distrust the metaphysics of vision and are trying instead to allow hearing to guide their thinking once again – read this anecdote as an indication of the bad conscience which all fanatics of vision have cause for.[15] They have indeed discovered a truth – but for this they have abandoned another, and falsely held their truth to be the whole truth.

Historically, however, as I've said, the supremacy of vision prevailed. The Aristotelian *Metaphysics* begins with a praise of vision and its model character for each and every insight and cognition; Neoplatonic and medieval light metaphysics is a singular ontology of visibility; Christian metaphysics even interprets the divine word in visual metaphors, and of course the saints are promised a *visio beatifica*; in the turn against the (as one was later to say) 'dark ages' the distinction of vision grew still further – such as when Leonardo da Vinci calls vision divine and accredits it with the apperception of the world's fundamental truths; the Enlightenment brings the metaphorics of light and visibility completely to bear; and modernity still knows no value higher than transparency.

The visual primacy also nests – as is commonly held to be self-evident – in countless details of our everyday orientation.[16] If someone hears voices then he's put in an asylum; but if he has visions then he is considered a forerunner, a prophet even. 'Knowing' is etymologically synonymous with 'having seen', and most of our other cognitive expressions – 'insight', 'evidence', 'idea', 'theory', 'reflexion', and so on – are visually tailored. Our political rhetoric and our private expectations are also visually determined: we expect openness and want to look into someone's very soul.

Of course the sciences too are practically bewitched by this visual primacy – more sharply formulated, by this ocular tyranny.[17] This extends to absurd details. Murray Schafer pointed out years ago that scientists handle and analyse even acoustic phenomena predominantly according to the type of visual appearances – acoustics to them becomes a matter of the eye instead of the ear.[18]

2.   Criticism of visual primacy: a plea for audition

Everyday reasons

But visual primacy has been coming under fire for decades. Everyday developments have had a considerable share in this. For although vision is continuing to expand in our everyday world, one shaped by advertising, television and video, visually dominated culture is nonetheless – in view of the manipulatory intentions of this pictorial world, of the possibilities for electronic image manipulation and of the transition to highly immaterial technologies – accompanied by a dissolution of trust in the visible at the same time.

Philosophical criticism

Philosophy too, which was traditionally a discipline for the assertion of visual primacy, has become an insistent critic of visual dominance in the twentieth century.[19] The two most important thinkers of the first half of this century, Heidegger and Wittgenstein, identified the visual orientation as being the *proton pseudos* of the history of occidental thought and brought to bear elements of hearing in opposition to this. As such Heidegger understood Plato's turn to vision as the Fall of occidental philosophy altogether.[20] Through this, the being (*Seiende*) was to have become from the very base an object of ascertainment (*Feststellen*) and production (*Herstellung*). With the turn to vision occidental rationalization was to have begun which makes the being (*Seiende*) calculable and which culminates in modern technology for which the being is only a disposable stock or a product to be cut to measure. Against this Heidegger pleads for a transition to hearing, interrogation (*Vernehmen*) and caring relations with things.[21] And Wittgenstein replaced the conventional theory of meaning, which was oriented towards the model of consciousness – with meanings being objects of a mental vision – with a usage theory of meaning: the sense of our expressions lies in their usage, and this is inseparable from social forms of communication and hence hearing.[22]

The transition from philosophy of consciousness to the paradigm of communication, such as has taken place in recent decades in various European and American schools of thought, means in every case a transition from the traditional favouring of vision to a new emphasis on hearing.

The 'Panopticon' and the surveillance society

That all of this is concerned not with philosophical glass bead games, but with a critique of culturally effective influences was shown by Michel Foucault. He demonstrated just how far vision has determined the institutions and architecture of modernity, and how liberation measures turned into surveillance and discipline scenarios.

The most striking example is Jeremy Bentham's 'Panopticon' from 1787, the ideal type of penal institution.[23] The cells are arranged in a circle around a central tower, and since – in contrast to earlier dungeons – they are afforded much light from outside, a single observation post in the centre suffices to watch over all the inmates perfectly. Every movement in the cells can be followed in silhouette. The Panopticon is perfect surveillance architecture. A very telling manifestation of the optical relationship to the world lies in this: an eye in the centre is the master of all appearances. What's more, it is revealing how light, the exalted symbol of the Enlightenment, functions here not as the medium of liberty, but as a trap, as a means of surveillance. The more light, visibility and transparency, the more surveillance, control and regimentation. This constitutes Bentham's ingenious exploitation of the dialectics of visibility. For Foucault it became a prime example of the 'Dialectic of the Enlightenment'. Visual primacy and the surveillance society form a consistent relationship. If you know you are exposed to continous transparency and supervisability, then you soon start to control yourself – in the end then even the one guard is no longer needed; rather we discipline ourselves, and the society of complete transparency becomes a society of complete surveillance.

Narcissus and Echo

Once you have been sensitized for connections of this type you discover them – with surprise and astonishment – in numerous older documents too. The dialectic, indeed the deadliness, of vision was already foretold to our culture in mythology – for instance in the story of Narcissus. When his mother asked the wise Tiresias whether her son would be blessed with a long life, Tiresias answers 'If he shall himself not know.'[24] – We know how the story ended. Narcissus died through the love of his own mirror image, which let him pay attention to nothing else. And yet that is only half of the story – significantly the only one commonly known, whereas the other has been kept quiet. For Narcissus fell victim to the deadly fascination of vision only after he had spurned, had failed to 'hear', the nymph Echo – that is, the mythical incarnation of pure tone. Thus mythology demonstrates to us in the story of Narcissus the double figure of vision's privilege and hearing's despisal along with its deadly consequences. It announces to the Occident the deadliness of a vision, which wants only to see and acts blindly towards hearing.

Greek and Jewish culture

Incidentally the Occident is familiar with a high ranking of hearing not only through its subsequently overshadowed early days, but because of its meeting with Jewish culture, which can be understood as an auditive culture. Jacob Taubes, who, as rabbi and occidental philosopher, was equally competent in both cultures, wrote 'if Hellas is called the "eye of the world", then perhaps it could be said that Israel is the "ear of the world"'.[25] Many of the present-day pleas for an auditive culture originate from intellectuals of Jewish provenance. Traditional visual primacy presumably contains an element of defence against Jewish culture – conversely the chance of a reconciliation might lie in the turn to hearing.

Reasons for caution

In spite of all plausible reasons to bid farewell to visual primacy and to plead for an auditive culture, a warning against a reversed one-sidedness should also be issued. With the transition to an auditive culture we associate the hope of putting behind us subject–object thinking and the twin pair of subjection of self and strangers, and of attaining structures of interposition, of symbiosis, of an ecological integration of human and world. But isn't a dialectic to be reckoned with here too? The culture of vision too had ultimately begun with promises of pure happiness – before then ending up in regimentation and self-endangerment. Might not something comparable await an auditive culture too?

The danger of subordination has already been pointed out. It is in no way completely distant. Heidegger's appeal to listen to Being (*Sein*) for example came dangerously close to being a call to heed the *Führer*. The other, much-taxed commendation of hearing, according to which genuine reason must be an interrogative, that is, a hearing, reason in contrast to calculating and calculative reason, is at the very least ambivalent. 'Interrogation' might well contain a reminder of hearing, but equally of interrogation by the police or a court of law, of the embarrassing questioning where one is – completely in the spirit of that imposing and calculative reason, which one wants to leave behind – compelled to answer. – It has to sound deeply concerning if the preachers of hearing are deaf to such ambivalences.

II. Typological differences between seeing and hearing

In this second section I want to set out some of the differences between the visual and auditory world which could both explain the motives for the traditional privileging of vision as well as make understandable the topical option for hearing.

1. The enduring – the disappearing

It is trivial to observe that vision refers primarily to spatial, hearing to temporal, phenomena. To look around oneself means to perceive spatial and corporal data which are available relatively constantly; to listen out, however, means to perceive sounds which will have disappeared in the next moment.

This difference has significant consequences. Imagine, just for once, that spoken words were not to fade away, but – similarly to visible things – persist further. No talking would then be possible, since all subsequent words would be absorbed by the continued presence of those preceding. This shows how consequential the difference is between optical and acoustic phenomena.

The mode of being of the visible and audible is fundamentally different. The visible persists in time, the audible, however, vanishes in time. Vision is concerned with constant, enduring being, audition, on the other hand, with the fleeting, the transient, the event-like.[26,27] Hence whereas rechecking, control and assurance belong to seeing, hearing demands acute attention to the moment, becoming aware of the one-off, the openness to the event. To vision belongs an ontology of being, to audition, on the other hand, a life born of the event. That is why vision also has an affinity to cognition and science, audition, on the other hand, to belief and religion.

Incidentally disparities which would otherwise remain incomprehensible also become explicable through such differences: for example, the fact that we take far more incisive measures when confronted with visible, rather than audible, environmental pollution. The visible is, after all, enduring, whereas the audible is temporary and represents a vanishing quantity in the literal sense. Apart from this our whole relationship to reality and actions is visually and objectively forged. We react to acoustic injuries only when they overstep the pain threshold and give rise to indignation and anger.

2. Distancing – insistency

Both hearing and vision are long-range senses, but vision is the sense which actually forms distance.[28] Vision sets things at a distance and holds them fixed in their place. It is the objectivizing sense through and through. In vision the world congeals into objects. Every glance has something of the look of Medusa: it causes objects to solidify, petrifies them. – It is completely different with hearing, which does not reduce the world to distance, but rather accommodates it. Whereas vision is a distancing sense, hearing is one of alliance.

From this it can be understood that vision was able to become the cognitive sense *par excellence*. It orders, distances and masters the world. Furthermore its data can always be rechecked and further investigated. For, since its objects are enduring, it can come back to them a second or third time. Hearing cannot do this. To listen out a second time would be of no use, the tone would have gone, the moment past, the chance wasted.

3. Inaffectuality – possibility

Vision is least influenced affectively by its objects. Tradition has always designated vision our most noble sense, and in so doing it had, alongside the universality of vision, its inaffectuality in view. In seeing we are affected least of all corporally.[29] In seeing we are the masters of the world.

Hearing, on the other hand, does not keep the world at a distance, but admits it. 'Tone penetrates, without distance.'[30] Such penetration, vulnerability and exposure are characteristic of hearing. We have eyelids, but not earlids. In hearing we are unprotected. Hearing is a sense of extreme possibility, and we cannot escape from acoustic congestion.[31] – That is why we are especially in need of protection acoustically.

4. Individuality – society

Vision is a sense of individuality, hearing is one of society. The evidence of vision as the sense for sovereign observation of the world extends from the ancient eulogy of theory and Leonardo da Vinci's description of the godlike, sovereign ocular human, through to the joy of viewing solitude. Vision always has something of the superior view at the end of the sixth day of creation – and of the solitude and self-sufficiency of the partaker of this view.

Hearing, on the other hand, is linked with people, with our social existence. We must hear so as to be receptive to language, and to be able to
speak ourselves. In this aspect, of course, audition has also been accorded
recognition in the tradition. If vision is designated the human's most noble
sense, then hearing – from Aristotle through to Kant and the present day –
has been esteemed as our most irreplaceable sense. But this recognition was
deceptive. For it was not hearing as such, but its servile function which was
valued. The eclipsing of the genuinely acoustic or sonorous dimension of
what is heard was in effect a precondition of this recognition. What matters
for linguistic communication is not the hearing of tones or sounds, but
solely the reception of linguistic meanings *by means of* the acoustic
signals.[32] The audible retreats behind its servile function for language. That
the phonetic elements as such mean absolutely nothing is in effect a
condition for their transmissive function.

III. Acoustic culture – against acoustic barbarism

1. Point of departure

Deliberations on an acoustic culture today take as their starting point the
particular unprotectedness of the sense of hearing and the structural
carelessness towards hearing of a visually shaped culture. The sensitivity of
the sense of hearing, which is, as such, admirable (physiologists tell us that
it is the most sensitive of all senses), turns into a blatant disadvantage in
surroundings which take no account of hearing. What could be a blessing
brings martyrdom and pain, makes us ill. It is this which initiatives in
favour of an environmental acoustics must oppose.

2. Equality of vision and audition

Alone the demand for equal rights for the acoustic will represent a
considerable reevaluation and challenge in a visually dominated culture. To
orthodox visualists it seems scandalous – and who would want to acquit
themselves completely of clinging to visual primacy here and there? Going
further, an occasional overloading of the acoustic side of the scales might
well be called for – as long as the concern is to redress the opposite
imbalance. (Something similar is familiar from the process of women's
emancipation; there too what demands equal rights must first of all seem to
be a one-sided challenge and in fact be prepared for one-sidedness from
time to time.) On the whole, however, the concern cannot be a primacy of
hearing, but merely a counter-manouevre against vision's conventional
hypertrophy, so as to attain a balanced equilibrium.[33]
  Hector Berlioz's project of a town in which music alone was to sound
cannot then be the paragon – 'Euphonia' was to be the name of this town

situated in the Harz mountains, its twelve thousand inhabitants were to dedicate themselves exclusively to their musical perfection.[34] For one-sided projects of this type Nietzsche once used the image of an 'inverse cripple'. Normally cripples are people who lack one thing whilst possessing everything else. Nietzsche calls an inverse cripple a person 'who ha[s] too little of everything and too much of one thing'. They consist, for example, of a single, giant eye or a gigantic ear. Nietzsche recounts how Zarathustra one day encountered an ear 'as big as a man'. Upon closer examination he then noticed that

> under the ear there moved something that was pitifully small and meagre and slender. And in truth, the monstrous ear sat upon a little, thin stalk – the stalk, however, was a man! By the use of a magnifying glass one could even discern a little, envious face as well; and one could discern, too, that a turgid little soul was dangling from the stalk. The people told me [. . .] that the great ear was not merely a man, but a great man, a genius. But I [. . .] held my belief that it was an inverse cripple, who had too little of everything and too much of one thing.[35]

Thus no one should argue for such inverse one-sidedness; we want to be ocular *and* auditive people – and not forgetting, of course, some other senses too.

3.   Reflexion of criteria

If the direction of the appeal is thus clear – it is a matter of revaluing audition – and the misunderstanding – that a predomination of hearing is intended – fended off, then it remains to name the demands and criteria of an auditive culture with equal rights.

Ideal claims?

In doing so one should not proceed from a false prerequisite, that from now on an ideal public world of sound is to be invented – as if we had a free hand, to wish everything anew and also to realize it straight away. The situation is not like this, and incidentally it would be – as paradoxical as this might at first sound – far more difficult to provide solutions for such an apparently ideal situation than for the real one. One should, however, make oneself aware of the reasons for this – if only because you can be sure to be confronted with such high-handed plans here and there.

Modern societies are highly differentiated and a variation in expectations, claims and schools of taste is legitimate and constitutive for them.[36] This cannot simply be brushed aside. In addition this plurality of demands is intensified further by receptive differences. What is harmony for one person can represent disharmony for another. One person's music – as Max Neuhaus put is – is another person's muzak.[37]

This variation in expectations cannot be avoided by a recourse to supposedly anthropological constants – as some would like to do in acoustic matters. Our cultural formations and differences are too strong and too legitimate for this. For example, for some people, consonances have in fact been poisoned since the emancipation of dissonance.

Whatever general norm one might want to suggest – whether a higher, spherically harmonic, or a lower, physiological one – it would always be fully abortive as a universal norm. In today's world there is no mono-criterion according to which the acoustic world could be ideally and universally constructed. The public sound world shaped according to a single paradigm would, as attractive as its model might at first appear to some, soon reveal itself to be the dictatorship of one group, of one taste, of one sonoric ideology to another ear.

Adjustment?

But of course the reverse, the straightforward acceptance of the factual sound world as it is, is also no solution. There is, however – even if I hesitate to say this – a cunning process which seems to teach us and commend to us this acceptation. I am thinking of the development of avant-garde music.

In the visual realm the futurists praised the beauty and speed of technical structures – say of the racing car.[38] And they were not alone in doing this: recent design on the whole had allowed itself to be inspired by technical innovations. Le Corbusier announced: 'We claim, in the name of the steamship, of the airplane, and of the motor-car, the right to health, logic, daring, harmony, perfection.'[39] In a similar manner the musical avant-garde attributed technical innovations and even downright noisemakers with exemplary function. Thus in 1913 Luigi Russolo praised in his manifesto *The Art of Noise* the fact that the noise of the city today triumphs over human sensibility, before then recommending to us as new acoustic pleasures the rumbling and rattling of machines, the harsh sound of mechanical saws and the orchestration of ironworks, power stations and underground railways.[40] John Cage finally proclaimed the equality of all sounds.

These recommendations of the musical avant-garde amount to the acceptation of sound and noise.[41] A lot could be said about this. I want to restrict myself here to a single aspect. Perhaps desperate attempts are to be seen in these tendencies to reconcile us once again with an acoustically intolerable world, to make it more bearable for us, and conversely make us more capable of living therein – say according to the motto 'If the music of your world doesn't suit you, then change your organs and your evaluations and you'll see that it works and helps.'

To be sure, art has always worked at altering our receptors and forms of reception, and this has influenced the everday world. In the case cited, however, it no longer seems to be about artistic extension, but only still about civilizational adjustment. How is this to be assessed? I fear that it is not mere adjustment, but over-adjustment which is being demanded of us, and, worse still (but in our culture not so unusual), an identification with the opponent – with that which is ruining us.

At any rate it seems certain to me that these experiments of the avant-garde cannot be used as a guideline for humane acoustic design and for an ethics of the acoustic environment.[42] Medical findings alone speak against this. Such avant-garde strategies can only be of supplementary interest, since we must of course always reckon with the chance that our aversions rest on stale motives which ought to be left behind.

Pragmatic perspectives

Our task, however, is not to invent an ideal situation, nor is it to leave a bad one as it is, rather it is to improve a damaging one. And the criteria-scenario for this is relatively simple. To determine what's best is always difficult, but to name something better when faced with a lamentable situation, such as the current one is, that can be done. To do this you need no absolute measures and no binding model; to do this plausible perspectives suffice.

4.   Guidelines

Reduction and differentiation

Certainly we need first of all a reduction in the amount of public noise. Unnecessary noise should be avoided. The manipulatory use of sound is the first to fall within this. I am thinking – under the heading acoustic environmental pollution – of muzak in department stores or of Brian Eno who lulls us at airports.[43]

The remaining, unavoidable amount of noise should – secondly – be consciously improved. Differentiation is a first means to do this. What other possibilities are on offer? Let us first of all talk about public areas. Here environmental acoustics and industrial design should be looking out for a desirable standard rather than for things wonderful and exquisite. Contemporary music might appeal as a paradigm, but it would be the wrong one. So as not to be misunderstood: I love this music, but it is an alternative to the everyday not an everyday standard. Certainly a transcendence of the existing and standardized belongs to our senses, and to hearing perhaps in particular measure. But to do this is not the responsibility of industry, it is rather that of art. Industry, on the other hand, which imposes sounds on us, which we all tend to have to hear, should offer us good standard sounds.

The distinction between public and private space is important in all of this. Sounds which are individually used can of course be made interesting; here industry can make use of opportunities for diversification. I somehow doubt that a shaver should play us hits, but why shouldn't the sound be consciously rugged for one model, gentle for the next, buzzing or gliding for a third? The social compatibility can be left here to electoral processes within the family circle.

But with sounds which affect public areas one should adhere strictly to the dictate of sensible noise avoidance, and the unavoidable noises should be so designed that they comply with the no-nuisance principle. Accordingly, sound which is less interesting for everyone is to be preferred to sound which is very interesting for a few. Obtrusion is to be avoided just as is pure monotony.

In public areas principles of solidarity apply. The freedom of one should not impair that of another, as Kant formulated it.[44] Translated into acoustic terms, the listening freedom of one may not impede the listening freedom of another. Democracy is a matter of being considerate already on the level of the senses.

The basic rule reads: what's unnecessary is to be avoided, what's necessary should be well designed. With this I am making an appeal not for noiselessness, but for the elimination of avoidable noise. We don't need to worry that absolute silence – which certainly would shock us[45] – could then break out. Absolute silence does not exist and we will not experience it in the present being.

Silent zones

A final point is particularly important to me: our senses need quiet zones too – as a complement to their natural curiosity. Hence acoustic frugality, wherever it is attainable, is necessary and beneficial. Indeed visually too we are living in a time of obvious excitedness and excessiveness. The aestheticization tendencies of recent years have spared hardly a corner of our being and our product world. Just as a reduction of this visual overstimulation is called for, one should not set about thoroughly acoustically styling everything. There should be no total acoustic styling as a complement to, or proof of equality against, rampant visual aestheticization! Acoustic improvement must rather take account of hearing's need for protection. Reduction of stimulation, the creation of areas without their own sound, and with little sound from elsewhere is needed. In the bombardment of the senses we need interruption zones, noticeable pauses, silence. – Botho Strauß once said of writers that they are 'in the midst of communication [. . .] responsible for [. . .] the interrupted contact, the dark phase, the break'.[46] I would wish that in future some acoustic designer would also feel responsible for this.

Notes

This essay was originally published as 'Auf dem Weg zu einer Kultur des Hörens?', in *Der Klang der Dinge. Akustik – eine Aufgabe des Design*, ed. Arnica-Verena Langenmaier (Munich: Silke Schreiber 1993), pp. 86–111. It has been revised for this volume. (First English publication.)

1. Joachim-Ernst Berendt, *Nada Brahma. The World is Sound*, trans. Helmut Brodigkeit (Rochester, Vt: Destiny Books 1987) as well as *Das dritte Ohr. Vom Hören der Welt* (Reinbek bei Hamberg: Rowohlt 1985). (Eng.: *The Third Ear. On Listening to the World*, Shaftesbury: Element 1988.)

2. Berendt, *Das dritte Ohr*, p. 283.

3. Friedrich Nietzsche, *Beyond Good and Evil*, trans. Walter Kaufmann (New York: Vintage 1966), pp. 182 and 183 resp. [246, 247].

4. Dietmar Kamper, 'Vom Hörensagen – Kleines Plädoyer für eine Sozio-Akustik', in *Das Schwinden der Sinne*, eds Dietmar Kamper and Christoph Wulf (Frankfurt a.M.: Suhrkamp 1984), pp. 112–114, here p. 112; Peter Sloterdijk, *Kopernikanische Mobilmachung und ptolemäische Abrüstung. Ästhetischer Versuch* (Frankfurt a.M.: Suhrkamp 1987), p. 95. Sloterdijk refers directly to Berendt in so doing (ibid., p. 85).

5. Cf. Marshall McLuhan and Bruce R. Powers, *The Global Village. Transformations in World Life and Media in the 21st Century* (New York: Oxford University Press 1989), p. 15.

6. Cf. Berendt, *Das dritte Ohr*, p. 59.

7. More notably in German given the similarity between *Hörigkeit* (subordination) and *Hören* (hearing) (trans.).

8. An overview of the subject area, suitable as an introduction, is provided by the reader *Welt auf tönernen Füßen. Die Töne und das Hören*, eds Kunst- und Ausstellungshalle der Bundesrepublik Deutschland (Göttingen: Steidl 1994).

9. Cf. Plato, *Republic*, 424c.

10. Hugo Kükelhaus and Rudolf zur Lippe, *Entfaltung der Sinne. Ein 'Erfahrungsfeld' zur Bewegung und Besinnung* (Frankfurt a.M.: Fischer Taschenbuch Verlag 1982), p. 120.

11. Egon Friedell, *Kulturgeschichte Griechenlands. Leben und Legende der vorchristlichen Seele* (Munich: Beck 1966), p. 138.

12. Cf. Franz Mayr, 'Wort gegen Bild. Zur Frühgeschichte der Symbolik des Hörens', in *Das Buch vom Hören*, eds Robert Kuhn and Bernd Kreutz (Freiburg i.Br.: Herder 1991), pp. 16–27.

13. Heraclitus, *Fragments*, Fragment 101a.

14. Ibid., Fragment 81a. – All the same Heraclitus himself still made use of musical metaphors from time to time, above all with a view to the cosmos.

15. Cf. Friedrich Nietzsche, *The Birth of Tragedy*, in *The Complete Works of Friedrich Nietzsche*, vol. 3, ed. O. Levy (Edinburgh/London: Foulis 1909), here pp. 111f.

16. Once you have started to listen out for the one-sided privileging of the visual amidst the dominant exclusion of the acoustic in our culture, then you discover this trap practically everywhere. If, for instance, you open a book with the title *Aesthetics of Architecture. Introduction to the Perception of Architecture* (Jörg Kurt Grütter, *Ästhetik der Architektur. Grundlagen der Architektur-Wahrnehmung*, Stuttgart: Kohlhammer 1987), then the talk there is in many chapters of culture and style, of aestheticization and beauty, surroundings and location, space and form, time and path, light and colour, part and whole. Only acoustics obviously comprise no part of this whole. Everywhere only visual elements are spoken of. Even when you finally come across a chapter 'Harmony', the talk is again only of visual harmony, of building proportions which are harmonically tuned. This can be explained historically: for the Pythagoreans musical relationships comprised the secret logic of the sensuous, and the Renaissance transferred this view to architecture. Just as Greek myth had already attributed to musical sounds the power to piece together stones into buildings (for example Orpheus is supposed to have erected a marketplace, and Amphion the walls of Thebes, by playing the lyre), early nineteenth-century thinkers understood architecture as 'frozen music' (Schelling, referring to the Amphion myth, called architecture 'solidified music', and Goethe, with reference to Orpheus, designated it a 'muted tonal art' and on another occasion 'mute music'; this before Schopenhauer criticized the excessive use of this topos, which Nietzsche nonetheless picked up again in designating Apollo's music 'architecture in tones' and remonstrated Wagner for fearing 'petrifaction [. . .] the transition of music into the architectonic'). But with all of this things remained a mere crypto-acoustics of the visual aspects of architecture. On the other hand, the factual acoustics of buildings was never dealt with sufficiently. Over and above the

dignified crypto-acoustics the day-to-day acoustics were forgotten – deep nobility and superficial ignoration formed a pair.

17. Thus Erwin Straus's pioneering work *On the Sense of the Senses. A Contribution to the Foundations of Psychology* (*Vom Sinn der Sinne. Ein Beitrag zur Grundlegung der Psychologie*, Berlin: Springer, 2nd edition, 1956), which offers brilliant analyses on the difference between the typicalities of visual and acoustic perception (pp. 390–409), of course contains in the index the heading 'vision', but no heading 'hearing'. Even in more recent times, when a fundamental critique of traditional conceptions of perception came about, a revision of the visual primacy – this Ur-dogma of our traditional doctrine of the senses – could still remain unaffected, in fact it could even come to a renewed securing of this primacy. The example for this is Merleau-Ponty. Although he pointed out to us the fundamental importance of perceptive feats for our existence and our thinking, and showed how the world is only given to us at all because we are corporal, sensible beings, even with all these revisions he left the fundamental primacy of vision untouched. Already the *Phenomenology of Perception*, trans. Colin Smith (London: Routledge and Kegan Paul 1962 [1945]) contains in the index the heading 'vision', but nothing of 'hearing', 'tone', 'note', 'sound', 'ear' or the like. In the later text *L'œil et l'esprit* (Paris: Gallimard 1964) Merleau-Ponty says, following on from Paul Valéry, that the painter brings in his body (ibid., p. 16) – but this body again remains for Merleau-Ponty only a potency of vision. The intellect remains coupled to the eye, this oldest, most traditional link remains intact. Only the relationship between visibility and invisibility thematized in Merleau-Ponty's late philosophy seems to give occasion for a transcendence of visual primacy. But this again is concerned only with a transcendence of the visual capacity, not, however, of the occidental prejudice, according to which all important relationships are to be dealt with in the context of visibility. The visible is transcended only towards the invisible, not say towards the audible or inaudible, tangible or intangible. In his criticism of Descartes Merleau-Ponty says very aptly that Descartes's theory was, like every theory of painting, a metaphysics (ibid., p. 42). But Merleau-Ponty never became aware of the converse: that metaphysics is a theory of visibility – and that what might matter is to go beyond this axiom. Even where Merleau-Ponty on one occasion speaks of voices he refers (following André Malraux) only to that of silence, namely to the 'mute language' of painting, that is, to the realm of visibility once again.

18. Cf. R. Murray Schafer, *Klang und Krach. Eine Kulturgeschichte des Hörens* (Frankfurt a.M.: Athenäum 1988), p. 167.

19. Romanticism – in contrast to the Enlightenment, which favoured light and vision – had already turned to the night and hearing. For Herder hearing was of higher standing than vision, and for Schlegel the sense of hearing was the 'most noble sense' (Friedrich Schlegel, *Philosophische Vorlesungen [1800–1807]*, in *Kritische Friedrich-Schlegel-Ausgabe*, ed. Ernst Behler, vol. 12, Munich: Schöningh 1964, p. 346). Following this hearing was even able to advance to being a model of philosophical activity. Thus Nietzsche said that the philosopher seeks 'to allow all the tones of the world to resonate within him and to express this entire sound outwardly in concepts' (Friedrich Nietzsche, 'Nachgelassene Fragmente. Herbst 1869 bis Ende 1874', in Nietzsche, *Sämtliche Werke, Sämtliche Werke. Kritische Studienausgabe in 15 Bänden*, eds Giorgio Colli and Mazzino Montinari, Munich: Deutscher Taschenbuch Verlag 1980, vol. 7, p. 442 [Summer 1872–Start 1873]). Likewise the hermeneutic tradition from Schleiermacher to Gadamer advocated the 'primacy of hearing over seeing' (Hans-Georg Gadamer, *Truth and Method*, trans. Joel Weinsheimer and Donald G. Marshall, London: Sheed and Ward 1989, p. 462). – The best survey of the questioning of visual primacy in the twentieth century is provided by Martin Jay's *Downcast Eyes: The Denigration of Vision in Twentieth-Century French Thought* (Berkeley: California University Press 1994); see also *Modernity and the Hegemony of Vision*, ed. David Michael Levin (Berkeley: University of California Press 1993); Don Ihde, *Listening and Voice: A Phenomenology of Sound* (Athens, Ohio: Ohio University Press 1976).

20. Cf. Martin Heidegger, *Platons Lehre von der Wahrheit. Mit einem Brief über den 'Humanismus'* (Bern: Francke, 2nd edition, 1954).

21. Heidegger most clearly formulated this opposition of auditive thinking and traditional thinking of reason at the end of his essay on Nietzsche's words 'God is dead'. The opposition

named is grasped by him as being in effect the opposition of thinking and non-thinking: 'And the ear of our thinking? Does it still not hear the scream? It will overhear this until it begins to think. Thinking first begins when we have learned to experience that the reason which has been glorified for centuries is the most obstinate adversary of thinking.' (Martin Heidegger, *Holzwege*, Frankfurt a.M.: Klostermann 1950, pp. 246f.) The 'reason which has been glorified for centuries' is precisely visually determined reason. This Heidegger contrasts with an interrogative (*vernehmendes*) or a contemplative (*besinnliches*) thinking. In *On the Way to Language* Heidegger designates hearing as 'the proper gesture of the thinking now requisite' (Martin Heidegger, *Unterwegs zur Sprache*, Pfullingen: Neske 1959, p. 180, cf. also pp. 176 and p. 179 [Eng.: *On the Way to Language*, trans. Peter D. Hertz and Joan Sambaugh, New York: Harper & Row 1971]).

22. Cf. Ludwig Wittgenstein, *Philosophical Investigations*, trans. G.E.M. Anscombe (New York: Macmillan 1958).

23. Cf. Michel Foucault, *Discipline and Punish. The Birth of the Prison*, trans. Alan Sheridan Smith (London: Penguin 1979), pp. 200ff.

24. Ovid, *Metamorphoses*, III 348.

25. Jakob Taubes, *Abendländische Eschatologie* (Bern: Francke 1947), p. 15. – Thorleif Boman elaborated on this opposition in remarkable detail and very knowledgeably. (Thorleif Boman, *Das hebräische Denken im Vergleich mit dem griechischen*, Göttingen: Vandenhoeck & Ruprecht, 5th edition, 1968 [Eng.: *Hebrew Thought Compared with Greek*, trans. Jules L. Moreau, London: SCM Press 1960]). He writes: 'The singular features and particularities of both [of the Greek and Hebrew modes of thought] are ultimately related to the fact that the Greeks experienced being by seeing, the Hebrews by hearing and feeling' (p. 9). Boman comes to the result 'that for the Hebrew hearing had to become the most important sense for experiencing reality [. . .], for the Greek vision. (Or *perhaps* the other way round: Because the Greeks were predominantly visually, and the Hebrews auditively inclined, the apprehension of reality of the two peoples gradually shaped itself so differently.)' (Ibid., p. 181.)

26. Hegel apportioned the phenomenal characteristics of tone with a speculative interpretation. To him hearing was the far more intellectual sense when compared with vision. Tone was namely to contain a double negation of externality and thus represents the beginning of a transition to inwardness, to subjectivity. For, first of all, in order to give off a sound, an object must vibrate in itself (first negation); and, secondly, the tone perishes with its sounding, ceases as something external (second negation). It can – just like a thought – linger on only in inwardness, in the medium of subjectivity. Thus in the acoustic sphere a transition from the material to the intellectual takes place (cf. Georg Wilhelm Friedrich Hegel, *Aesthetics. Lectures on Fine Art*, vol. 2, trans. T.M. Knox, Oxford: Clarendon Press 1975, pp. 889f.). – Adorno, again proceeding from the fact that tones, unlike visual phenomena, free themselves from the object, saw the advantage of music in that it is not, as is vision, a medium of dominance, but one of freedom: music is 'free from the start of that bind to objectness: the ear does not perceive the things. Hence it must neither undo objectness as something heteronomous to it, nor retract its dominance over the objects.' (Theodor W. Adorno, 'Zum Verhältnis von Malerei und Musik heute', in Adorno, *Gesammelte Schriften*, vol. 18, Frankfurt a.M.: Suhrkamp 1984, pp. 140–148, here p. 145.)

27. Correspondingly vision directs itself to attributes of things, hearing, however, to the activity of things. Erwin Straus said about this: 'In seeing we grasp the skeleton of things, in hearing their pulse' (Straus, *Vom Sinn der Sinne*, p. 398).

28. Cf. Dieter Hoffmann-Axthelm, *Sinnesarbeit. Nachdenken über Wahrnehmung* (Frankfurt a.M.: Campus 1984), p. 36.

29. Cf. Immanuel Kant, *Anthropologie in pragmatischer Hinsicht* (1798), A 50. (Eng.: *Anthropology from a Pragmatic Point of View*, trans. Mary J. Gregor, The Hague: Nijhoff 1974.)

30. Helmuth Plessner, *Anthropologie der Sinne*, in Plessner, *Gesammelte Schriften* (Frankfurt a.M.: Suhrkamp 1980), vol. 3, pp. 317–393, here p. 344.

31. Elias Canetti designated the process of hearing as bordering on rape.

32. Herder constitutes an exception. According to him hearing is not merely a necessary medium of communication, rather it is, prior to this, constitutive for linguistic activity as such.

33. Insofar as the sense of balance is concerned with the ear, a particularly attentive listener could of course object that the demand for a balanced culture of eye and ear underhandedly gives preference to the logic of the ear. This would, however, be done in a reasonable sense, and no longer an oppressive one.

34. Hector Berlioz, *Euphonie, ou La ville musicale. Nouvelle de l'avenir* (Paris 1852).

35. Friedrich Nietzsche, *Thus Spoke Zarathustra.* trans. R.J. Hollindale (London: Penguin 1961), p. 160.

36. Cf. my *Unsere postmoderne Moderne* (Weinheim: VCH 1987; Berlin: Akademie Verlag, 5th edition, 1997).

37. Cf. Max Neuhaus, 'Klanggestaltung von Signalen und Sirenen', in *Der Klang der Dinge. Akustik – eine Aufgabe des Design*, ed. Arnica-Verena Langenmaier (Munich: Silke Schreiber 1993), pp. 62–76, here p. 62.

38. 'We declare that the splendour of the world has been enriched with a new form of beauty, the beauty of speed. A race-automobile adorned with great pipes like serpents with explosive breath . . . a race-automobile which seems to rush over exploding power is more beautiful than the *Victory of Samothrace.*' (Marinetti, *The Foundation and Manifesto of Futurism*, 1909. Quoted from: *Theories of Modern Art. A Source Book by Artists and Critics*, ed. Herschel B. Chipp, Berkeley/London: University of California Press 1968, p. 286.)

39. Le Corbusier, *Towards a New Architecture* (Oxford: Butterworth 1987), p. 19.

40. Russolo was influenced by Marinetti. One of his compositions is significantly entitled *Convegno d'automobili e d'aeroplani.*

41. Helmuth Plessner's judgment in this respect was harsh: musical modernity does not shy 'before aesthetic suicide' (Plessner, *Anthropologie der Sinne*, p. 350).

42. It is also worth thinking about that muzak too was to begin with a positively intended invention of the avant-garde. Schafer named the origin: Erik Satie's *Musique d'ameublement*, which was first performed in 1920 in a Parisian gallery and was meant as 'entertainment during an interval'; the spectators were supposed to walk around and not be consciously aware of the music, but perceive it solely as decoration (cf. Schafer, *Klang und Krach*, p. 149).

43. There has been a special guide to London since 1991 listing more than four hundred restaurants, pubs and shops in which you are not burdened by muzak.

44. Kant defined the purpose of civic legislation as 'freedom for each man, his happiness itself, in whatever he might set it, to ensure that he does not impair the equally lawful freedom of another.' (Immanuel Kant, Letter to Heinrich Jung-Stilling, March 1789, in Kant, *Briefwechsel*, Hamburg: Meiner, 3rd edition, 1986, pp. 367f., here p. 368.)

45. Pascal spoke of the shock when faced with the eternal silence of infinite space: 'Le silence éternel de ces espaces infinis m'effraie.' (Blaise Pascal, *Pensées*, in Pascal, *Œuvres Complètes*, ed. Louis Lafuma, Paris: Editions du Seuil 1963, p. 528, no. 201.)

46. Botho Strauß, 'Die Erde – ein Kopf', in *Büchner-Preis-Reden 1984–1994*, ed. Deutsche Akademie für Sprache und Dichtung (Stuttgart: Reclam 1994), pp. 126–137, here p. 130.

10

ARTIFICIAL PARADISES?

Considering the World of Electronic Media – and Other Worlds

People dream of paradise. This dream is a double one: it refers backwards to a lost state from the beginning of time, it aims forwards at a new, utopian state of happiness, at a new paradise, one to be achieved through human history. From Kleist comes the famous phrase that we must 'eat from the tree of knowledge' a second time in order to win back paradise; this is to be 'the final chapter in the history of the world'.[1]

Has this chapter begun today with electronic media? Have we, in the meantime, eaten so successfully from the tree of information technology knowledge that now – in keeping with the turn of the millennium – the 'final chapter in the history of the world' is commencing, bearing the auspicious title 'electronic paradise'? Many seem to think so.

Marshall McLuhan, the original electronic media theorist, had already in 1964 spoken of how the new media would bring us 'a Pentecostal condition of universal understanding and unity'.[2] Henceforth we would be able to understand one another in the universal language of electronic communication. We would then regain the state which preceded the building of the Tower of Babel – thus, although not paradise as such, a nonetheless comparatively paradisiacal state.

For other theorists this doesn't go far enough. Ihab Hassan hoped in 1975 for the fulfilment through the electronic media world of the old gnostic dream of universal communication not only between people, but between man, matter and cosmos altogether.[3] The new paradisiacal state is to be more perfect still than the old one, since in it everything material is to be transposed into the spiritual. We humans will in the end have become not mere original humans, but angels, purely spiritual beings.

The deliberations by Hans Moravec, perhaps the most suggestive AI enthusiast in the USA, currently point in this direction too. Moravec thinks that we should transfer our mind on to a data-processing machine – he calls this 'downloading'.[4] In this way 'our thoughts could be completely freed from every trace of our original body and of any body altogether. The bodyless intellect arising in this way would be [. . .] something wonderful with respect to the clarity of its thoughts and the depth of its insight.'[5] It would no longer be 'human', since it would have overcome the body and attained a purely immaterial condition. – Thus, in this most advanced branch of research too, the transition to pure intelligence constitutes the goal.

Is this a vision only of the most recent technologies? No, it was already the innermost dream of modern science. In its beginnings Francis Bacon had spoken of how the mind's work would in future 'be done as if by machinery',[6] and Descartes believed the new science 'would facilitate our enjoyment of the fruits of the earth and all goods we find there'[7] – right through to the overcoming of the usual *conditio humana*.[8] Medicine, for example, was to find not only antidotes to various illnesses, but eventually a remedy against death. Through the new science and its technology people would be able to know everything, put everything right, arrange everything in accord with the intellect. Even then people had started to dream that in the end there would be no more frail humans, but only pure intelligences.

Today, as I've said, these hopes appear to be being fulfilled – or even over-fulfilled – through the media technologies which emerged from that modern science in a sort of quantum leap. Since electronically we seem to be becoming not just an angel's, but even God's, equal. The divine mode of being has been traditionally defined as 'interminabilis vitae tota simul et perfecta possessio', that is, as the 'all-embracing, instantaneous and perfect possession of an unlimited life'.[9] Something like this is supposed to be being afforded us today telecommunicatively. For amidst the league of electronic media all the realities of past and present are becoming accessible and all thinkable forms of creativity are becoming possible interactively. The electronic Superhighway will, so they say, make highly active 'couch commanders' out of passive 'couch potatoes' – who until now had moved as far as the fridge at best – in an inexhaustible reservoir of interactive information and entertainment possibilities. Al Gore is obviously understating things when he far too prosaically calls the data highway just an instrument which 'promotes democracy, saves human lives and creates new jobs'. He should have spoken about new creativity by means of computer graphics and computer animation, about the morphing of the spouse or the real-time simulation of coitus, about the extension of consciousness through multimedia, or about the trend towards virtual experience also in the realms of taste, smell and touch. For here too, so we are assured, the first initial successes will be followed by the universe of possibilities, a ubiquity of fulfilled experiences – that is, according to the old formula, a divine condition.

Baudelaire had spoken of 'artificial paradises' in 1860, of 'exceptional states of the mind and of the senses', in which the 'penchant for the infinite' awakes.[10] But he complained of the insufficiency of traditional means for this. Opium and hashish had the disadvantage that the hallucinations are considered real and are linked with a weakening of the will. – On the other hand, how greatly would Baudelaire have admired electronic media, which perfectly suggest a reality without denying their own artificiality, in which the virtuality of the hallucination is far more transparent and the freedom of imaginative play remains intact?

Put briefly, Baudelaire's dream, the dream of the modern age, the dream of
gnosis and humanity's dream of paradise on earth, appear to be being
fulfilled, now and in the future, in the artificial paradises of electronic
media. – And if some things are being redeemed in ways other than
expected, then one shouldn't complain: redemptions never occur in a 1:1
relation. Moreover, potential deficits in redemption are compensated for by
unexpected surpluses in redemption.

Following these preliminary remarks I would like, in the first section of
my exposition, to set out some thoughts on the concepts of the world and
artificial worlds, in the second section to expand on the phenomenological
peculiarities of electronic-media worlds, and in the third section to set out
several counter-accentuations.

I.   Worlds between naturalness and artificiality

What are worlds? And what are artificial worlds? How do these relate to
non-artificial worlds?

The world is – according to Kant – the 'sum-total of all appearances'.[11]
However, such worlds of appearance can be very different in type. Their
typology depends on the respective guiding basic forms of intuition and
conceptuality. These will impress themselves on all objects of the world
concerned. Sensory beings live in worlds considerably different from those
of intellectual beings.

And what are artificial worlds? You will say, worlds contrasting with
natural worlds. What, however, is a natural world? The world of physics
maybe – and are we to understand by this the world of Aristotelian,
Galilean, or quantum physics? Or is the natural world the world of
experienced nature? Or the everyday environment?

1.   World as an interpretative complex

Modern philosophy – in its hermeneutic just as in its analytic versions –
speaks of a multitude of worlds. This is a consequence of the fact that a
direct, an interpretation-free, access to reality doesn't exist. And this is not
because such access is denied to us, but because the seemingly self-evident
idea of an interpretation-free access to reality is in truth contradictory in
itself and untenable. Whoever advocates this thesis of a world-in-itself does
something other than they believe. They believe they are talking about a
world independent of interpretation. But they obviously give this world a
certain rendering at the same time – in the very sense of its transcendence
over all interpretations. They thus make anything but an interpretation-free
statement. This dilemma – that even the intended independence from
interpretation can occur only as interpretation – cannot, as a matter of
principle, be escaped from. The postulated world-in-itself too is

unavoidably a world *interpreted* and *described* as transcending description. And other than in interpretations and descriptions of this type there can be no conception of the world – no matter how it may be comprised in detail. Interpretation or description thus proves to be the more fundamental horizon, *within* which alone apprehensions of reality or references to reality altogether are possible. Put briefly: not realism, but interpretationism is the principle of our cognition.[12]

I have just presented this view that the idea of a strictly independent reality-in-itself is untenable in connection with recent hermeneutic and analytic philosophy – following on from Rorty or Goodman[13] – but this view is of far older origin. It was already the great doctrine of Nietzsche, whose principal understanding of man was as an *animal fingens* – as a being which creates fictions;[14] it was the doctrine of Hegel, who showed that the distinction between in-itself and for-us, between object and consciousness, falls within consciousness itself;[15] and it was of course already the doctrine of Kant, who comprehended our reality as a construction within the framework of transcendental prerequisites (forms of intuition and categories);[16] indeed this view already belonged in fact to the whole approach of the scientific modern age, which from Descartes onwards aimed not for the representation of an existing reality, but for – *more geometrico* – a construction of reality.[17]

But back to the present day: today's philosophy considers complete worlds – be it the everyday world, or the physical world, or a literary world – to be constructions and, to this extent, at least in part to be artefacts. Artistic or fictional feats inhere in all worlds, starting with the fundamental schemata of perception, via modes of symbolization, through to the forms of evaluation of objects. And it cannot be said that any of these procedures and criteria could be straightforwardly derived from a reality-in-itself. – All worlds are basically artificial worlds.

2. *Degrees of artificiality*

But even if artificiality thus prevails as a matter of principle, the distinction between more natural and more artificial worlds retains a valid sense on a subordinate level. Some worlds are obviously more artificial than others. The world of novels, for instance, is in general more artificial than the everyday one, and our everyday world is more artificial than the world of archaic forms of life. The telephone, means of mass transport, fitness centres – certainly defining elements of our everyday culture – are obviously not natural products, but artefacts to a high degree. But the archaic world too had its artificiality – its inventions and rituals. It too was not simply given over to nature, nor did it simply arise from nature.

Generally this means that one can always go back from something artificial to something a little less artificial, to something comparatively natural. But this too will present itself as something artificial when faced with something more natural. What's called 'artificial' is often quite simply the new in contrast to the old – but this, in its turn, was already something artificial compared with a predecessor. Our woods and meadows, for example, seem natural to us, but they are highly artificial compared with the primeval forest of the Tertiary – whereas they do look natural compared with the Manhattan skyscraper-jungle, which will of course in turn appear natural in comparison to an artificial computer simulation of the city of tomorrow.

In short, artificiality and naturalness are reflexive concepts. They denote not objects, but aspects, perspectives, relations. That's why one and the same object can appear to be natural in one respect and artificial in another. There exist no artificial and natural worlds *per se*, but only comparatively natural or artificial worlds. Artificiality and naturalness form – just as other reflexive concepts too – a pair.

3.   Double reflexion as a duty

These determinations must then also be treated as coupled. The logic of the expressions 'artificial' and 'natural' demands that when speaking of one side the other must always be considered at the same time. This seems to me – and this is what I'm leading to with these points – to be particularly of importance with regard to the current talk of artificial media worlds. You can only talk about these worlds satisfactorily if, at the same time, you cast an eye on those worlds from which they set themselves apart – and which have already changed conceptually as well as factually merely as a result of the advent of artificial worlds. Later on I will expand on such recursive effects in detail, for example by asking how the coordinates of everyday perception alter under the influence of media, or how virtual and real reality influence one another.

In emphasizing this duty to double reflexion I am distancing myself from one-sided descriptions such as the simple plea for the complete transition to virtual electronic worlds. Whoever demands such things fails, in my view, to recognize the tandem nature of the development and impregnation of one strand by the other. The fascination of artificial worlds is always an anti-fascination with the banal accustomed reality too, and the joy of the new worlds is a joy of over-fulfilment, outdoing or supersession of traditional desires. Conversely, numerous elements of the accustomed reality are experiencing a change and re-evaluation in contrast with the electronic worlds. The old forms of experience and perception don't simply die out, as some electronics enthusiasts propagandize or wish.[18] The Gutenberg galaxy is not just fizzling out, but is changing its meaning. Book readers are not simply fossils in the electronic age, as the propagandists of a new monoculture of artificial worlds – paradoxically in books – would have us believe.[19]

Only in a double, in a dialectic consideration of the new and old worlds – such is my thesis – can current conditions be adequately grasped. Of course, whoever wants to conceptualize the present day (and as a philosopher one is always mindful of Hegel's dictum that the 'task of philosophy' is 'to comprehend *what is*', to comprehend one's own time '*in thoughts*'[20]), of course whoever plans to do such things must above all grasp the determination of our world through media. But such reflexion liquidizes itself wherever it is thought that it will succeed by merely acclimatizing to the new media methods and by just stringing together incoherent scraps of ideas. Some new media theorists, however, actually seem to reach the point of delirium and to want to engender a lack of awareness in what they write and say (so that their thesis – that rational reflexion is outdated on principle in the age of electronic media – is proved at least in their own doings).[21] I approach things differently. I stick – rather more conservatively towards the value of reflection – to efforts toward rational clarification and insight. This seems to me, precisely in the face of ecstatic tendencies toward the dissolution of the discursive, to be not outmoded but rather imperative.

II. On the phenomenology of electronic worlds

In this second section I want to try to name some characteristics of media worlds. In doing so I proceed phenomenologically – not, however, transcendentally phenomenologically like Husserl, but more perceptively phenomenologically like Merleau-Ponty and several others who, proceeding from phenomenology, arrived at aesthetic thinking. – Wherein lies the novelty and alterity, the fascination – and in particular the aesthetic fascination – of electronic worlds?

1. Television: an unusual physics

Let's start with television, the medium known to us all. It is a most amazing experience when – say in the trailer for a programme – a stripe rears towards us from the depths of the picture space, then transforms itself into a three-dimensional body, which, as if by a ghostly hand, is subsequently raised, rotated, flipped and turns into a two-dimensional structure. Perhaps we are used to such processes by now; to begin with, however, they were absolutely fascinating. Things like this don't exist in the real world. Or, put more precisely: such stripes, bodies and surfaces are also known to us from the real world, but there they are subject to different laws from those in the space of electronic media. The physics of matter doesn't permit such weightless movements and enchanting transformations. In reality three-dimensional things can only seemingly, not really, become two- or one-dimensional. This is possible more in mathematical construction, to which the world of electronic imagery is closer than it is to the everyday world.

On the other hand, with such methods the media physics lives up to old aesthetic dreams. Surrealism, for example, had dreamt of such transformations, but was only able to realize them rudimentarily and relatively clumsily. Electronic image manipulation, on the other hand, executes them filled with elegance and as a matter of course. How perfectly, for instance, would Yves Tanguy have been able to give form to his visions with today's electronic equipment![22]

If one were to name the phenomenal peculiarities of the electronic world, then the talk would be primarily of lightness, of free mobility, of the free play with dimensions and forms. Movements in the synthetic picture space resemble those in conditions of weightlessness. Bodies have lost their inertia, resistiveness and massivity. They have become light; they float and carry out bizarre and enthralling motions. The electronic picture space has something of the weightlessness of a spaceship. Free mutations take the place of constancy, and the contents can be modelled at will. Moreover the appearances, even when they relate to things real, retain everywhere the flair of the pictorially virtual. They might suggest reality, but this suggestion is linked with an index of freedom throughout – everything could also be or become different. If there is a 'lightness of being' anywhere, then it's in electronic space.

2.   *The digital ontology of the PC world*

Hyperspeed

Let's move on to a different device, to the foremost fossil of our epoch, to the PC. What's fascinating here, above all, is the speed with which even the largest sets of data can be processed. In a few minutes, for example, the works of many occidental philosophers can be scoured for a particular term, and you get the source references displayed in full. With the old cultural technique of reading you would have needed years for this and the error rate would have been high.

The momentariness of the appearance is similarly astonishing. All of a sudden the whole set of data is there, and all of a sudden it's gone. The world of electronic media is a world of instantaneity. Not only does the arithmetic unit operate binarily, the ontology too is binary. The signs are not formed slowly as in an organic process, but are instantly to hand. – And, just as instantly, they've vanished.

The completeness of this disappearance is as unusual as anything at all. From the likes of you and me there remains at least a corpse, of the cigarette the ashes, and of petrol the stench. But here everything is completely clean, clinically clean. The appearance was already the entire substance, there's nothing behind it and nothing to follow. There is only the opposition of being and non-being. But even this is only a momentary one. The touch of a key – and what was just caused to disappear is immediately and agelessly there again. Even years later. There is no ageing here, rather everything retains the freshness of its first day, of the original. The whole world is of razor-sharp precision and extreme lightness at the same time. – Certainly a fascinating world.

Beyond everyday ontology

Let us consider additionally the form of existence of documents. They exist twice over: analogue on the monitor screen and digital in the medium of memory. Most PC users are familiar only with the analogue form of existence. They move themselves around the user environment. The software, on the other hand, is to them a book with seven seals, a black box. Few of us have a command of programming languages. Most are digital illiterates – a group to which I also belong.

The named doubling of known forms of appearance and hidden structure seems to be analogous to conditions in the real world. We know and value flowers for example. But few of us know how these are constituted in their physical and chemical structure. The inner life of phenomena is a black box for us in everyday life too – not only in the electronic world. All the same there exists a major difference between the two worlds. If you leave a document (that is, an object of the electronic world), then it remains not in analogue but in digital form in the medium of memory. If, however, you turn your back on objects of the everyday world then these remain intact in the phenomenal form. Here the phenomenal form is the enduring form of the appearances. On the other hand, in the realm of data the analogue mode of being is only a temporary state. The true existence is analogue in one case, digital in the other.

But what does 'true existence' mean here? Can the distinction between appearance and essence be retained at all in the electronic realm? For the everyday world this difference is entirely meaningful. The classic ontology – the doctrine of being and the appearances – was an unflinching treatment of this relationship.

In the electronic world, on the other hand, the distinction between appearance and essence is invalidated. Monitor existence and memory existence are completely congruent. The appearance is a perfect representation of the 'essence'. It lacks nothing. The 'essence' contains nothing more and nothing less than the appearance. The whole factual content is identical, the form of presentation alone is different – sometimes analogue, sometimes digital.

In fact even more: the essence is even subject to the operations in the realm of appearance. For if you alter a document then you alter – in a strict 1:1 relation – its 'essence' too. The essence is a copy of the appearance. In the everyday world things are the other way round: the appearance is a copy – mostly a bad one – of the essence.

That in the electronic world there exists no matter of fact difference between appearance and essence deprives every application of the conventional ontology to electronic media of its basis. By relying on the classical categories one could only misunderstand or misrepresent electronic worlds. The traditional ontology had always criticized the appearances in the name of the difference between essence and appearance. The essence was supposed to be the paragon, the appearance merely its imperfect realization. To be sure, classic ontology had also dreamt of the appearances and essences becoming identical, and in its final phase – with Hegel – it believed it was witnessing the entry of this identity before it. In the electronic world, however, such an identity exists from the start – without any differences ever having been to hand, and without an inadequacy of the appearances having been able to act as a spur or impetus in the direction of identity. Appearance and essence are identical at every moment. – From which, incidentally, it follows that the digital illiterate, the merely analogue PC user, is in the right too; he actually lacks nothing.

Unforeseeable extensiveness

Is the electronic world, because it lacks the *vertical* difference of being and appearance, perhaps worse off than the everyday world? Quite the contrary: in a *horizontal* direction it possesses an openness for alterations, mutations and innovations unknown to the everyday world. On the Internet data alliances can proliferate from one moment to the next, regenerate themselves; they can be combined and hybridized. You can amend a single document, can modify its manner of representation, can cross it with other documents, can network it in various ways. Think of hypertext.

The electronic world might well be completely flat, but it is an infinitely wide world.[23] To it belong an unforeseeable multitude of lateral connections and extensions – from the proliferation of the same, through to complex networkings. The digital's room to unfold is inexhaustible.

Mediality and philosophy

Since this ontology of electronic media is of the utmost philosophical interest I shall interpose a digression. The media-ontology is obviously anti-classical, is of a quite different type from the conventional everyday ontology and its noble form, the metaphysical ontology. Instead of a hierarchically organized world, it unfolds a world of lateral connections, of crossings and networkings, as well as of rhizomatic proliferations and transformations. Changeability dominates in place of stability, surface instead of depth, possibility instead of actuality.

These traits converge in an astonishing way with some of the most advanced descriptions of reality which have been put forward from the philosophical side in recent decades, and in particular from poststructuralist authors such as Jacques Derrida and Gilles Deleuze.[24] According to them, reality and rationality are characterized by transitionality, by openly networked chains, permanent shifts of meaning and an on-principle incon-cludability in processes of meaning. Derrida and Deleuze have been unfurling this view since the late sixties – that is, shortly after the beginning of the spread of electronic media. In so doing Derrida has made explicit reference to this context.[25]

These new philosophical descriptions of reality imply an incisive correction of traditional philosophy. Faced by media the fundamental significance of mediality within philosophy has been recognized for the first time and philosophy has thereby been freed from one of its oldest mistakes. For philosophy had traditionally believed itself to be completely free from a shaping of thought through the media used – be it orality or be it textuality. The meaning was supposed to exist primarily in a medium-free originary state and to experience only subsequently a dissemination and alienation through being fed into a medium – that's how one thought from Plato through to Hegel and far beyond.[26] Since the mid-sixties, however, Marshall McLuhan's media-related dictum that 'the medium is the message' has also been made fruitful in a philosophically relevant way. Eric Havelock, McLuhan's Toronto colleague in ancient philology, was the first to do this by demonstrating the potency of the Greek alphabet in shaping the development of Greek philosophy.[27] The effect was then pioneering as Jacques Derrida proved that meaning is always due to the inscription in media, and that the mediality doesn't first ensue subsequently and exter-nally, but is constitutive for meaning from the outset, that it has *productive* significance for processes of meaning. Meaning is not, as the metaphysical tradition had thought, 'tarnished' or faked through the connection with the materiality of the medium; rather without this connection there would be no meaning at all. The pure, sign-free meaning which the tradition had dreamt of was a phantom. Today this is – thanks to media experience – the state of reflection in philosophy.

Following this digression on the central importance of the subject of media for philosophy I return to the course of the considerations of this second section in which, commencing from television and the PC, I attempted to take a few steps towards tracing the phenomenology of electronic worlds. Technological development is continuing today with new processes such as multimedia, the Internet, the World Wide Web and cyberspace.[28] Here too hyperspeed, lightness, transformability and virtuality are characteristic. On top of this comes an extension of the scale of participating senses. Alongside the visual enter the auditive and tactile, and experts in this field assure us that in regard to the senses of smell and taste there exist only temporary factual, but in principle no, limits.[29] – For present purposes I would like to leave it with the points named. I will supplement further aspects in the next section, in which I want to look on the other side and portray the repercussions of media worlds for forms of experience in the non-media world.

III.   Repercussions of electronic worlds for the everyday world

How does the influence of electronic worlds alter our understanding of everyday reality and our day-to-day experience of the world?

Some say that through the advent of artificial worlds our experience simply becomes broader and richer. But whoever talks like this overlooks the fact that the addition of the new always changes the old too. For instance, the extension of possibilities is always linked with a devaluation of the singular possibility: this one possibility no longer matters so much, since it can always be evaded, other possibilities can be turned to; the mere accumulation theorem calculates too simply. The preceding possibilities are changed qualitatively; their arrangement and their standing experience modifications.

The changes today are mainly of a dual nature. Firstly a *virtualization*, that is, a derealization of the real, or of our comprehension of reality, comes about. And secondly – complementary to this – comes a *revalidation* of non-electronic experience of reality, and moreover particularly of those aspects which are peculiar to these realities alone – in contrast to the electronic ones – and which hence, from now on, seem specific to these non-electronic realities and are accorded particular value.

1.   Virtualization

To begin with virtualization. It results – put generally – from the fact that media laws are increasingly permeating the everyday world too.

In media, as I've said, a different physics applies and a different logic of appearances and run of events than in the everyday. This begins on the television screen with the rotating objects previously mentioned and assumes fully unaccustomed dimensions through videos and cyberspace. From now on different versions of reality belong to the realm of our everyday experience. The existence of such alternatives suggests one thing at least: that the exclusivity and massivity of the customary understanding of reality could be unjustified, that other versions of reality are possible too. With this our apprehension of reality begins to open up to a potential multitude of worlds. Even if, to begin with, one only wants to understand this as meaning that there exist other artificial world constructions alongside the one, the actual real world, then the accustomed experience of the real at least loses its claim to exclusivity – if not yet its priority too.

Interpenetration of media reality and everyday reality

However, matters are made more complicated by the fact that everyday reality crops up within media reality, which leads to repercussions for everyday reality. From this point onwards a clean separation of everyday reality and media reality can no longer be carried out. I want to name some stages of the interpenetration.

Firstly, media presentation has become a seal of authenticity for everyday reality. Only what is transmitted is considered completely real. Karl Kraus wrote (in the pre-electronic age): 'In the beginning was the press, and then appeared the world.' Günther Anders updated this in 1956 in televisual conditions, reducing it to the sarcastic formula: 'In the beginning was television, for which occurs the world.'

With its media presentation the everyday world is being modelled increasingly according to media laws. It is, for example, being submitted to the demands of the quick cut, of pictoriality, of rhythmic sequencing. This results, at least in those cases where we know reality only through its media presentation, in the intermingling of media and everyday logic. And these cases are numerous; most of what we know about the world, as Niklas Luhmann has noticed, we know from television. In this way media logic is increasingly inscribing itself in everyday reality – and furthermore into precisely those portions of reality singled out and found worthy of television transmission.

Secondly, this has repercussions for the arrangement of reality itself. Many real events are today staged from the start with a view to their media presentability. This applies to protest actions just as to cultural fixtures. Something similar can be noted with regard to the self-fashioning of individuals. Since the formation of personality in the modern world results predominantly by means of ideal media images, we are increasingly coming across typically media-styled figures in everyday life. Media peculiarities are thus forging the real inventory of reality outside media too. Not only the media *portrayal* of reality, but the media-external *reality itself* is henceforward permeated by elements of media determination.[30]

Thirdly, telecommunications are leading to a general assault on the basic coordinates of our accustomed reality. Space and time, the basic dimensions which underpin everyday reality, are being increasingly drawn in telecommunicatively. Where the speed of light dominates, interspatial distances lose significance. The distinctiveness of locations disappears since electronic media equipment manages to outmanoeuvre all local peculiarities: you can effect the same communications from all locations. Equally the past, through its data-based presentation, and the future, through its computational extrapolation, are becoming more and more available and tendentially the contents of a telematic present.[31] A collapse of spatiotemporal differentiation is coming about, a structure of omnipresence without distinguished presence. Space and time, the conventional base coordinates of our world, are becoming comparatively marginal. The electronic communications world has to this extent changed the real world in its base coordinates.

If you bear in mind this collapse of spatio-temporal differentiation in the world of telematic communication, then the result is once again that several versions of reality coexist in our reality. Space and time no longer have a trenchant separative function everywhere, but only in certain areas; in other areas, however, their relevance is telematically neutralized. Such contrasts between versions of reality are today becoming everyday experience. Or, put another way, as a result of media-induced changes in reality, what I presented in section I with reference to philosophical developments is becoming more and more standard experience for contemporaries: that straightforward reality doesn't exist, that things either exist so or otherwise, that reality in each case is a construction.

Blurring of boundaries between reality and simulation?

New approaches to television consumption as well as the use of micro-electronic design and production techniques also contribute to the weak-ening of the obligatory character of reality. The televisionary reality is obviously not binding and inescapable, but selectable, changeable, dis-posable, can be fled from. If something doesn't suit you, then you change channels again. In zapping and switching between channels the advanced television consumer practises the same derealization of the real which also applies elsewhere.[32] And for whoever works frequently with computer-aided design the far-reaching pliability and virtuality of reality is everyday experience.

But how far does the blurring of reality and virtuality go? Some theorists believe not far at all. Rather reality and simulation remain clearly distin-guishable in their view. No one, for example, has yet mistaken the marital strife in an ongoing soap opera for the unpleasantries at their own breakfast table.[33] This is indeed true, but falls short as a diagnosis. For we certainly continue to succeed in distinguishing between simulation and reality in the short term, but what's decisive are the long-term effects of interaction with media. And in this respect studies show that modes of behaviour which are practised in the guiding electronic world are increasingly impregnating everyday behaviour.[34] The virtualization of reality is a long-term effect of media worlds.

Let me illustrate this with an example. In the USA an eight-minute tape with interactive components is sold under the name 'Video Baby'. A birth certificate and health certificate are included in the package. The user has their dream baby in front of them on the screen and can delight in it without interruption. It responds to sentences such as 'eat your pudding', 'smile at mummy'. And as you can imagine: *this* child's obedience is perfect. At the end of eight minutes you can sing it to sleep.[35] On the packing it states: 'The full, rich experience of parenthood without the confusion and bother of the real thing! Do you love children, but lack the time to look after them? "Video Baby" is for you!'

Of course the user knows of the distinction between simulation and reality. But the critical point is that this difference *means* less and less. Simulation is taken as reality's substitute straight away, even valued as the more perfect version of the real – precisely because it offers 'the full

[. . .] experience of parenthood without the [. . .] bother of the real thing'. The experience of simulation is being made more and more the matrix of real behaviour: babies are being perceived of increasingly as Video Babies and their deviations from the ideal electronic image are considered not a sign of humanity but as burdensome imperfections. In media conditions originals – in the case of babies as well as elsewhere, say in art – tend to be disappointing. The real is being measured more and more against ideal media conceptions.[36]

You might find such developments dreadful – certainly they are highly problematic. However, it's not by denying the coalescence of reality and simulation, but by making oneself aware of this *status quo* and learning to take a stand within it that you arrive at different, and possibly more humane, options. I will come back to this. – Before I do, one last point on today's fusion of virtuality and reality.

Cyberspace

The focus of the interfusion of virtuality and reality is currently found in cyberspace technology. To be sure, what's concerned here is a fashionable subject as well as a point of crystallization for rhetorical exaggeration and a hyped-up hit for PR strategies. All the same this technology and its resonance also have a hard core worth thinking about. This is what I want to examine.

Cyberspace introduces an element to electronic worlds which is indeed completely new: in cyberspace you no longer face a picture at distance, but you step into it and, by means of headset and datagloves, can move around in the picture's virtual world just as in a real one. The being-before-the-picture-world – this very conventional trait of electronic worlds so advanced in other respects – becomes a being-in-the-picture-world. The presence in front of and facing the picture transforms itself into presence within the picture – into what is called telepresence. What's interesting about this is not so much the in truth fairly limited perfectability of these cyberworlds (you see, here too you can only realize forms of behaviour accommodated for by the program and not say random variations),[37] rather the effect on consciousness which such cyberspace experiments bring about is important. In entering the virtual world like a real one you have the concrete experience that the virtual can also be real, and from this the suspicion might grow that perhaps everything real could also be virtual in another respect. The world-view of someone like Leibniz or Borges, according to which what counts as real to one conscious state could in truth be the vision of another conscious state,[38] becomes the general supposition about reality. The borders between reality and virtuality are becoming definitively uncertain and pervious.

Enlightening effects of media experience

It has often been observed and lamented that electronic media lead to a virtualization of our awareness of reality in the way described. I consider this diagnosis correct, but its negative evaluation wrong. In my view an almost enlightening effect of media and artificial worlds lies in the media-induced change in our customary understanding of reality. Faced by the new media the fundamental constructivist character of reality, the interpretivity of all our apprehensions of reality, comes to our attention more clearly than ever before.[39] As a result of this our commonplace view of reality too is transferring from realism to constructivism, from being given to being made, from the singular to the plural, and from reality to virtuality. Thanks to the interaction with media realities we are comprehending that reality always was (at least in important respects) a construction – that previously one just didn't like to admit this to oneself.[40]

2.   Revalidations

This might all sound like an apologia for electronic worlds and their artificial paradises – but finally I want to follow up something else, to cast a different emphasis. Because in fact, it seems to me, the present day is characterized by a *double* figure: predominantly, of course, by the fascination with electronic worlds, but, on the other hand, and complementarily, also through a new turn to different, non-electronic, forms of experience. This point has received too little attention in the discussions of recent years. – I would like to bring it to the fore.

Contrasting experiences

If all realities are – individual, social or media – constructions, then the choice between them is no longer one between being and appearance or between true and false, but a choice between versions potentially having equal rights according to varying preferences. And then, first of all, we are responsible for our choices. And, secondly, one version of reality can lead to a new evaluation of another. Its virtues can be made noticeable in contrast and this other version can hence become a desideratum.

This applies particularly in the relationship between electronic and non-electronic worlds. The electronic worlds revalidate forms of experience of the non-electronic worlds – which admittedly, according to law of contrast, they have also altered.

It is precisely when Marshall McLuhan's thesis that the medium is the message applies (and I don't doubt that this is the case) that electronic media must, for systematic reasons, lack the forms of experience peculiar to other media. Electronic media might well be able to take hold of *all objects*, but – just as every other medium too – *only in their own way*.[41] In that the same objects become accessible, sometimes in the one medium, sometimes in another, the specifity and restrictedness of the respective medium can be experienced. Put another way, electronic media too are specific. They certainly offer wonderful opportunities. But not all opportunities. And it's not only the possibilities of media which are today becoming interesting, but also, in contrast to these, some of the qualities which they lack and which are reserved exclusively for other forms of reality.

Counter-options

Thus we are today learning anew to esteem inertia as opposed to hyper-speed, resistibility and unchangeability as opposed to universal moveability and changeability, persistence as opposed to free play, massivity as opposed to suspension, constancy and reliability as opposed to mutability. Touch-of-a-key instantaneity revalues in contrast slow, autonomous development; arbitrary repeatability awakens the desire for uniqueness. Electronic omni-presence and the universe of virtual opportunities lead to the yearning for another presence, for the unrepeatable presence of *hic et nunc*, for the singular event. Importance is regained by opaqueness as opposed to com-plete transparence, by the sovereign ignorance of matter as opposed to the intellectuality of processors.

The counter-values named can be assembled conceptually under headings such as 'matter', 'body', 'individuality', 'uniqueness'. What claims its own space and time, what's not exchangeable, but rather unrepeatable is becoming important to us again. Accordingly Botho Strauß pointed out that in the midst of overwrought communication it's the poet who is responsible 'for the unmediated, the strike, the interrupted contact, the dark phase, the break. The foreignness.'[42] Similarly, in Bertolucci's *Last Tango in Paris*, the situation of namelessness – in contrast to rampant gossip – created the setting for a unique love.

We have good grounds to defend silence against being deafened; to esteem our own imagination, one unavailable to others, higher than social and mutual electronic imaginary; and equally to appreciate afresh our ageing and vulnerable bodies against the perfection and agelessness of synthetic bodies.

Telematic and natural experience

Telematic and natural experience stand in contrast. Their disparity is irrevocable. Distances are today vanishing telematically, but this doesn't mean that our bodies are shrinking too. Processors are becoming ever faster, but not our sensors and our motor and psychic abilities. The processing capacity of computers is growing ever more gigantic, but not our lifetimes, our reaction times, our comprehension times.

The body is a conservative element, and it remains a condition for our every operation. From the philosophical side the significance of corporality as a counter-balance to the electronic tendencies of immaterialization has been expounded repeatedly in the last few years. Lyotard posed the question as to whether one can think without body – and this he denied.[43] From the phenomenological perspective Dreyfus has pointed out that there is no understanding without linkage back to corporality and everyday experience.[44]

Similarly, starting from anthropological premisses, Virilio and Baudrillard have defended our physical bodies against the project of their metaphysical, technological re-equipment.[45,46]

Corporality, individuality and materiality are not merely to be put
forward as the preconditions or limits of our thinking; they are not only to
be asserted defensively – and also not simply offensively. All of these are
still forms of a functionalization. Rather these aspects should be
acknowledged and asserted in their own right.

Of course, our bodies are also after changes and are open to extensions.
The classical *citius–altius–fortius* (faster–higher–stronger) was the sporting
formula for this. Today we are enhancing our bodies in league with
technical arrangements and electronic media. And bodies do not simply say
no to this. The fascination of electronic media previously outlined is one
not only for the intellect or the imagination, but one also for our yearning
and unsatisfied bodies.

But there is also a media intangibility, a sovereignty and obstinacy of
bodies. These we are rediscovering today in a counter-move to the
mediatization of the world. Think, say, of Nadolny's 'discovery of
slowness'[47] or of Handke's praise of weariness.[48] Amidst the turbulences of
a world increasing its electronic potency the uniqueness of an unrepeatable
hour or encounter is becoming important to us anew – or the inertia and
the joy of a touching hand or of a pair of eyes. We are remembering the
self-sufficing perfection and autonomy of simple actions – of a stroll, a
meal, looking at a landscape, or of solitude too, the media-free solitude far
from all communications machinery.

To be sure, the rediscovery and new evaluation of such actions results
only against the backdrop of a world determined by media and its
turbulences. It cannot be separated from this. The media world bubbles on
the horizon of such experiences. But the named experiences also keep the
media world in check and are at best intensified by it.

Complementarity

In order not to be misunderstood: of course I don't intend this revalidation
of the corporal and the individual as a simple counter-programme to the
artificial paradises of electronic worlds, but rather as a programme complementary to them. These counter-aspects do not negate the fascination of
electronic worlds; nor is it simply a matter of a return to sensuous
experience, such as this might have been in pre-electronic times. The
revalidations are far more coloured by experience of the electronic world
too. And there are obvious links between the two. Sometimes natural
experience is just the thing lovers of virtuality are after too. My favourite
example are the electronics freaks from Silicon Valley who in the evening
drive to the coast to observe those indeed incomparable Californian sunsets
before returning to their home computers and diving into the artificial
paradises of the Internet.

What I am turning against is far more the simple opposition which media freaks set out for and their historical teleology, according to which only electronic forms of experience are advanced and all others are merely antiquated and rightly condemned to extinction. Against this I am pointing out the revalidations named and the tandem nature of the development.[49]

In doing this, however, I do not want to fall victim myself to the dichotomization of intellect and electronic communication, on the one side, versus body and natural communication, on the other, which is prescribed by electronics freaks. This schism of pure intellectual experience and bodily sensation (remember Moravec) is obviously wrong. There is (the references to Lyotard and Dreyfus stood for this) no intellectual experience without bodily participation and also no electronic experience without the body. You notice this at the very latest when you return to everyday life after a three-hour trip into virtual reality – and in so doing, at least to begin with, have great physical difficulties, for instance extended feelings of dizziness: the body has been taken along on this journey and feels the worse for wear.

There are, as I said, also transitions and reciprocal influences between electronic and non-electronic worlds of experience. But above all there exists a reciprocal unsubstitutability. That natural experience cannot simply replace electronic experience is familiar to us. The fascination of electronic worlds – which also thrives on the very contrast with usual forms of experience – feeds on this fact. That, however, electronic experience cannot replace natural experience either, and does not simply overcome it, but rather sometimes lacks something peculiar to natural experience, this seems – at least within the electronic enthusiasts' club – to be something which people don't want to perceive, and this is what I wanted to point out.

There remains a difference in walking through a building – say St Peter's cathedral – really or virtually. The difference in experience is a blatant one (as difficult as it may be to accommodate conceptually). Or in seeing a statue of Buddah in front of you on the monitor, or approaching it in real life and experiencing such a 25-metre-high colossus with the entire body. Or in experiencing a sunset sitting on a clifftop in Big Sur or watching a video of it at home.

Revalidations and counter-validations

In one respect, however, my talk of 'revalidations' is in need of a supplement. One could rightly object that *re*validations of the type mentioned can only occur with people who grew up non-electronically, who are non-electronically socialized. Since for them – the elder members of today's population – relatively natural modes of experience stood at the start, with them there can be a return to forms of experience such as those which seem, in the meantime, to have been overtaken electronically, but whose own value is now being esteemed anew. With the cyber-kids, however, things must be different. For them the turn to 'natural experience' cannot mean a return to elementary experience at all, but an alternative mode of experience at best. What's more it's highly questionable whether, for someone electronically socialized, 'natural' experience can ever attain particular significance or ever be anything other than a weak and less interesting modification of electronic-media experience.

It is obvious, however, that young people today possess an astonishingly high awareness for the alterity of forms of experience – even when only differences within the electronic world between one form of experience and another are concerned, say between television, video games, on-line chat, Web-surfing and virtual reality. Young people are far more aware than their elders of the specifity of such different media and modes of experience, and they know how to use them ably and in a calculated manner. As a result of their early media training (their electronic socialization) they experience counter-validations: they value the alterity and specifity of different media and utilize their contrasts.

Whether revalidations or counter-validations, in both cases it holds that by taking several tracks our life becomes more contemporary and more invigorating. I think generally that people today are becoming something which traditional metaphysics never thought highly of and always rejected: they are becoming nomads – with this, of course, I have in mind less a geographical, but far more a mental, psychic, so to speak everyday nomadism. We are starting to move to and fro between different forms of reality as if it were natural to do so. Our cultural formation is becoming increasingly transcultural,[50] our behaviour follows several options, and our reason is becoming transversal.[51,52] A person today should, I think, live in both the types of reality outlined. You should be able to enjoy moving around in electronic worlds – but not *only* in them, rather in other worlds as well.

Modernity's dual character

Does all of this ultimately amount to a rejection of modernity, so far as this has always made technological development its guiding line? Yes and no. Modernity had two origins – two very different origins. Stephen Toulmin elaborated on this in his 1990 book *Cosmopolis*. There was, on the one hand, in the seventeenth century, the modern science of Descartes which aimed for pure intellectuality and transparency. But there was also, from the sixteenth century onwards, the humanism of Erasmus or Montaigne which distinguished itself through a 'concern for human life in its concrete detail'.[53] Toulmin traces both strands through to the present day. My account here converges with his view. In the artificial electronic worlds the Cartesian scientific tradition culminates or explodes. In the complementary re-evaluation of the finite, the corporal, the individual, however, the basic motifs of humanism recur once again. Toulmin too states that what is needed today is to 'reappropiate the wisdom of the 16th-century humanists'[54] – without, of course, abandoning the achievements of the Cartesian tradition.[55] This is precisely my viewpoint. We should not abbreviate the dual figure of modernity to one pole, neither through media euphoria nor through body fanaticism. We should retain – or regain – our binocularity.

Notes

This essay was originally delivered as my Inaugural Lecture, 'Künstliche Paradiese? Betrachtungen zur Welt der elektronischen Medien – und zu anderen Welten', at Otto-von-Guericke University Magdeburg, Germany (8 June 1994). It has been revised for this volume. (First English publication.)

1. Heinrich von Kleist, 'Über das Marionettentheater', in Kleist, *Sämtliche Werke und Briefe*, vol. 2 (Munich: Deutscher Taschenbuch Verlag 1987), pp. 338–345, here p. 345.
2. Marshall McLuhan, *Understanding Media: The Extensions of Man* (London: Routledge 1964), p. 80.
3. See Ihab Hassan, 'The New Gnosticism: Speculations on an Aspect of the Postmodern Mind', in Hassan, *Paracriticisms. Seven Speculations of the Times* (Urbana, Ill.: University of Illinois Press 1975), pp. 121–147.
4. Cf. Hans Moravec, 'Geist ohne Körper – Visionen von der reinen Intelligenz', in *Kultur und Technik im 21. Jahrhundert*, eds Gert Kaiser, Dirk Matejovski and Jutta Fedrowitz (Frankfurt a.M.: Campus 1993), pp. 81–90, here pp. 84f. For a detailed account of Moravec's views, see his *Mind Children* (Cambridge, Mass.: Harvard University Press 1988).
5. Ibid., p. 89.
6. Francis Bacon, *Novum Organum*, in *The Works of Francis Bacon*, vol. 4, eds J. Spedding, R.L. Ellis and D.D. Heath (London: Longman and Co. 1860), pp. 39–248, here p. 40.
7. René Descartes, *Discourse on Method*, in *The Philosophical Writings of Descartes*, vol. 1, trans. J. Cottingham, R. Stoothoff and D. Murdoch (Cambridge: Cambridge University Press 1985), pp. 111–151, here p. 143.
8. Cf. ibid.
9. Boethius, *De consolatione philosophiae*, Book V, 6th verse.
10. Charles Baudelaire, *Les paradis artificiels* (Paris 1860).
11. Immanuel Kant, *Critique of Pure Reason*, trans. Norman Kemp Smith (New York: St Martin's Press 1965), pp. 323 and 449 [A 334 and 506].
12. For the epistemological concept of interpretation see Günter Abel, *Interpretationswelten. Gegenwartsphilosophie jenseits von Essentialismus und Relativismus* (Frankfurt a.M.: Suhrkamp 1993).
13. Rorty, for example, says that there exists only 'reality-under-a-certain-description' (Richard Rorty, *Philosophy and the Mirror of Nature*, Princeton: Princeton University Press 1979, p. 378). Similarly Goodman explains that 'We are confined to ways of describing whatever is described.' (Nelson Goodman, *Ways of Worldmaking*, Indianapolis: Hackett 1978, p. 3.)
14. Cf. Friedrich Nietzsche, 'On Truth and Lies in a Nonmoral Sense', in *Philosophy and Truth. Selections from Nietzsche's Notebooks of the early 1870's*, trans. and ed. Daniel Breazeale (Atlantic Highlands, NJ: Humanities Press 1979), pp. 79–91.
15. Cf. Georg Wilhelm Friedrich Hegel, Introduction to the *Phenomenology of Spirit* (1807), trans. A.V. Miller (Oxford: Oxford University Press 1977), here pp. 56–57.
16. This being the fundamental idea of the *Critique of Pure Reason* of 1781.
17. This is expressed almost emblematically – *pars pro toto* – in Descartes's elevation of the blind man, probing with a stick, as a model of someone seeing (cf. René Descartes, *La Dioptrique*, 6th Discourse: On Vision, in Descartes, *Œuvres*, eds Charles Adam and Paul Tannery, Paris: Vrin 1964–7, vol. VI, pp. 130–147).

18. 'The last dinosaurs of the Gutenberg galaxy [. . .] are threatened with extinction.' (Norbert Bolz, *Chaos und Simulation*, Munich: Fink 1992, p. 135.) Kittler differentiates more: 'New media don't make old ones obsolete, they assign them a different place in the system.' (Friedrich Kittler, 'Geschichte der Kommunikationsmedien', in *Raum und Verfahren* [*Interventionen* 2], eds Jörg Huber and Alois Martin Müller, Basel: Stroemfeld/Roter Stern 1993, pp. 169–188, here p. 178.)

19. The euphoric reversal of Postman's one-sidedness is no less wrong than his Cassandrian sentiment.

20. Georg Wilhelm Friedrich Hegel, *Elements of the Philosophy of Right*, ed. A.W. Wood, trans. H.B. Nisbet (Cambridge: Cambridge University Press 1991), p. 21.

21. An example: 'The media text [. . .] forgets dialectics and seeks ecstasy because it understands itself to be part of the medium. [. . .] Its stirring will to text is systematically random in dealing with all concepts and information which come drifting by.' (Agentur Bilwet, *Medien-Archiv*, Bensheim: Bollmann 1993, p. 15.)

22. In the history of art one must in general reckon with an excess of visions over the feasible. By no means all of the fantasies of artists have been realizable with the means then available. Think, for instance, of how Leonardo da Vinci continually ran up against the boundaries of feasibility and sought technical and media innovations. – I have dealt more closely with aspects of art in a world determined by electronic media in 'Künstliche Welten? Blicke auf elektronische Welten, Normalwelten und künstlerische Welten', in *Synthetische Welten, Kunst, Künstlichkeit und Kommunikationsmedien*, ed. Eckhard Hammel, Essen: Die Blaue Eule 1996, pp. 157–189, esp. pp. 180ff.)

23. 'The digital can extend itself only flatly.' (Holger van den Boom, 'Digitaler Schein – oder: Der Wirklichkeitsverlust ist kein wirklicher Verlust', in *Digitaler Schein. Ästhetik der elektronischen Medien*, ed. Florian Rötzer, Frankfurt a.M.: Suhrkamp 1991, pp. 183–204, here p. 203.)

24. Cf. Jacques Derrida, *Of Grammatology*, trans. G.C. Spivak (Baltimore/London: Johns Hopkins University Press 1976) as well as Gilles Deleuze, *Difference and Repetition*, trans. Paul Patton (London: Athlone Press 1994).

25. See Derrida, *Of Grammatology*, p. 10.

26. Nietzsche constitutes (here as in so many things) an exception. He was the first philosopher to use a typewriter and wrote on this: '[. . .] our writing tools work along with us on our thoughts' (Letter to Heinrich Köselitz, end of February 1882, in Friedrich Nietzsche, *Sämtliche Briefe. Kritische Studienausgabe in 8 Bänden*, eds Giorgio Colli and Mazzino Montinari, Munich: Deutscher Taschenbuch Verlag 1986, vol. 6, p. 172).

27. Eric A. Havelock, *Preface to Plato* (Cambridge, Mass.: Harvard University Press 1963).

28. Within the scope of this essay I cannot individually expand on the specific aspects of the Internet and in particular the World Wide Web, which because of their novelty and cultural significance require a longer treatment. See the essay 'Information Superhighway or Highway One?' in the present volume.

29. See Derrick de Kerckhove, 'Cyberdesign – Interaktion mit virtuellen Realitäten', in *Das Verschwinden der Dinge. Neue Technologien und Design*, ed. Arnica-Verena Langenmaier (Munich: Design Zentrum München 1993), pp. 32–58, here p. 52.

30. Our modes of perception have always been shaped by cultural determinants. We never have a simple 1:1 relationship to the real. In earlier times religious fabrications or aesthetic discoveries were the main designers of our modes of perception. What's new today is that electronic media have taken over this role.

31. 'The time category of the future will be done away with and replaced by that of an extended present.' (Helga Nowotny, *Eigenzeit. Entstehung und Strukturierung eines Zeitgefühls*, Frankfurt a.M.: Suhrkamp 1989, p. 53.)

32. For derealization see also the essay 'Aesthetics beyond Aesthetics: For a New Form to the Discipline' in the present volume.

33. See Hans Magnus Enzensberger, 'Das Nullmedium oder Warum alle Klagen über das Fernsehen gegenstandslos sind', in Enzensberger, *Mittelmaß und Wahn. Gesammelte Zerstreuungen* (Frankfurt a.M.: Suhrkamp 1988), pp. 85–103, here p. 91.

34. See Joshua Meyrowitz, *Die Fernsehgesellschaft. Wirklichkeit und Identität im Medienzeitalter* (Weinheim: Beltz 1987).

35. Quoted from: Hans Ulrich Reck, 'Imitieren? Klar, immer. Aber wie?', in *Basler Magazin*, No. 47, 25/11/1989, pp. 1–5, here p. 2. See my analysis in *Ästhetisches Denken* (Stuttgart: Reclam 1990), p. 22. (Forthcoming in English as 'Aesthetics and Anaesthetics', in *Aesthetic Thinking*, trans. John Bailiff, Atlantic Highlands, NJ: Humanities Press 1998.)

36. The restoration of Michelangelo's frescoes in the Sistine Chapel was tellingly sponsored by a television company (Nippon Television Network Corporation) – the frescoes were then rebuilt perfectly telegenically.

37. See here Florian Rötzer's revealing account: 'Ästhetische Herausforderungen von Cyberspace', in *Raum und Verfahren*, pp. 29–42, pp. 41f., as well as his 'Virtuelle und reale Welten', in *Cyberspace. Zum medialen Gesamtkunstwerk*, eds Florian Rötzer and Peter Weibel (Munich: Boer 1993), pp. 81–113, esp. p. 106.

38. '[. . .] nor is there anything to prevent certain well-ordered dreams from being the objects of our mind, which we judge to be true and which, because of their accord with each other, are equivalent to truth so far as practice is concerned.' 'Indeed, even if this whole life were said to be only a dream, and the visible world only a phantasm, I should call this dream or this phantasm real enough if we were never deceived by it when we make good use of reason.' (Gottfried Wilhelm Leibniz, 'On the Method of Distinguishing Real from Imaginary Phenomena', in *Leibniz, Philosophical Papers and Letters. A Selection*, trans. and ed. Leroy E. Loemker, Dordrecht: Reidel 1969, pp. 363–365, here p. 364.) Borges' story 'The Circular Ruins', in which a man dreams of a youth at another location so precisely that the latter becomes real – and there are unambiguous reports of the success (the youth is even able to walk through fire without being harmed) – ends with the man himself, when he survives a test by fire unharmed, discovering to his surprise that he too was due only to the dream activity of another: 'With relief, with humiliation, with terror he understood that he, too, was all appearance, that someone else was dreaming him.' (Jorge Luis Borges, 'The Circular Ruins', in *Jorge Luis Borges. A Personal Anthology*, ed. Anthony Kerrigan, London: Jonathan Cape 1968, pp. 68–74, here p. 74.)

39. Significantly the constructivist character of reality – following the named philosophical preparations – has been developed in recent decades by a school of thought calling itself 'constructivism' which has stood in intensive contact with cybernetics from the beginning.

40. Once again we run into a congruence between the modes of experience conveyed by new electronic media and central philosophical theorems of the present day. I have explained this above with regard to the anti-hierarchical ontology of media as well as with regard to the mediality of thought; this has now demonstrated itself once again with regard to the insight into the constructivist character of reality. Media experience has an enlightening effect for philosophy and beyond.

41. Put another way, media can very well be universal, but not total. They can contain everything, but not in every way.

42. Botho Strauß, 'Die Erde – ein Kopf', in *Büchner-Preis-Reden 1984–1994*, ed. Deutsche Akademie für Sprache und Dichtung (Stuttgart: Reclam 1994), pp. 126–137, here p. 130.

43. See Jean-François Lyotard, 'Can Thought Go on without a Body?' in Lyotard, *The Inhuman. Reflections on Time*, trans. Geoffrey Bennington and Rachel Bowlby (Cambridge: Polity Press 1991), pp. 8–23.

44. See Hubert L. Dreyfus, *What Computers Can't Do: The Limits of Artificial Intelligence* (New York: Harper & Row 1972).

45. See Paul Virilio, 'Verhaltensdesign: Vom Übermenschen zum überreizten Menschen', in *Das Verschwinden der Dinge*, pp. 73–95, as well as Jean Baudrillard, 'Überleben und Unsterblichkeit', in *Paragrana. Internationale Zeitschrift für Historische Anthropologie*, 3(1), 1994, pp. 95–111. With similar aims in mind, Dietmar Kamper paid tribute to the body as an organ critical of the advancing process of civilization (cf. Dietmar Kamper, 'Die Wiederkehr des Körpers. Notizen zu einer Bestandsaufnahme des Zivilisationsprozesses', in Kamper, *Zur Geschichte der Einbildungskraft*, Munich: Hanser 1981, pp. 39–46).

46. The dream of some contemporaries who fancy themselves as particularly advanced – they can be found particularly in the field of design – that of a world as free as possible from hardware, as objectless as possible, is misguided on principle. This inverted vision of a neutron bomb – whereas this wipes out all human life, people here want to eliminate objects completely – belongs in the arsenal of error of futuristic imaginations.

47. Sten Nadolny, *Die Entdeckung der Langsamkeit* (Munich: Hanser 1983).

48. Peter Handke, *Versuch über die Müdigkeit* (Frankfurt a.M.: Suhrkamp 1989).

49. And there is cause to emphasize this tandem nature expressly, because the tendency is always towards what's advanced in the spirit of the age – and today that means towards the electronically advanced. This tendency triumphs for instance wherever we in fact recognize our corporality's own rights and its needs, but where again we comply with this only by means of instrumental or media prostheses: from fitness studios and bungee-jumping through to electronic sex. We should resist this technological pressure; we shouldn't, whenever it sprouts within us, mistrust the need for the named counter-values, but pay attention to its genuine forms and practise them.

50. See section III of the essay 'Cities of the Future: Aspects from Architectural Theory and Cultural Philosophy' in the present volume.

51. See my *Vernunft. Die zeitgenössische Vernunftkritik und das Konzept der transversalen Vernunft* (Frankfurt a.M.: Suhrkamp 1995, 2nd edition, stw 1996).

52. Botho Strauß advocates a similar perspective to that of the double option of electronic and non-electronic experience developed here: 'I would hope that a flexible double nature emerges for the future man, so that he can exist simultaneously and in alternation as one sensitive to technology and as an intensified sensuous man. [. . .] For the individual it will be a matter of experiencing a kind of cultural schism as a balance and not as a tensile test.' (Botho Strauß, *Die Fehler des Kopisten*, Munich: Hanser 1997, p. 173.)

53. Stephen Toulmin, *Cosmopolis. The Hidden Agenda of Modernity* (Chicago: University of Chicago Press 1990), p. xi; for the double origin see also pp. 23, 42–44.

54. Ibid., p. xi.

55. Cf. ibid., p. 174.

11

INFORMATION SUPERHIGHWAY OR HIGHWAY ONE?

Introductory remarks

1. Two kinds of highway

I intend to combine thoughts on the US information superhighway with deliberations about another type of highway, California's Highway One. The information superhighway is a project of the nineties: a US-wide digital communication system combining computer, TV and phonelines in order to provide interactive access to all sorts of information. Highway One is California's most beautiful highway, running from Northern California to Mexico, mostly along the Pacific coast, with wonderful scenic views.

Connecting the prospect of the information superhighway with a look back to the Interstate highway system is not unusual. Ralph Smith, who as early as in 1971 – in his book *The Wired Nation* – was the first to conceive of an 'electronic highway system', was also the first to draw parallels with the Interstate highway system.[1] And recently Al Gore, the country's leading advocate of the information superhighway, suggested: 'One helpful way is to think of the national information infrastructure as a network of highways – much like the Interstates begun in the '50s.'[2] In the case of Al Gore, the comparison even has a personal aspect: his father, former Senator Al Gore, Sr, helped shepherd the Interstate highway system through Congress in the 1950s.[3]

The analogy usually serves to promote the new system. As the older of the two, the Interstate highway system, has proved such a success – realized as it was in the face of many mental and emotional obstacles – the parallel might help to overcome obstacles to the new system too.

But I am going to connect reflections on these two kinds of highway for a different reason. I neither want to justify the new system by looking at the old one, nor will I suggest that we should simply move on to the new system for reasons of contemporariness. My aim is rather to compare the types of experience linked to these two systems and to suggest that we should combine them, should cruise along both kinds of highway.

2.   *The concept of the information superhighway*

Once fully established (hopefully around the year 2000) users of the information superhighway will have access to the greatest libraries, will be able to participate in lots of virtual communities, design their own TV programme, teleshop and telecommute or have telemedicine – a list which, of course, is not comprehensive. The Government calls the new system the 'National Information Infrastructure' (NII). But its use will, of course, be transnational, with the information superhighway providing access to a global network.

Basically two origins and two visions are combined by the superhighway. The first is a cerebral highway, where information and communication are the key commodities. The second is an entertainment highway, where movies, TV shows, interactive games and home-shopping offers prevail. The first, the information-based vision of the information superhighway, has grown out of the country's experiences with computer online services and especially the Internet; by connecting a personal computer to this network of networks, people can tap into innumerable storehouses of information – including news, research papers, books, business statistics, government reports, health care tips, and so on.

In contrast, the entertainment-based vision sees the superhighway as an extension of cable TV. Instead of waiting for movies or programmes to come on, people will be able to watch just about anything they want, any time they wish. The programme also includes interactive fare – movies where you can choose the outcome and game shows where you can be a participant.

The goal of the superhighway project is to merge these two visions. As the National Research Council points out, 'a national information infrastructure should be capable of carrying information services of all kinds, from suppliers of all kinds, to customers of all kinds, across network providers of all kinds, in a seamless, accessible fashion'.[4] There are, however, not only considerable obstacles which this proud vision would have to overcome – technological as well as financial challenges and obstacles arising from the conflicting interests of different groups – but there are also several problems being discussed with respect to the information superhighway, for instance: Will it produce anything but a never-ending cacophony of information noise? And if not: Doesn't it produce an information overload which confuses, disorientates and finally disables the user in finding what he or she wants? Doesn't the freedom of choice in conditions of overchoice turn into a lack of freedom? Doesn't the information system widen the gap between society's information-rich and information-poor? Will it not threaten personal privacy? Doesn't it increase narcissism and the loss of a sense of community and shared values? Will it not increase the difficulty for teenagers mesmerized by the new technology in developing social skills and managing in the real world? This catalogue of questions too is of course not comprehensive.

3.   Structure of the essay

In the following considerations I'd like to address some of these questions. First the question of information overload and of a supposed loss of freedom (I). To answer this question, I will look at the Internet, the furthest developed information system so far. Then, I will discuss the question of narcissism and of the loss of a sense of community (II). For that purpose, I will consider the so-called virtual communities. Up to this point I will engage in a sort of defence of the superhighway enterprise by refuting some all-too-common objections arising from ignorance or a sheer unwillingness to recognize what is really going on – an attitude which is closely connected with traditional attitudes of cultural critique. But I will not merely advocate the new tendencies, or even praise them as the only tendencies we should follow at present and in the future. My considerations will rather highlight the emergence of a counter-tendency which I call the revalidation of non-digital forms of experience (III). In the third section of my essay I will focus on this aspect and take a glimpse at current ways of wandering between different types of reality.

I.   Using the information superhighway – and using Highway One

1.   The Internet: information overload or increase in individual freedom?

Globality and individuality

The Internet provides people with access to an immense variety of information. You can get news or headlines or information about banks, entertainment, environment, sports, markets, copyright, medicine, Supreme Court decisions, and so on. You can read *Der Spiegel* or *L'Espresso* or various low-budget publications.

Of course, using the system requires specific competences in order to find not just anything, but the thing you really want. Even after working with the system for only a few hours, however, you will have achieved a certain degree of competence. The system is highly self-explanatory.

The variety of information creates one effect which every conventional library-user also appreciates: that the book next to the book you are looking for is the right one. Internet allows one to browse through information, and to have unintended effects of this kind as a by-product of your search.

Using the system, people soon develop certain habits in selection, a personal way of reducing the complexity of the information offered. Competent users are not at all lost in the system. And they get considerable help from expert systems. Software programs called 'intelligent agents' use artificial intelligence to alert us to sought-after information, and eliminate the choices that would just bog us down. This software even sorts out the 'need to know' from the 'nice to know'.

The system also offers the opportunity to define an individual selection of news, your personal news-collection. Using a service called First, you can define the type of news you are interested in, and each evening an expert system will search through the 15,000 news stories it has received during the day for the subjects you have specified, and you will get your news the next morning. Another service called Newscast even provides you with personalized news twenty-four hours a day. And soon people will be able to get their selections not only on their computer screens, but on their TV screens, too.

There is in fact neither disorientation through information overload nor mere information-noise. And there is just as little reason for complaining about dangers of uniformity (which are all too often associated with the digitalization of information by people who follow the old lines of cultural critique). Just the opposite is true: the totality of available information enables you to make perfectly individual information-choices.

The advantages for scholarly work are immense. Not only is the completeness of available data wonderful, but searching along headwords the system even provides you with many unexpected stimuli. It is comprehensive and creative at once.

Hence the new technology doesn't threaten, but increases the freedom and individuality of information. But you should be a competent user. However, this was already the case for radio and TV use. In the case of the Internet you even get every help you may want along the way.

The postmodern perspective put into practice

At the end of *The Postmodern Condition*, Lyotard mentions, among his proposals for the information age, the demand for free public access to all sorts of data banks.[5] This is, I suppose, precisely what's put into practice by the Internet. Everybody gets access and can use the information for his or her own, unsupervised purposes. The in-built interactivity – which allows users not only to receive but also to send messages to a potentially broad range of other interested users – supports the same purpose.

What needs to be effectively guaranteed, however, is the openness of different information sources and low user's costs.

Government responsibility

This, of course, is a political issue, and the present US Government seems aware of its responsibility in this respect. Accordingly, Al Gore says: We have to 'provide open access to the network'.[6] 'The most important step we can take to ensure universal service is to adopt policies that result in lower prices for everyone.'[7] And the democratic claim 'to avoid creating a society of information "haves" and "have-nots"' is, as Al Gore points out, 'the outgrowth of an old American tradition. Broadcasts, telephones, and public education were all designed to diminish the gap between haves and have-nots.'[8]

The belief in the liberating and democratic effects of communication generally is an old American belief. In 1835 de Tocqueville wrote:

> I know of but one single means of increasing the prosperity of a people that is infallible in practice that I believe one can count on in all countries as in all spots. This means is naught else but to increase the ease of communication between men [. . .] America, which is the country enjoying the greatest sum of prosperity ever accorded to a nation, is also the country, which, proportional to its age and means, has made the greatest efforts to procure the easy communication I have spoken of.[9]

With regard to this, the information superhighway is a contemporary way to pursue an old American dream.

Information gap and democracy

The gap, then, will not be one between information haves and have-nots, but one between people requiring and not requiring information. This, in my view, is concordant with democracy. Free access at very low costs is what democracy needs and what the Government has to take care of. But the question whether or not somebody makes use of the possibilities offered, is strictly and completely *his* or *her* decision. If there were a gap between users and non-users – not for reasons of cost, but of interest – then there would be nothing wrong with that. Democracy has to provide equal access, not to impose equal use – or to limit the use to the average. Such tendencies arise from an erroneous concept of equality. The equality has to be that of opportunities, not of usage.

In these aspects, I think, we can advocate the liberating and individualizing effects of the new technology. Those who use it will encounter not information noise, but information gains; and those who only find information noise will not use it. The old-fashioned fear of uniformity is groundless. Here, as in many other respects today, universalization is accompanied by an increase in individuality and diversity. And the possibilities for individual choice exist not only for an elite, but on all levels: from the advantages for scholarly research to the many choices of personal entertainment.

2. *Using Highway One: an example of the contemporary revalidation of non-electronic forms of experience*

Sunset tourism

Now, I will change the type of reality I am speaking of. I will tell another story from the heart of California, of that state which – due to its leadership in microelectronics – is so addicted to the development of the information superhighway.

Every evening, people get into their cars and drive to Highway One, in order to watch the sunset at the Pacific coast. I witnessed this on several occasions in the Stanford area, but the same procedure takes place in other regions too. From Stanford, it takes you about half an hour to reach Highway One and to visit your familiar place on the rocks or to walk along the beach and watch the sunset. Some people do the shorter version; they drive to a viewpoint on top of the hills between Silicon Valley and the ocean and watch landscape and sunset from there. – Why do these people do this?

There is an obvious explanation. Californian sunsets are unique. Once you have seen them, you will never forget them. What is fascinating is not only the incredible change of the colours of the sea – turning from white and all sorts of grey to blue, pink and black – but above all the sky with its metal clearness and its tones of yellow, green, orange and pink, enriched by tiny clouds and fog-streaks. In my personal view, it is the most wonderful premonition of our final experience, of the impression we will have when we die.[10] Sure, people may usually just enjoy the wonderful spectacle of nature without thinking about death. But I feel certain Caspar David Friedrich would have loved these Californian sunsets.

Living in two wonderlands

Whatever people may experience in their personal perspective, my point is that this sort of sunset tourism doesn't decrease but increases in the age of electronic wonderland. And what's more, the *same* people are addicted to both kinds of experience: to good old nature and to electronic virtuality, to both Highway One and the information superhighway. Having returned home, many of these people sit down at their PCs and turn to the virtual realities of Internet.

Are these people schizophrenic? Not at all. Both forms of reality can very well coexist and be combined. They even seem to challenge and provoke each other.

One way to understand this correspondence would be that of analogy: both types of experience transcend narrow locality, strive towards wider horizons, long for a universal perspective. Another explanation would follow a model of contrast: the experience of virtuality seems to be increasingly accompanied by a desire for full reality – which normally remains unsatisfied. This provokes a turn to primary reality and an intensification and altogether a revalidation of primary experience. In this sense, watching the outstanding Californian sunsets becomes an opportunity to fulfil this desire. Watching the sunset is just the kind of fulfilment you sometimes need when spending most of your time pursuing virtual reality.

II. Virtual communities

In the second part of my essay I will discuss another standard reproach: the supposed narcisissm and the loss of a sense of community caused by the increasing use of electronic communication.

1. Virtual communities in cyberspace

Standard reproach versus obvious advantages

Sure, electronic communication is currently increasing in use. 'Chat' is the most common online activity today. People talk to each other – writing on their keyboards and watching their screens for replies. They communicate on all kinds of matters – private as well as public, expert as well as banal. Some explanations for the attractiveness of electronic communication are obvious. I will mention only three.

Firstly, there are advantages for specific groups: people whose physical handicaps make it difficult to form new friendships find that in electronic communication they are treated as they always wanted to be treated – as thinkers and transmitters of ideas and feeling beings, not fleshy vessels with a strange appearance and an inappropriate way of walking or talking.

Secondly, there are general advantages: online you can cross national and cultural borders without difficulties; you meet people of numerous ethnic and religious backgrounds, from all corners of the globe, young and old, straight and gay. Not real America, but electronic America – or the electronic globe – is today's melting pot.

And a third reason: in virtual communication, you can always decide how far you want to reveal or to hide yourself, which side of your personality you present or which image of a person you build. In acting out yourself in both everyday life and electronic communication you may more fully realize yourself.

Life in cyberspace generally seems to correspond to another element of the old American dream. It is shaping up exactly as Thomas Jefferson would have wanted it: founded on the primacy of individual liberty and a commitment to pluralism, diversity and community. The conventional cultural criticism of electronic media, however, objects to the arbitrariness and irresponsibility of this type of communication, deplores its presumed singularization effects and even blames it for the decrease in the sense of community in everyday life. Electronic communication, these people say, may be 'modern' in the sense of furthering individualism, but what we need is a 'postmodern' turn to communitarianism. We should fight the consequences and limit the use of electronic communication – this, at least, is what communitarianists say.[11]

The case of the WELL

I don't partake of this criticism. I want to show its falseness by taking a closer look at virtual communities.

There are different sorts of virtual communities. You all know that the cutting edge of scientific discourse today is migrating to virtual scientific communities, because through e-mail you can read the electronic pre-printed reports of molecular biologists and cognitive scientists long before they are published in reviews – after having become outdated.

But I'm going to speak about everyday, not scientific, virtual communities. I refer above all to Howard Rheingold's very informative report on one of these communities, the WELL.[12] The community is located in the Bay area around San Francisco and mostly comprises people of this region, but it is open to other users too, as its name indicates, for 'WELL' means 'Whole Earth 'Lectronic Link'. Similar systems exist all over the world: TWICS, for example, in Tokyo, CIX in London, CalvaCom in Paris. Millions of people on every continent participate in bulletin board systems of this kind; in the US alone there were probably sixty thousand such systems in 1993 – only fourteen years after the first had been launched in Chicago and California. Each of these systems comprises between a dozen and several thousand participants.

The important and amazing thing is the great solidarity between the members of these communities. Although virtual, these communities are very effective communities in everyday life. Let me quote three examples from the WELL: there is a parenting conference, where parents can immediately profit from the experience of other parents; when you find a tick on your child's head, you get advice as to how to get it off faster from these people than from the paediatrician, and these people you trust, because you know them through several conversations. Another example: one day, a person reported that some members of his family had leukaemia. The other participants replied both emotionally and intellec-tually. Within a few weeks, most of them became – by virtue of the exchange of information on the subject – experts on blood disorders and learnt to understand how parents can stand up for their children in the medical system without alienating the care givers. A third example: when a former member of the community who had later moved to Asia was reported to be in a hospital in New Delhi, suffering from severe hepatitis and liver failure, the community organized the best available help to be in place within a few days and then transferred funds to get the patient to a hospital in the San Francisco region for further treatment. – You see: from everyday problems to emergency cases, the community is extremely helpful and shows a remarkable sense of and practice of solidarity. Whereas the cultural criticism speaks of narcissism and isolation and of a loss of the sense of community, nothing of this sort really is the case, but precisely the opposite is true: virtual communities are communal in a way which the so-called real communities have long since lost.

Regaining community and democracy

Perhaps we have generally to think the other way round in these matters. If conservative criticism blames virtual communities for the loss of real community feeling, it mistakes the effect for the cause, for indeed the hunger for virtual forms of community seems to be a consequence – not the origin – of the fact that informal public spaces have more and more vanished from our real lives.

And in principle virtual communities are less a threat to democracy, but could rather be contemporary means to rebuild democracy. – I will just mention three arguments for this.

Firstly, electronic communication in some ways re-establishes the public sphere, whose goal and decline has been described by Jürgen Habermas.[13] Electronic communication can become a sphere of free communication and underpin discussion of ideas among citizens. The information networks really constitute a sort of 'electronic agora'.[14]

Secondly, virtual communities are largely the arbiters of a sense of community, the disappearance of which has so often been deplored. Robert Bellah, for example, bemoans America's loss of a sense of a social commons, and advocates a need for rebuilding community.[15] Virtual communities are, in my view, at least to a certain extent proper ways of rebuilding solidarity and community. Therefore it would make much more sense to explore their democratic potential than to damn them through mere ignorance.

Thirdly, virtual communities – in contrast to politics and the mass media – can reinforce democracy. Politics has taken the turn from public discussion and participation to party-management and autonomous administration and has thereby lost the soul and almost the façade of democracy. And the public media at the end of the twentieth century will – according to Ben Bagdikian's prediction – be dominated by five to ten corporate giants who will control most of the world's important information-channels, and these media lords are not likely to donate the use of their privately owned and controlled networks for all the kinds of information that unfettered citizens and non-governmental organizations tend to disseminate. In this situation, the alternative local and planetary information networks in virtual communities properly function to reinvent and revitalize citizen-based democracy. Of course, I am not saying that the virtual communities provide *the* or even a sufficient solution to the current problems of democracy – how, for example, could they integrate the manifoldness of such communities on the level of a state? – but I am opposing the all too self-satisfactory and blind denial of the democratic potential of such virtual communities.

To sum up this point: blaming the turn to virtual communities for the loss of the sense of community is mistaking the effect for the cause and completely fails to recognize the proper communal and democratic content of these communities.

2.   *Virtual communities re-entering real space*

Let me turn to another point. Having argued that the common reproaches against electronic communication are silly and ungrounded, I'd like to point to an aspect which I've mentioned before, when contrasting the use of the superhighway with the fascination by sunsets. – What about the relationship between virtual communities and everyday reality?

Re-entry

Virtual communities do not have to remain in cyberspace. They can re-enter real space. There is even a tendency to do just that.

Rheingold reports that the WELL community sometimes has parties at one of its member's homes.[16] Virtual conversation becomes a real encounter. The members of the WELL also have a regular annual picnic in the San Francisco Bay area. Other communities all over the world do the same.

This is surprising for the common deprecators of virtual communication, but in fact it is quite natural. There is no necessary or definitive separation between cyperspace and real space. As the examples mentioned before demonstrate, electronic communication is often highly devoted to problems in real life.[17] The amount of solidarity between these people even renders it more likely that they want to meet in real life too.

I'd like to underline two aspects. Firstly, virtual community doesn't exclude ordinary reality at all. And, secondly, real communication even seems to constitute a sort of fulfilment – perhaps the ultimate fulfilment, the very completion – of electronic communication.

Returning to ordinary experience

In a way, the members of virtual communities, when meeting in real life, do the same as the sunset lovers I described before. In both cases, a return from virtual to real experience takes place ('real' in the sense of ordinary reality). Or, to put it more sharply: what's really going on there is an obvious revalidation of ordinary experience through virtual experience. – This, to my knowledge, hasn't been sufficiently recognized in the discussions of recent years.

Real experience is a quite extraordinary thing, when you meet people whom you know pretty well from their messages, including private messages, but whom you have never met in person before. Rheingold describes this as 'one of the oddest sensations of my life'.[18] And a student who had met her boyfriend through Internet Relay Chat reports: 'The first time I actually touched him was one of the biggest rushes in my life. To walk into the airport and see him sitting there, in Real Life, it was scary and it was wonderful.'[19]

We have long been used to virtualizing our personal relationships – by the use of letters or phonelines. In the cases I mentioned, people proceed in the opposite direction: they turn from virtuality to ordinary reality. None of these types of reality is any longer closed in itself. We can move from one type to the other, and they also affect and interpenetrate each other. Remember my description of the sunsets: in some sense, these Californian sunsets too are real and virtual at once. Though being natural phenomena, they imply a high degree of virtuality on the aesthetic level – and this, of course, is what we appreciate and what makes us drive over to see them.

In order not to be misunderstood, I conceive of the turn to ordinary reality neither as a simple counter-programme to the artificial paradises of electronic worlds nor as a return to sensuous experience, such as it may have been in pre-electronic times. Its revalidation is a *complementary* move to the appreciation of electronic worlds, and the 'natural' points of reference are tinted and etched by experience of the electronic world. There is interchange between these two types of reality, and therefore natural phenomena are not just traditional counterparts, but can also become contemporary partners to electronic or virtual experience.

III.   Revalidation: two-way perspective

My defence of the steps towards electronic communication and virtual communities follows a two-way perspective. All too often we think of defending or furthering these tendencies as being equivalent to denying the relevance of the natural or everyday forms of experience – by declaring them to be lesser or outdated. But this is not what I have in mind at all. I'd rather draw attention to the fact that the highly developed electronic world goes hand in hand with a new appreciation and revalidation of non-digital forms of experience. The network-freaks in Silicon Valley are also prone to the fascination of sunsets, and the WELL-beings in the Bay area extend their interaction to real life.

It is this two-way-model that I would advocate as being both descriptively adequate and normatively promising. Electronic experience doesn't simply overcome or absorb the more traditional forms of experience, but also revalidates them and recognizes them as an unsubstitutable limit, and even as defining a desirable goal. It is by following both types of experience – cruising along both the information superhighway and Highway One – that we achieve a fuller and contemporary realization of our existence.

Notes

This essay, written in 1994, was originally presented at the International Workshop 'Media Transforming Reality', Magdeburg, Germany (15–18 December 1994).

1. Ralph Lee Smith, *The Wired Nation; Cable TV: The Electronic Communications Highway* (New York: Harper & Row 1972), p. 83.

2. Quoted from Reid Goldsborough, *Straight Talk about the Information Superhighway* (Indianapolis: Alpha Books 1994), p. 4. Goldsborough's book was very helpful to me in preparing this essay.

3. Ibid., p. 11.

4. Quoted from ibid., p. 7.

5. Cf. Jean-François Lyotard, *The Postmodern Condition: A Report on Knowledge*, trans. G. Bennington and B. Massumi (Minneapolis: University of Minnesota Press 1984), p. 67.

6. Quoted from Goldsborough, *Straight Talk about the Information Superhighway*, p. 19.

7. Ibid., p. 18.

8. Ibid., p. 18.

9. Alexis de Tocqueville, *De la démocratie en Amérique* (Paris 1835). (Source: Goldsborough, *Straight Talk about the Information Superhighway*; no page given by Goldsborough.)

10. Of course, I am not going to propose that we will see an ocean and a heaven at the moment of sunset in our last seconds, but we will probably experience – maybe by quite different means – a similar kind of infiniteness, of a move towards the universe, of being freed from all borders and of being absorbed in a kind of final redemption.

11. Communitarianism is fiddled in many aspects. Its claims might have better prospects today in virtual than in real communities – in inventions of community rather than in rejoicing roots. What's puzzling, incidentally, is the coincidence of the rise of communitarianism and the decline of communism. Perhaps communitarianism's unrecognized purpose was to establish semi-communist claims within Western culture – in order to be prepared for the imminent loss of the foreign enemy, this beloved and constitutive part of our identity.

12. Howard Rheingold, *The Virtual Community: Homesteading on the Electronic Frontier* (New York: Harper Perennial 1994; first published Reading, Mass.: Addison-Wesley Publishing Company 1993).

13. Cf. Jürgen Habermas, *The Structural Transformation of the Public Sphere: An Inquiry into a Category of Bourgeois Society*, trans. Thomas Burger with the assistance of Frederick Lawrence (Cambridge, Mass.: MIT Press 1989).

14. Rheingold, *The Virtual Community*, p. 14.

15. Cf. Robert Bellah, Richard Madsen, William Sullivan, Ann Swindler and Steven Tipton, *Habits of the Heart* (Berkeley: University of California Press 1985), *The Good Society* (New York: Knopf 1992).

16. Cf. Rheingold, *The Virtual Community*, p. 2.

17. 'In real life' is a common expression in electronic communication, abbreviated as IRL.

18. Ibid.

19. Goldsborough, *Straight Talk about the Information Superhighway*, p. 121.

INDEX